Direct Democracy in the Baltic States

Studien des Instituts für Ostrecht München

Begründet von Professor Dr. Reinhart Maurach
Herausgegeben von
Professor Dr. Friedrich-Christian Schroeder,
Dres. h.c., Regensburg

Band 76

PL ACADEMIC RESEARCH

Evren Somer

Direct Democracy in the Baltic States

Institutions, Procedures and Practice in Estonia, Latvia and Lithuania

PL ACADEMIC RESEARCH

Bibliografische Information der Deutschen Nationalbibliothek
Die Deutsche Nationalbibliothek verzeichnet diese Publikation in der Deutschen Nationalbibliografie; detaillierte bibliografische Daten sind im Internet über http://dnb.d-nb.de abrufbar.

Library of Congress Cataloging-in-Publication Data
Somer, Evren, 1980- author.
Direct democracy in the Baltic states : institutions, procedures and practice in Estonia, Latvia and Lithuania / / Evren Somer.
p. cm. -- (Studien des instituts fur ostrecht munchen ; Band 76)
Includes bibliographical references.
ISBN 978-3-631-65298-5
1. Direct democracy--Baltic states. 2. Constitutional law--Baltic states. 3. Referendum--Baltic states. 4. Comparative law. I. Title.
KJC5049.S66 2014
328.2'309479--dc23
2014012444

ISSN 0073-8492
ISBN 978-3-631-65298-5 (Print)
E-ISBN 978-3-653-04440-9 (E-Book)
DOI 10.3726/ 978-3-653-04440-9

PL Academic Research ist ein Imprint der Peter Lang GmbH.

Peter Lang – Frankfurt am Main · Bern · Bruxelles · New York · Oxford · Warszawa · Wien

Diese Publikation wurde begutachtet.

www.peterlang.com

To my grandfather – Dedeme

Outline

Contents

Preface

When I embarked on the research project that resulted in the present volume, I did not expect to find such a wide range of direct democratic instruments in the Baltic states, and in Latvia and Lithuania in particular. This relative ignorance on my side might, in part, be attributed to the existing literature on the subject – or rather the lack thereof. While there are some studies on direct democracy, they either do not address direct democracy in the Baltic republics at all or in a superficial manner. But apart from this dearth of research, the limited use made of these instruments so far has also contributed to their relative obscurity. The Baltic States are comparatively young democracies that became independent (once more) when throwing off Soviet rule at the beginning of the 1990s. It seems that considerable time is required for citizens to get used to direct legislation.

In order to make a reasoned comparison of direct democracy in three republics, this book not only investigates the legal basis of each direct democratic institution, but also addresses the practical experiences of referendums held between 1991 and 2014. By discussing each referendum, the study examines both the development of direct democracy and as well as its functioning respectively *dysfunctioning* in each country.

The preparation of this study on Direct Democracy in the Baltic States would have been impossible without the help of many friends and colleagues. First, my gratitude is extended to Prof. Dr. Andreas Auer and Prof. Dr. Herbert Küpper, who encouraged me to pursue this project. In addition, I would particularly like to thank Dr. Uwe Serdült, Dr. Jonathan Wheatley and Dr. Lorenz Langer from the c2d-team for their valuable comments on the manuscript and highly useful suggestions. I would also like to acknowledge the helpful support from Arne Koitmäe of the Elections Department Chancellery of the Riigikogu of Estonia, Vita Brižе of the Central Election Commission of Latvia and Kristina Ivanauskaitė-Pettinari of the Central Electoral Commission of Lithuania. I am especially indebted to them for having offered me also linguistic support since I do not speak any of the languages of the Baltic states. Further, I would like to express my gratitude to my partner Mischa for his valuable assistance, visual illustrations, infographics and particularly for his patience during the entire time. And finally I would like to thank the *Centre for Research on Direct Democracy Aarau (c2d)* and the *Institut für Osteuroparecht München (IOR)*. Without their generous financial support this book would not have been possible.

Zurich, 30 October 2014

I. Introduction

Within the last decades there has been a considerable rise in the use of direct democratic institutions around the world and provisions for direct democracy have increasingly been added to the constitutions of new or re-established democracies.[1] Such an increase in the importance of direct democracy has also been seen in the Baltic states of Estonia, Latvia and Lithuania.[2]

Indeed, the three neighbour countries do not refer to the same ethnic group nor should they be treated as a unity. However, apart from their geographical location along the Baltic Sea, they share many properties and experiences with each other that were decisive in solidifying their common Baltic identity.[3] For centuries they were part of the Polish-Lithuanian Commonwealth and later the Russian Empire. In the aftermath of World War I and the breakup of the Russian, Ottoman and Habsburg empires, they became parliamentary democracies supplemented by different institutions of direct democracy. However, as in other European countries, Baltic democracies proved too fragile. In the context of divided societies, weak institutions and poor economies, they lasted only for a short time. In each country, crises paved the way for authoritarian regimes.[4] Until the Soviet occupation in 1940 and 1944, none of these three countries seized the opportunity to return to democratic politics.[5] With the Soviet incorporation, the Baltic states had become constituent republics within the Soviet Confederation for over fifty years (1940–1991) and thus subject to the Soviet Union's ideological discourse. Not nationality, but class was the source of legitimacy for all government decisions relating to political and economic life.[6] At the end of the communist era, all three countries marched towards democracy together and in each country

---

1 Butler/Ranney, *Growing Use*; Qvortrup, *Continued Growth;* LeDuc, *Politics of Direct Democracy;* Auer/Bützer, *Direct Democracy*; Auer, National Referendums; Pallinger et al., *Direct Democracy*; Kaufmann/Waters; Altman; Hug/Tsebelis; Serdült/Welp; Ewert, Potentiale; Neumann/Renger.

2 Ruus, Estonia; Ušacka; Krupavicius/Zvaliauskas.

3 Kasekamp, History, p. IX.

4 Ruled by Antanas Smetona in Lithuania, Karlis Ulmanis in Latvia and Konstantin Päts in Estonia; see Komáromi, Popular law-making, p. 72f.

5 Duvold, *Making Sense*, p. 150; Evert, Potentiale, p. 49f.; for more history see Kasekamp, History; Tauber, Geschichte, pp. 17–33; Rozenvalds, Baltische Staaten, pp. 55–74.

6 Mole, pp. 81–119; see also Hoffmann, Baltikum pp. 309–327; Rozenvalds, Baltische Staaten, p. 59f.

referendums were an essential tool in carrying this transition through peacefully. In 1991 and in the immediate post-independence period, referendums did not only pave the way for independence but they also served to restore the statehood of the Baltic states and to re-establish national identities. In Estonia and Latvia, however, this entailed excluding very sizeable Russian-speaking minorities. At present, around a quarter of Estonia's people and 27 percent of Latvia's are native Russian-speakers. The number of native Russian-speakers is, however, much lower in Lithuania. It stands at 6 percent of the population.[7]

Today, all three countries have attained membership in the NATO and the European Union. But twenty years after the fall of Communism, their democracies are relatively young and in the process of becoming consolidated.[8] Estonia, Latvia and Lithuania are still exposed to Russian pressure, for historic, geographic, linguistic and economic reasons. Furthermore, after Russia's annexation of Crimea in March 2014 and the continuing Ukrainian crisis the Baltic trio feels increasingly uneasy and vulnerable.[9] As some referendums also illustrate, Baltic emotions are occasionally driven by fears of assimilation by Russia.

Currently, in addition to parliamentary mechanisms, there is indeed a large set of direct democratic instruments available to the citizens of the Baltic states, and within the last two decades, they have been variously applied at national level. Despite this, experience with direct democracy and its institutions is comparatively limited in the Baltic context. Nevertheless, considering their historical past, we must say that democracy has been more of an exception than a rule in each country. As such, compared to Western democracies, these three countries have relatively little experience with democracy at all. Regarding direct democracy at local level neither the constitution nor legislation provide for local or regional referendums. There might be opinion polls on decisions made by local governments or meetings to discuss administrative issues or topics

7 Echoes of Sudetenland. The Baltics look to NATO for protection, *The Economist* [from the print edition, online], http://www.economist.com/news/europe/21599828-baltics-look-nato-protection-echoes-sudetenland#sthash.nfC8KPsE.dpbs (accessed on 01.04.2014).

8 See also DUVOLD, *Making Sense*, p. 244.

9 Echoes of Sudetenland. The Baltics look to NATO for protection, *The Economist* [from the print edition, online], http://www.economist.com/news/europe/21599828-baltics-look-nato-protection-echoes-sudetenland#sthash.nfC8KPsE.dpbs (accessed on 01.04.2014); Die Ukraine-Krise wirft ihren Schatten auf Lettland, *Neue Zürcher Zeitung*, 26 September 2014, p. 5.

concerning territorial planning.[10] In May 2009 and June 2012 there were two initiative launches on introducing the initiative right for local referendums in each administrative unit in Lithuania. However, the proponents of the proposal were not able to collect the minimum number of required signatures within the given time frame.[11]

Of the referendums held between 1991 and 2014, only a small number succeeded; the majority were ineffective in bringing about policy changes. For the most part, referendums had been implemented by political parties to promote their particular interests. The literature on referendums in the Baltic states provides some possible explanations for such kinds of uses and the success of referendums.[12] But in many cases, a confusing classification of referendums has been used and less attention has been paid to the institutions regulating direct democracy in the Baltic states. It should be known that the notion of a referendum can cover diverse phenomenon within a direct democracy. Depending on who can frame the question and who can trigger the process of popular decision, the character and democratic quality of a referendum can vary widely.[13]

By taking such facts into account, this book presents a systematic comparative analysis of Baltic direct democracy from a legal perspective by specifying the political actors controlling these. It further pays attention to specific rules determining the procedures and practices of referendums and gives some possible explanations by comparing them. It has to be stressed that the present work does not aim to cover all historical events that may have shaped the current state of direct democracy in the Baltic republics. Nor does it try to explain its functioning by considering the socio-cultural aspects prevalent during the last 25 years or so. Rather, the book aims at bringing direct democratic institutions to light by classifying them systematically. It further attempts to examine formal shortcomings which are prevailing in the respective referendum mechanism, and makes some possible proposals that could contribute to better working. Thus, the book will hopefully serve as a useful starting point to scholars interested in conducting further research on direct democracy in those post-Soviet countries.

In order to meet the book's objective, a theoretical conceptualisation of direct democracy and of its three mechanisms – required, top-down, bottom-up – in combination with the veto player model[14] is first needed (chapter II). Following

10 VANAGS/VILKA, Local democracy, p. 133.

11 See chapter V-B-15.

12 See HOFFMANN, Baltikum, p. 312f.; FELDHUNE, pp. 77–83; MØLLER, pp. 281–293.

13 BIAGGINI, Demokratietheorie, p. 11.

14 HUG/TSEBELIS, pp. 465–515.

this conceptualisation, a systematic legal framework of all current direct democratic institutions at national level and their practical use from 1991 to 2014 is provided for each of the three Baltic states. Here, possible causes of variation in the use and success of referendums are also discussed (chapters III, IV and V). Furthermore, to better understand the performance of direct democracy, the book makes a comparison of referendums held in Estonia, Latvia and Lithuania. By using the situation in Switzerland as a kind of quality control, chapter VI provides a comparative assessment of the quality of direct democracy in each Baltic state. The book ends with some concluding remarks in chapter VII.

II. Definition and classification of direct democracy

A. Popular sovereignty through referendums

The modern concept of democracy is based on the idea of popular sovereignty. Popular sovereignty means that actions and institutions of the state must be legitimised by the people.[15] In a representative democracy, this legitimation generally occurs at parliamentary elections. Thereafter, for period of four or five years, the will of the people is represented by the elected national legislative body. In contrast, within a direct democracy the people exercise their sovereignty directly. Indeed, direct democracy does not replace the standard pattern of representative law-making. It is rather a sensible complement to the parliamentary process. Compared with the framework of representative systems, direct democracy offers the people greater opportunities for participation in which they can exercise their sovereignty within the political decision-making process in the most direct manner. Such a political act can be implemented by the adoption of constitutional or statutory provisions. Besides substantive issues the recall of representative bodies can also be part of the realm of direct democracy.

A referendum, as one possible form of decision-taking, may have two different meanings. First, it is used as a synonym for a popular vote. Second, it is an institution or a procedure of direct democracy that empowers citizens to reach political decisions on issues with which the political elite may disagree. More precisely, it is a popular right of eligible citizens to either accept or reject a specific public issue that may originate from a decision or proposal made by the authorities or from a citizens' initiative.[16] At that point, a link between representative and direct democracy is made, wherein the citizens not only share the decision-making process but also have the final say in the outcome. Thus, direct democracy introduces the people as an additional political actor into the decision-making procedure whose agreement is required to make a policy change possible.[17] Whether the popular decision on the public issue submitted to vote is positive or not, referendums have a legitimising effect because they reflect the will of the people. In addition, referendums work as correctives to

15 Marxer/Pállinger, System, p. 13; Hangartner/Kley, p. 132.

16 Kaufmann/Büchi/Braun, p. 240.

17 See following explanations, Hug/Tsebelis, pp. 465–515; Linder, Schweizerische Demokratie, p. 267f.

the shortcomings of purely representative legislation and serve as instruments of power sharing by integrating a variety of new actors into the decision process. This is especially crucial for those minorities whose interests are represented either inadequately or not at all through the representative organs.[18]

However, in order to assess such effects, it is important to consider which direct democratic mechanisms are available to the people and how well designed their procedures are. Referendums do not necessarily provide a higher quality of democracy. How and to what extent the people's will can be converted into legal norms of the state depends on the institutional arrangements (rules in form) that a country provides for direct democracy. Indeed, there are several ways to involve citizens in the law-making process. Yet citizen participation does not always enhance democratisation in public politics. Depending on the mechanism, referendums can also serve as a strategic tool for political elites to legitimize or sustain their own power.

B. Mechanisms of direct democracy and veto player

A *mechanism of direct democracy* is a set of procedures allowing citizens to make political decisions directly.[19] Within these procedures it is important to determine who *controls* the vote, because the common term referendum is often used to describe all kinds of popular decision-making processes. As AREND LIJPHART states, a referendum can be grouped according to its *initiator*, which can either be controlled or uncontrolled.[20] A controlled mechanism occurs if citizens have to decide – through a facultative or mandatory referendum – on a parliamentary decree that it had pre-passed. An uncontrolled mechanism occurs if a certain number of people initiate and submit their own proposal to a popular vote, irrespective of the state authorities.

To give a more systematic comparison of direct democratic institutions and procedures in the Baltic states and to show their possible effects, it is essential to classify direct democracy according to its possible mechanisms. My classification is based on DAVID ALTMAN's typology, which groups direct democracy into three main mechanisms according to their initiator (automatic, from above, from below), character (binding, nonbinding) and intention (proactive, reactive,

18 For functions and effects of direct democracy see KAUFMANN/BÜCHI/BRAUN, p. 71. LINDER, *Schweizerische Demokratie*, pp. 266, 268, 285; LINDER/LUTZ, *Direkte Demokratie*, p. 119; VATTER, *Politisches System*, pp. 358–364, 373–377.

19 SERDÜLT/WELP, p. 70.

20 LIJPHART, *Democracies*, p. 203f.

or even delaying).[21] Here it should be noted that in some cases these three mechanisms can overlap. In addition to ALTMAN's conceptualisation, I also pay attention to the normative level (constitution, law, statutory), or to the subject matter (policy issues) of a referendum that can vary within a single mechanism. Furthermore, I combine ALTMAN's 'procedural typology' with the 'controlling-model' of SIMON HUG and GEORGE TSEBELIS that is based on the theory of the veto-player. As the authors note, it is the information about the control options that is crucial when it comes to assessing the effect of institutions allowing for referendums. The 'controlling-model'[22] explains differences between referendums, depending on who is empowered to *ask the question*, or, rather, to frame or determine the content of the popular vote, and who exactly *triggers the process of a referendum*.[23] According to this classification, we can generally distinguish between four main direct democratic institutions: *required referendums*, *authorities' referendums* (e.g. plebiscites, parliamentary referendums or extraordinary referendums), *citizens' facultative referendums* (popular veto) and *citizens' initiatives* (popular initiative).[24]

1. Initiator of referendums

a) Referendums required by the constitution

I identify *referendums required by the constitution*, or 'mandatory referendums', as they are also called, as the first mechanism of direct democracy. Here a popular vote on an amendment to the constitution or law must be held automatically since the referred issue cannot otherwise be amended.[25] For required referendums, the term automatic referendum can also be used.

Theoretically, constitutional or legal regulations are the 'initiators' of automatic direct democratic mechanisms. Nevertheless, the activation of the referendum

21 See also ALTMAN, pp. 8–18.

22 I use this term for their 'multi-dimensional model of referendums on the basis of veto player theory'.

23 HUG/TSEBELIS, pp. 477–488; see also SMITH, *Functional*, p. 6f.; BIAGGINI, *Demokratietheorie*, p. 11; HANGARTNER/KLEY, p. 156f.; SERDÜLT/WELP, p. 70; VATTER, *Politisches System*, p. 378f.; MARXER, *Wir sind das Volk*, p. 15f.

24 HUG/TSEBELIS, p. 478.

25 In the federal system of Switzerland, for instance, any amendment to the constitution requires a mandatory referendum. In addition, joining an organisation for collective security or a supranational community and urgent federal legislation without the required constitutional basis are also necessitating a referendum. For approval, both the majority of the participant electorate and the majority of the cantons are needed (double majority).

procedure does not occur automatically, as the name of the mechanism per se suggests; it must be initiated by a political actor. In general, framing the question in the sense of adopting a new law, amending, or repealing an existing law is a political result of a legislative activity that is caused by current economic, societal or political events both within and outside the borders of a state.[26] How the question is framed can also depend on the willingness of the political establishment to carry out a revision of the constitution or a law. In addition, a group of citizens that may wish to effect an alteration to a specific constitutional norm or a law can be the source of legislation.

Required referendums are mostly used for constitutional amendments since they refer to the most significant issues concerning the existence of the state and the nation. But international treaties can also belong to this type of referendum. In some states or at some second tiers of federal systems (regions; states; cantons; *Länder*), there are also specific laws and other public issues that can only be altered by a popular vote. Furthermore, a required referendum can be held if a legislative resolution has not been approved by the required qualified parliamentary majority.[27]

Within an automatic mechanism, it is essential to note what central role is automatically given to the citizens. As the authors SIMON HUG and GEORGE TSEBELIS state correctly, the possibility of a [required] referendum enables the citizens to become a veto player and thus to have the final say in decision-making.[28] According to GEORGE TSEBELIS, veto players are individual or collective actors whose agreement is required for a change in the legislative status quo.[29] Depending on the model of the political system, the number of veto players (presidential or parliamentary regimes, uni-cameral or bi-cameral parliament with equal competencies, parties, citizens, and federalism) can vary. The possibility of a referendum introduces the people as an additional veto player into the decision-making process. As the number of these actors and the ideological gaps between them increase, a significant change in the status quo becomes more difficult to achieve and policy stability increases. Mandatory referendums thus have a delaying effect

---

26 See, MÜLLER/UHLMANN, p. 73, n. 102.

27 For example in some Swiss cantons such as the Canton of Aargau, art. 62 par. 1 lit. b, Constitution of Canton of Aargau of 25 June 1980 (Cst-AG) and Canton of Solothurn, art. 35 par. 1 lit. d, Constitution of Canton of Solothurn of 8 June 1986 (Cst-SO).

28 HUG/TSEBELIS, p. 479; KAISER speaks here of legislatorial veto points, see KAISER, Types, p. 436.

29 TSEBELIS, Decision Making, p. 289; TSEBELIS, *Veto Players*, p. 17f.

by postponing the final say from the parliamentary to the popular stage. And depending on the popular decision, such a referendum can either be confirmatory or refusing.

Required referendums automatically add the hurdle of popular support. With other direct democratic mechanisms (referendums from above or citizen-initiated referendums), the formation of the popular veto player is optional and, depending on the criterion of a referendum, the nature of the popular veto player can vary. As HUG/TSEBELIS state, a veto-player may only trigger a referendum on a proposal that was framed by another actor, such as parliament. Another option is that a referendum is framed and triggered by the same veto player. If he or she *controls* both: asking the question of the popular vote and triggering the process of the referendum, he or she would become the one actor who individually determines the outcome, because others would lose their ability to veto it.[30] However, this actor would still have to make every effort (e.g. campaigning) to ensure that the majority of the deciding body is convinced of his/her position. And he or she would also have to consider that within a legal framework, there may be some additional specific rules and provisions that could restrict his or her power.

b) *Referendums from above*

The second type of direct democratic mechanism includes referendums that are derived from the *top down*. Top-down referendums refer to 'plebiscites' to 'authorities' referendums' respectively.[31] In contrast to a required referendum, they are optional. That is to say, they depend on the will of the authorities in power (executives or legislators) who are in full control of both the formulation of the question (adoption, alteration, repeal) and the triggering of the referendum. The citizens are being included into the law-making procedure only at the end of the whole legislative process. Therefore, the authorities' referendum represents a right of the authorities rather than the people.

Generally, it is the parliament or a part of the parliament that both frames the proposal and triggers the referendum. Parliamentary-initiated referendums can be divided into such plebiscites that are either triggered by a majority[32] or

30 HUG/TSEBELIS, pp. 466f., 477–487.

31 Here, the term authority does not only refer to governments or administration; it also includes the parliament as a legislative body, SCHMID, Unbekannte, p. 130.

32 The so-called extraordinary referendums [ausserordentliches Referendum] in some Swiss Cantons, such as Basel-City, Glarus, Graubünden, Jura, Schaffhausen, Solothurn,

minority[33] of the parliament's members.[34] The latter is more democratic, since it gives parliamentary minorities the opportunity to bring the issue to be decided at the popular stage. Asking for and triggering a top-down referendum can also be carried out by two different actors of the political establishment: the president and parliament. In a few cases, a public authority can also trigger a referendum in combination with signature collection by the people (joint action with citizens).

Independently of the actor that is responsible for triggering of the authorities' referendum, the referendum can refer either to a resolution that was enacted by parliament itself or to any matter falling within the jurisdiction of parliament, which has been chosen by the triggering actor himself.[35]

For some scholars, it is disputable how far a plebiscite can be part of the realm of direct democracy. According to Bruno Kaufmann and M. Dane Waters, 'plebiscites have nothing to do with referendums and initiatives; on the contrary, they are often used by governments who want to get a special legitimacy on their policies by bypassing laws and constitutional rules'[36], or to avoid the consequences of political responsibility, which may result from the adoption of a sensitive issue. Thus, plebiscites would have a greater legitimising than democratizing effect, as they do not empower the citizens. The authors' reservation

---

Thurgau and Uri, have a rather plebiscitary character because they are triggered by parliamentary majorities. Here, the parliamentary majority triggers ad hoc a referendum on its own decree that is otherwise not subject to a referendum and submits the parliamentary draft directly to popular vote (extraordinary mandatory referendum). Alternatively, the parliament can allow citizens to trigger a referendum on a parliamentary proposal that was not subject to a referendum (extraordinary optional referendum).

33 For instance, in Canton of Zurich (Switzerland) one fourth of the members of parliament (45/180) are entitled to launch a referendum [Kantonsratsreferendum] on parliamentary decrees that are subject to facultative referendums, if they so wish, according to art. 33, par. 2, lit. c of the Constitution of Canton of Zurich of 27 February 2005 (Cst-ZH). In other Cantons, such as the Canton of Zug, not less than one-third of the members of parliament can trigger a referendum [Behördenreferendum] on a decree that has been passed by the parliamentary majority ante, according to Art. 34, par. 4 of the Constitution of Canton of Zug of 31 January 1894 (Cst-ZG). Another six cantons that also have such an instrument are the Cantons of Aargau, Thurgau, St. Gallen, Fribourg, Appenzell-Ausserrhoden and Obwalden.

34 Schmid, Unbekannte, p. 127f.

35 Marxer, Wir sind das Volk, p. 16; Schmid, Unbekannte, pp. 130f., 135–141.

36 Kaufmann/Waters, p. XIX; see also Kaufmann/Büchi/Braun, p. 91.

towards plebiscites stems from instances in which plebiscites are used within a political regime with authoritarian tendencies and the constitution contains such provisions that empower a single (executive) state authority, such as the president, to formulate any proposal and at the same time to trigger a referendum on it. In such cases, he would clearly bypass the parliament, which is in fact the legislative authority. In countries with a weak civil society, ambiguous separation of powers and missing principles of the rule of law, plebiscites would open a Pandora's box. The consequences are clear; such situations lead to abuses of power and are far removed from anything resembling popular sovereignty.[37]

In consolidated democratic countries with well-framed systems of checks and balances, it may still be advisable to consider authorities' referendums as part of direct democratic mechanisms, especially if a resolution is drafted and submitted by two different authorities.[38] First of all, citizens are involved in challenging the legislative status quo, and depending on the issue, they may prefer another outcome than that of the actor who triggers the referendum – there is no guarantee that voters follow the state authority that launches the popular vote. There might also be specific constraints on the authority itself (e.g. a negative outcome could lead to a premature ending of a term) that limit the actor's ability to trigger a referendum. In addition, as mentioned above, plebiscites that are triggered by parliamentary minorities have another meaning, given that they are submitted to popular vote by the majority of the parliament or the president. Referendums from parliamentary minorities reveal an oppositional character. They rather serve to resolve disagreements within the parliament by a popular decision than to legitimize a critical parliamentary decree.[39] Therefore, it is essential to distinguish between who exactly formulates the question and who triggers the process of a referendum.

Considering these aspects, it is advisable to include plebiscitary referendums in direct democratic systems. Within the context of this work, understanding the function of plebiscites is particularly important in achieving this book's aim, as it enables us to make an adequate comparison of direct democratic mechanisms and instruments in the Baltic states.

---

37 For example, consider the former Soviet republics of Belarus, Kazakhstan and Azerbaijan, where referendums have been used to prolong or augment presidential powers.

38 Similar Marxer, *Wir sind das Volk*, p. 16.

39 See Schmid, Unbekannte, p. 151.

c) *Citizen-initiated referendums*

The third direct democratic mechanism refers to referendums that are derived from the bottom up. One can distinguish between two main types of *citizen-initiated referendums*: the 'citizens' facultative referendum'[40] and the 'citizens' initiative'. Both institutions are triggered by the people and thus require a collection of a certain number of signatures from the electorate. And both instruments work as oppositional tools of the people. However, the main difference between them is caused by the responsibility of drafting legislation. In addition, citizens' facultative referendums and citizens' initiatives have different functions: facultative referendums are reactive and they serve to maintain policy stability; whereas citizens' initiatives are proactive, as they seek to change the status quo. Aside these two instruments, the 'recall' and so-called 'agenda initiative' are also popular rights. However, as we will see, they have other functions than the ordinary direct democratic instruments.

(a) Citizens' facultative referendum

The citizens' facultative referendum is a direct democratic instrument enabling a certain number of citizens to call – by a formal demand – a popular vote on a constitutional provision or a law which has been *adopted, altered or repealed* (i.e. framing of the question) by the parliament. To avoid misunderstandings, within this conceptualisation the term 'facultative' or 'optional' has nothing to do with a 'consultative' or 'advisory' referendum. In contrast to the terms consultative and advisory, the terms facultative and optional do not refer to the result of the referendum. They are rather applied to the mechanism that triggers the referendum. The adoption of such referendums is as legally binding as the result of mandatory referendums. That is to say, such referendums also create decisive popular decisions that come into force.

Accordingly, a citizens' facultative referendum can be understood as a popular veto that is occasionally used by a group of the electorate to sustain the status quo by breaking the policy change effectuated by the representative body. In addition to constitutional or legal provisions, other parliamentary decisions and public issues such as public finances or international treaties can also be subject to a popular veto. It is a reactive popular instrument that allows latent veto players

40 To avoid confusion, I use this terminology because facultative referendums can also emanate from a state representative body, such as parliament, government or the president. In such cases, we speak of optional plebiscites.

such as the people to veto a resolution of the parliament in order to force a return to the status quo ante.

Aside from the immediate direct effects that citizens' facultative referendums manifest in ballots (possible rejection of parliamentary resolutions), in the long term they should also have indirect effects on the entire system. At least in Switzerland, facultative referendums on laws have lead to an integration of different groups from outside parliament into legislation. To avoid those groups with particular interests vetoing a parliamentary draft at the end of the legislative process, they are consulted at the beginning of the process (Vernehmlassungsverfahren).[41] Accordingly – at least in Swiss case – we can state that facultative referendums have an 'immunization' function. In fact, it is an 'immunization' in two respects: First, in the sense that the draft law is able to weather the threat of referendum triggering by groups that are potentially (negatively) affected by the specific law and second, an immunization in the sense of drafting qualitatively better laws. If there is any consultation procedure wherein associations and interest groups can state their position and submit improvement proposals to the draft, it is, as a consequence, expected that those laws are being put better into practice. The immunization effect can be empirically supported by the fact that in Switzerland for instance, of all laws that were passed by parliament only around seven percent were submitted to a national referendum[42] and from 1874 to 2014 less than half (44%) of all submitted draft laws (100% = 176 resolutions for which a referendum was called) were rejected by the people. In other words, the facultative referendum causes decisions that are both broadly supported and balanced so that only a little more than three percent of all enacted laws fail to enter into force. However, it is worth mentioning that further power-sharing institutions such as a two-chamber parliament with equal competences, federalism, proportional representation as well as broad coalitions are key contributing factors to this low quota and thus to wider integration of potential groups from outside parliament.

Within the procedure of citizens' facultative referendums, authorities maintain responsibility for the formulation of the referendum question (which is the parliamentary resolution on a law or other public issue) while triggering the referendum remains a matter for citizens. Therefore, the facultative referendum causes nothing more than switch the actor responsible for final decision-making

---

41 See Linder, Schweizerische Demokratie, p. 268; Vatter, Politisches System, p. 358; Kriesi/Bernhard, Referendumsdemokratie, p. 5f.; Neidhart, Plebiszit.

42 Kriesi/Bernhard, Referendumsdemokratie, p. 7f.

on a public issue from the parliament to the people. On the ballot, the outcome is either confirmed or rejected.

In the sense of substantive law, adoption by means of the referendum implies that the majority of the citizens who participated in the ballot give their consent to parliament's resolution regarding the adoption, alteration or repeal of the specific law. It is a final signal to go ahead on a policy change launched by the parliament. A negative outcome of the ballot, in contrast, is a popular confirmation for the proponents who had triggered the citizens' facultative referendum in bringing a final decision on the issue to the popular arena. Such a result is a final answer in favour of the proponent's preferred status quo and a rejection of parliament's proposed policy, which will thereby not come into force. Nevertheless, some confusing results can appear if the referendum question put on the ballot is formulated or phrased in a confusing or ambiguous manner. Therefore, to avoid such results, the question, regardless of the issue the referendum addresses, must be formulated in official yet comprehensible language so that it is understandable to every voter.

(b) Citizens' initiatives

The second instrument of the bottom-up mechanism refers to the *citizens' initiative*. It is a political right that enables a certain number of citizens to submit a proposal for an alteration of the legal norms and principles, which are within the jurisdiction of parliament. By contrast to citizens' facultative referendums, full control of the popular vote with regard to its framing and triggering properties is gained through this direct democratic institution. It is a proactive instrument that allows for a certain number of the electorate to both put their own draft on the political agenda (framing the question) and to submit it to a referendum (triggering). Citizens' initiatives can generally be distinguished between *citizens' constitutional initiatives* and *citizens' legislative initiatives.* However, as in the Baltic states, it is also possible to hold citizens' initiatives on other public issues. Initiatives can either be submitted as an elaborated draft or a general suggestion. They both aim to alter the status quo by adopting a new law, or by amending or repealing existing ones. With regard to the direction of impact, it formally effects a change of legal settings; this change, however, can also materially intend to preserve the status quo.

Theoretically, a citizens' initiative should enable certain minorities to push forward a specific issue that the authorities might otherwise not raise themselves. Since the citizens' initiative is framed and triggered exclusively by the people, it should in turn cancel out the remaining veto players in the legislative arena.[43] As

43 See also HUG/TSEBELIS, p. 489.

such, the people do not only define the content independently from parliament but also the time when the issue will be submitted to a popular decision. This is one of the reasons why the citizens' initiative has also been called the radical institution of direct democracy.[44] Nevertheless, it is not unusual that this radical institution is applied more frequently by organized interest groups or elites than by the citizens themselves.

(c) Recall

In addition to the citizens' facultative referendum and the citizens' initiative, there is a third institution, namely the *recall,* which can be included in the group of referendums 'from below'. However, it must be noted that direct democracy makes decisions about substantive issues and not about people or public bodies. The right of recall is a popular right to dissolve the parliament or to recall another state authority before the end of their term in office. It is important to note that such an institution must thus also be triggered by the people by gathering an appropriate number of popular signatures.[45] The outcome of a recall is more than an adoption, alteration or repeal of a certain issue; it is aimed at single authorities or whole public bodies and has larger consequences for the political establishment.[46]

(d) Agenda initiative

Further bottom-up instruments such as the 'citizens' agenda initiative' or the 'collective addresses' are excluded from the third mechanism of direct democracy. They are indeed popular rights, but not necessarily direct democratic ones. Agenda initiatives or collective addresses permit a group of citizens to force the parliament to consider a proposed action or a bill. As a petition, however, they have no legally binding force to oblige the parliament to adopt the proposal or cause it to be submitted to a popular vote. At least their application can be useful in promoting collective learning and trust in participatory democracy.

2. The character of referendums

In addition to the three main mechanisms that have been classified according to their initiators, further attention must be paid to the legal *character* of referendums.

---

44 Hangartner/Kley, p. 156f.
45 See also Serdült/Welp, p. 71.
46 Altman, p. 16.

The outcome of a popular vote can either be consultative or binding.[47] Binding decisions are final and mandatory for all state authorities. The appropriate state body is legally compelled to implement the passed proposal. By contrast, nonbinding referendums do not have any legal consequences, even if the majority of the voters has approved them. Such decisions are indeed 'non-decisions' since they create an uncertain and unfair democratic procedure.[48] Advisory referendums put some political pressure on authorities. Nevertheless, the final word on the approval of public issues still depends on the volition of the parliament. In order to limit the power of such state organs, binding decisions on referendums are absolutely necessary within a direct democratic system.

A distinction between binding and nonbinding referendums is also of great significance in the application of the veto-player approach, which has been integrated into the classification of referendum mechanisms. It should be noted that there is no additional veto player as long as referendums are consultative – even if the referendum has been framed and triggered by the same political actor.

Regardless of whether a referendum is binding or not, to avoid disruptive consequences, popular votes face an important hurdle: the constitutionality check. In general, referendums must be in accordance with the constitution of the country. Depending on the country, international treaties of preeminent importance may also apply. Constitutional courts are therefore permitted to assess the compatibility of submitted drafts with the norms of higher legal forces. However, in some countries such as Switzerland, the legal assessment of referendums is carried out by the parliament. Another aspect that one may also take into account is the timing of a compatibility check. In some countries, referendums are submitted to the court or to the parliament before the ballot in order to be allowed to proceed. In other instances, such as the U.S. state of California, a judicial review can also be implemented after the approval of a referendum.[49] This may also occur in Swiss cantons if the cantonal parliament declares an initiative admissible, despite its doubtful content, and the initiative is appealed against before the cantonal or federal court after it passes and is effectuated.

---

47 ALTMAN, p. 8.

48 KAUFMANN, Monitor, p. 23.

49 California permits pre-election judicial review of the constitutionality of the substance of an initiative only in specific and limited circumstances. A review is permissible if the initiative is both facially and patently unconstitutional. Judicial review of an initiative for compliance with content and subject matter restrictions is also regularly conducted after elections in California (despite the option of conducting these beforehand); see NOYES, *Law of Direct Democracy*, p. 146, 150.

3. The intention of referendums

It is also important to pay attention to the third criterion of referendums, namely their intention, which can either be proactive or reactive. Proactive referendums are used to alter the status quo by submitting a new idea to a popular vote. In contrast, reactive referendums aim to sustain policy stability.[50] A mandatory referendum can either be proactive or reactive depending on the citizens' decision. At first, such a tool has a delaying effect of the legislation. There are two types of reactive referendums. The first type refers to facultative referendums, as described above. Facultative referendums can be requested by a group of citizens or by another representative body as a reaction to a policy change introduced by the governing majority. It is a democratic tool to veto a parliamentary resolution in favour of the status quo. The second reactive referendum is related to *counter-proposals*, which are very common in Switzerland.

A counter-proposal is a reaction of the establishment to an alteration of the status quo initiated by the citizens. However, in some cases counter-proposals can also originate from a given number of citizens as a response to a parliamentary decree, which is subject to the facultative referendum.[51] Indeed, a counter-proposal must be seen as an alternative rather than an opposite vote on a referendum. It aims to alter the status quo too, but in a different and generally less radical way than the original initiative. For the decision, a counter-proposal is presented together with the citizens' initiative (or with a parliamentary decree that is subject to the facultative referendum), and the electorate has a choice between the original initiative, counter-proposal or both proposals. In such cases, a tiebreaking question is used to determine which version should be implemented, should both proposals be approved. Accordingly, voters have to decide either in favour of the initiative or in favour of the counter-proposal.

It is important to note that the possibility of a counter-proposal is a clear sign of the existence of an indirect initiative procedure in which the parliament and proponents of the citizens' initiative interact together. At this procedural stage, a link between direct and representative democracy is established, which is indeed to be welcomed since direct democracy can better realise its full potential.[52] In such a procedure, the parliament and the government are obliged to debate the citizens' initiatives before they are placed on the ballot. The parliament is free to

---

50 Altman, p. 8, 14.

51 The so called 'Volksvorschlag' in Canton of Bern, see art. 63 par. 3, Constitution of Canton of Bern of 6 June 1993 (Cst-BE).

52 Rohner, pp. 249–257.

accept or to refuse a citizens' proposal. In case of a rejection, the initiative must be submitted to the popular vote. And in case of parliamentary approval of a popular proposal, there is no popular vote on the citizens' initiative unless the popular proposal is subject to required referendums, for which a popular vote is then mandatory.

Another effect that an indirect initiative procedure is that it may result in a withdrawal of the citizens' initiative. Depending on the formal institutionalisation of citizen-initiated referendums (e.g. the existence of a withdrawal clause), the parliament may propose a counter-proposal and that may lead the proponents of the initiative to withdraw their proposal due to the partial fulfilment of their demand by the legislature. And even if a counter-proposal by the authorities does not cause a withdrawal of the citizens' initiative by the initiative committee, voters can still choose between at least three substantive options: citizens' initiative, counter-proposal or tie-break question in support of one of these two options.

In contrast to the indirect procedure described, with a direct initiative procedure, the citizens' initiative bypasses the legislature and is placed directly on a ballot; there is no mutual give and take between the parliament and citizens.[53]

4. The normative level of referendums

Referendums refer to the jurisdiction of parliament. This means an issue can only be subject to a popular vote if it is within the remit of the parliament. Regardless of the initiator of a single mechanism, the issue of a referendum can affect an amendment of constitutional or statutory (law) provisions. Furthermore, parliamentary decisions (decrees) and questions on the budget or public credits may also be the object of a referendum. In addition to these referendums that concern substantive issues, popular votes are also used for recalls in some countries, in which an official elected public body (or official) can be removed from office before the end of their term.

C. Constraints on mechanism of direct democracy

From these theoretical explanations, we can see that the current model of direct democracy is a complementary set of legislative processes on public issues that enables citizens to make political decisions in conjunction with (plebiscites, authorities' referendums, mandatory referendums), against (citizens' facultative

53 See also: KAUFMANN/BÜCHI/BRAUN, p. 232, 233, 234, 237; KAUFMANN, Monitor, p. 28.

referendums) or without their elected representatives (citizens' initiative). It can be argued that the more citizens are able to control a referendum mechanism (asking and triggering) and the more binding its result, the greater the popular sovereignty can be realised in a democracy.

Which different mechanisms of direct democracy a country has, if any, depends on its constitutional arrangements (rules in form). How some of these tools are used (rules in use) results from the strategic context in which political actors act. The effect of referendums differs not only according to their initiator, character, intention, normative level and controlling features, but also according to their further precise formal arrangements. Some procedural provisions can affect the implementation so strongly that even a veto player (mainly the citizenry, by citizens' initiative) who is in full control of the referendum (asking/triggering) loses the ability to veto the legislative outcome even before it is possible to cancel out the other veto players from the political game. In other words, procedural details can create an additional institutional framework in which a veto player's nature of full control becomes superfluous. It is therefore important to note that within a single type of mechanism of direct democracy, further procedural differences and formal hurdles with significant consequences can exist. To borrow DAVID ALTMAN's words, the devil is in the institutional detail.[54] Any detailed institutional provision, such as restrictions on turnout and approval, time limits, signature collection, specific rules for consideration of a referendum or even on the exclusion of some policy areas from being subject of a popular vote, might be further factors that diminish the potential for policy change. The more formal restrictions there are within a direct democratic mechanism, the more referendums are ruled out and the greater the constraints on popular sovereignty.

It can therefore be assumed that any additional obstacle to direct democratic procedure leads to disappointment and, consequently, to a lack of interest in direct democracy among the people. In some countries, obstacles such as quorums, for instance, are established to foster both participation and legitimacy of the vote. However, they are more counterproductive than conducive to referendums and to direct democracy as a whole. For the opponents of a referendum, quorums create an incentive to not participate in the corresponding ballot in order to void the outcome. By avoiding the referendum, the counterparty also evades the political discourse, which is indeed essential for a participatory culture in a democracy. Within a direct democratic system, it is crucial that not only the result of the referendum but the whole procedure are legitimate because a legitimate procedure

54 ALTMAN, p. 18.

that allows every single eligible citizen to be part of direct legislation automatically generates legitimate outcomes.

Thus, in the following chapters, I not only consider the mechanisms of direct democracy in the Baltic states according to their initiator, character, intention, normative level and controlling features but also according to further precise formal requirements that may diminish the people's will. Tables (*Table 1 for Estonia, Table 2 for Latvia and Table 3 for Lithuania*) have been created to outline all current direct democratic institutional arrangements for each of the Baltic states. Each table presents a structured overview of both the formal rules and the use of direct democracy since the beginning of 1990s (last column of tables 1–3).

III. The legal framework and practice of direct democracy in Estonia

A. Direct democratic instruments in Estonia

Direct democracy is not new in Estonia. At the national level, the right of referendums and even of citizens' initiatives were already provided for in the 1920 constitution, but in 1935, the interim president Konstantin Päts abolished these provisions from the constitution, leaving only the provision of the presidential plebiscite.[55] At the end of the 1980s, as disengagement from the Soviet Union was underway, Estonian direct democracy underwent a revival. The implementation Act of the 1992 Constitution also contained provisions for quasi-citizen-initiated referendums, but only for a limited time of three years.[56] The wave of transition was not strong enough to maintain it beyond this period.

Today, it is true that the current constitution requires the supreme power to be exercised by citizens with the right to vote by electing the Estonian Parliament [Riigikogu] and through referendum.[57] However, a referendum as it has been framed in the new constitution can only be activated automatically or top down (see *Table 1*).[58] The constitution still does not provide for referendums initiated by citizens. The people (around 903,000 enfranchised citizens[59]) are introduced into the decision-making process as an additional veto player as long as there are parliamentary plebiscites or referendums that are required by the constitution.

How and according to which procedure such referendums have to be held is provided by the Estonian Referendum Act (ERA) that entered into force on 6 April 2002.[60] This law itself may be passed and amended only by a majority of the members of the Riigikogu.[61] Lastly, it was amended on 17 October 2012.

---

55 Ruus in Kaufmann/Waters, p. 54; Komáromi, Volkswille, p. 452f.

56 Art. 8, par. 2, Law on the Application of the Constitution of 28 June 1992 (LAC); Mikkel/Pridham, p. 728.

57 Art. 56, par. 1 and 2 of the Constitution of Republic of Estonia of 3 July 1992 (CE).

58 See also Ruus, Estonia, p. 48f.

59 See http://www.vvk.ee/voting-methods-in-estonia/engindex/statistics (accessed on 05.06.2014).

60 See art. 106, sec. 2 CE.

61 Art. 104 CE.

The management of the administration of direct democracy mechanisms is conducted by the National Electoral Committee (NEC).[62]

Before we consider the particular referendum mechanisms, it should be noted that Estonia is a unicameral parliamentary system with 101 representatives, elected according to the principle of proportional representation.[63] The president of the state is elected by the parliament or under specific cases by the electoral college, which consists of members of the parliament and representatives of local authority councils.[64] The president has a ceremonial role and the executive power is instead vested in the government of the republic.[65] As in the other two Baltic states, Estonia has fairly weak presidential institutions, however, as DUVOLD in his research on Baltic democracy illustrates, many Baltic citizens still express a certain degree of support for elitist rule – at the expense of participatory democracy. According to his survey results, the idea of strong and efficient executive power in the hand of one leader still enjoys strong support across the Baltic countries. This might be explained both by the performance of parliamentary regime and even by the communist legacy. As DUVOLD shows, people who are satisfied with the way democracy works also tend to trust and support its institutions.[66] Even if there is still significant support for presidential system among the citizens in the Baltic states, it is not compatible with the demographic constellation of all three republics. As AREND LIJPHART also acknowledges, a presidential system is characteristic of majoritarian democracies consisting of homogenous societies. It concentrates the executive power in one authority. Such a majority rule for Baltic states with multi-ethnic entities (e.g. Russian-speaking minorities) is less advisable since it does not cause power sharing. Instead, it denies access to (executive) power for minorities. And as long as some groups are continually excluded, they may lose their allegiance to the regime and cause conflicts within their society.[67]

---

62 Art. 12, par. 1, sec. 1 Estonian Referendum Act of 6 April, 2002 (ERA).

63 Art. 60, par. 1 CE.

64 Art. 79 CE.

65 Art. 86 CE.

66 DUVOLD, Making Sense, p. 151f., 166, 177, 182, 257; for Lithuania in particular see EWERT, Potentiale, p. 71f; see also KNEUER, Transformationsstaaten, p. 90.

67 LIJPHART, Patterns, pp. 31–33, 93f.

1. Referendums required by the constitution

a) The mandatory constitutional referendum

According to article 162 of the constitution of Estonia (CE), any change of provisions of chapter I (Art. 1–7) 'General Provisions', which establish the legal basis of Estonia as a democratic independent state, and any amendment of provisions of chapter XV (Art. 161–168) 'Amendment of the Constitution' of the constitution require a mandatory referendum. This means that the Riigikogu is automatically obliged to submit such modifications to a popular vote. Indeed, the automatic referendum introduces voters into the decision-making process as one additional veto player. However, it does not authorise them to ask the question nor does it enable them to trigger the referendum. It is a popular right with delaying effect. Depending on the people's decision it can either change or maintain the status quo at the highest normative level.

The range of automatic referendums in Estonia that are open to a direct democratic process, is relatively narrow; only a few constitutional provisions have to be submitted to popular vote. There are no further procedural restrictions that constrain the sovereignty of the people. No specific threshold is needed for the participation, and in order to be passed, the referendum proposal has to be supported by a majority (over 50 percent) of those who vote.[68] The decision of the citizenry is binding for all public bodies and can later only be amended by a referendum.[69] In the case of a negative outcome, the corresponding issue cannot be re-initiated within one year after its rejection.[70]

2. Referendums from above

In addition to the mandatory referendum that is needed to amend chapters I and XV of the constitution, there is also a top-down direct democratic mechanism in Estonia, namely parliamentary *plebiscites* for draft acts to amend the constitution, other draft acts and other national issues.[71] As article 105, sec. 1 CE states, the parliament is entitled to submit a bill or other issue of national importance to a referendum.[72] Following this wording, the referendum can either be proactive

68 See art. 2, par. 1 ERA.
69 Art. 4 ERA; Art. 162 CE.
70 Art. 168 CE.
71 See art. 1, par. 1 second sentence ERA.
72 See also art. 65, par. 2 CE; Liivik, Legitimacy, p. 89; Lagerspetz/Maier, Estland, p. 95.

(to allow a policy change) or reactive (to keep the status quo).[73] In conjunction with article 65, par. 2 CE, the authority to triggering a referendum lies exclusively with the parliament. That means it is up to the Riigikogu to decide whether to hold a referendum or not.[74] This option for a top-down referendum becomes clearer when we consider article 163 CE. Due to this provision, the constitutional chapters (excluding chapter I and XV[75]) shall either be amended by an act that has been passed by a referendum or by two successive sessions of the parliament. For such plebiscites, the parliament is the one public authority that is also enabled to frame the proposal and to put it forward for the people to vote. One exception to this rule is the right of the president. According to the constitution, the right to initiate (in the sense of asking for) a constitutional amendment is also vested in the president.[76]

Despite the possibility of holding parliamentary plebiscites over these issues, there are still some restrictions on the range of its objects: 'Issues regarding the budget, taxation, financial obligations of the state, ratification or termination of international treaties, the declaration or termination of a state of emergency, or national defence' as declared under article 106 CE shall not be submitted to a referendum.[77]

For the approval of parliamentary plebiscites, formally there is no minimum participation requirement necessary.[78] A law that passes by a majority must promptly be proclaimed by the president of the republic. The decision of the referendum is binding for all state institutions.[79]

a) *The parliamentary constitutional plebiscite*

The parliamentary constitutional plebiscite is an instrument to amend the constitution by popular vote in regular cases. According to article 161, section 1 CE, initiating constitutional amendments rests with not less than one-fifth of the membership of the Riigikogu and with the president of the republic.[80] One should be aware that initiating a constitutional draft act does not necessarily

---

73 See also art. 128, par. 2, sec. 1 and 2 of the Riigikogu Rules of Procedures and Internal Rules Act of 11 February, 2003 (RRPIRA).

74 Art. 6, par. 1 ERA.

75 See Hoffmann, Baltikum, p. 311.

76 Art. 161, sec. 1 CE.

77 See art. 1, par. 1 and 2 ERA.

78 See also Mikkel/Pridham, p. 728.

79 Art. 105, sec. 2–3 CE, see also art. 2, par. 1 and Art. 4 ERA.

80 See also art. 78, par. 8 CE, art. 103, par. 5 CE and art. 122, par. 1 RRPIRA.

mean submitting it at the same time to a referendum. The triggering can automatically happen if such an initiated draft act is subject to the 'General Provisions' and to the chapter on the 'Amendment of the Constitution'.[81] Otherwise three-fifths of the parliamentary votes are necessary to submit the proposal to amend the constitution to a referendum.[82] A popular vote can be held no earlier than three months after the passage of a resolution to this effect by the Riigikogu.[83] The constitutional proposal that is subject to the plebiscite must be adopted by a majority of voters. An amendment to the constitution regarding the same issue that has been rejected by the parliament or by a referendum may not be re-launched within one year.[84]

As stated, constitutional amendments can also requested by the president. However, he or she is not entitled to submit the proposal to a referendum. For the triggering, he/she needs the cooperation of the parliament. This division in controlling the parliamentary constitutional plebiscite is an essential characteristic of a system of checks and balances. The mutual control exists even within the parliamentary constitutional plebiscite mechanism since the framing and triggering require two different quotas of members of parliament.

b) *The parliamentary plebiscite for other draft acts and national issues*

Except for constitutional plebiscites, the Riigikogu can also submit other draft acts or national issues to a referendum, as indicated previously.[85] Initiating a referendum in order to pass a draft act or to decide on other national issues rests with members, factions and committees of the parliament.[86] In addition to the parliamentary organs, the government of the republic is also entitled to initiate laws.[87] In order to submit a draft act for laws or other national issues to a referendum, a majority of the votes of the members of the parliament in favour is required.[88] As in the case of parliamentary constitutional plebiscites, there is no unique political actor who has full control over the referendum procedure. Asking and triggering are performed by two different parliamentary groups.

81 See art. 162 CE.
82 See art. 164 CE.
83 Art. 164, second sentence CE.
84 Art. 168 CE.
85 Art. 105, sec. 1 CE.
86 Art. 128, par. 1, section 1–3 RRPIRA; see also art. 103, par. 1–3 CE.
87 Art. 103, par. 4 CE.
88 Art. 129, par. 7 and art. 130, par. 2 RRPIRA.

A plebiscite for draft acts and other national issues has to be supported by the majority of the participants in the vote.[89] However, there is a confusing provision for a referendum on draft acts. The fourth section of the article 105 CE establishes that 'if a bill which is submitted to a referendum does not receive a majority of votes in favour, the president of the republic shall declare extraordinary elections to the Riigikogu'.[90] This means that in case of a negative outcome, the entire parliament has to be dissolved and new elections must be set. Such a provision does not exist for referendums on other national issues.[91]

As Liivik and many Estonian scholars correctly note, section four of article 105 CE curbs the parliament's enthusiasm and leads to its hesitation to put any draft acts to a referendum.[92] For a parliamentary member, it is risky to support a triggering of a plebiscite since he or she does not know if the people will approve the issue on the ballot. Otherwise a rejection would cause the dissolution of the parliament and set new elections. There is then no guarantee that the parliamentary members will be elected again. Given such uncertainty, a deputy would seldom dare to put an issue to a popular decision of his own volition. Considering these possible consequences, it can be ascertained that the fourth section of article 105 CE makes the rest of article 105 CE superfluous.[93] It is also important to note that the fourth provision, which may precipitate pre-term elections, clearly goes far beyond any sense of direct democracy. Such weighty political consequences of a negative outcome of a single referendum do not appear to be appropriate, especially when it deals with an issue that is of lower importance in respect of its material content. Furthermore, it is to be expected that the consequences of the dissolution of parliament will outweigh those negative effects caused by the rejection of a single referendum.

3. Citizen-initiated referendums

a) Initiative rights in the Constitution of 1920

Citizen-initiated referendums were present in the Estonian constitution until September 1935.[94] In addition to mandatory referendums, articles 30, 31, 32 and 87 of the Constitution of 15 June 1920 (Basic Law of the Republic of Estonia)

---

89 Art. 105, sec. 2 CE.

90 See also art. 78, par. 3 CE and art. 64 ERA.

91 Liivik, Referendum, p. 26.

92 Liivik, Legitimacy, p. 89; Liivik, Referendum, p. 25.

93 See Liivik, Legitimacy, p. 89.

94 Liivik Referendum, p. 19.

also provided for three different bottom-up instruments (e.g. semi-plebiscite on repealing a passed law, popular legislative and constitutional initiative) for the Estonian people. But, until their abolition from the constitution by the interim president KONSTANTIN PÄTS in September 1935, they had seldom been applied in practice.[95] Between 1920 and 1935 there was one facultative referendum triggered by the joint action of the parliamentary minority and church-related circles (semi-plebiscite) to abrogate the law on the repealing of religious education in public schools that was previously passed by the majority in the State Assembly. The referendum of 19 February 1923 was supported by 72 percent of voters and accordingly, religious education remained as a voluntary subject of public schools. The next bottom-up referendum was not held until ten years later. The constitutional initiative of the *League* of *Veterans* providing a semi-presidential system with a parliament of only 50 deputies was adopted by the people on 16 October 1933 and the amendment came into force after its promulgation in the Official Gazette on 28 October 1933.[96]

After the adoption of the 1992 Constitution, the Implementation Act enabled 10,000 eligible citizens to initiate amendments to the constitution for a three-year period.[97] Within this period, one draft act on amending the constitution with two aims (fixing the retirement age and the popular election of the president) was proposed by Estonian citizens. However, the parliament rejected their proposal[98] since, legally, it was not obliged to submit it to a popular vote.[99]

Currently, there is no provision for citizen-initiated referendums in the constitution. Estonians do not possess the right to initiate their own proposals or to veto parliamentary decrees by gathering a certain number of signatures. They can only participate in either required or top down referendums. From this point of view, it can be argued that the Estonian people have limited authority in terms of direct democratic politics. Indeed, thanks to required referendums or possible parliamentary plebiscites, Estonians are introduced into the legislative procedure as one additional veto. However, this occurs only occasionally. The existing arrangement of direct democratic rules in the Republic of Estonia is not strong

95 RUUS in KAUFMANN/WATERS, p. 54; KOMÁROMI, Popular law-making, pp. 69–71, 73f.; KOMÁROMI, Volkswille, pp. 452–454.

96 KOMÁROMI, Popular law-making, pp. 71–73; see also c2d database, http://c2d.ch/detailed_display.php?lname=votes&table=votes&page=1&parent_id=&sublinkname=results&id=131061 (accessed on 20.06.2014).

97 Art. 8, par. 2 LAC.

98 LIIVIK, Legitimacy, p. 91.

99 Art. 8, par. 1 and 2 LAC.

enough for citizens to exercise supreme power, and hence Estonians continue to remain theoretical holders of political power.

Recently, several attempts have been made by different parts of the parliament to reintroduce citizen-initiated referendums, but all these attempts have been blocked by the governing parties or by lack of interest. The submitted draft of an amendment to the constitution sought to enable citizens to initiate a draft act or question for vote by gathering 25,000 signatures. An amendment to the constitution by popular initiative was not foreseen. As for parliamentary plebiscites for draft acts, some issues listed under article 106 CE would also have been excluded from the range of issues of a popular vote. However, after eight years, the parliamentary draft act on the introduction of citizens' initiative failed to be completed.[100]

b) The 'collective adresses to Riigikogu'

Currently there are no plans to introduce the possibility of citizen-initiated referendums. The only new development is the adoption of the 'collective addresses to Riigikogu', introduced in the 'Response to Memoranda and Request for Explanations and Submission of Collective Addresses Act' (CAA), which entered into force on 11 April 2014.[101] Art. 2 par. 3 defines a collective address as 'a proposal made by public initiative and submitted to the Riigikogu to amend the current regulation or improve the community life, the exercise of which is within the competence of the Riigikogu.' For such a collective address, at least 1000 signatures of support must be collected for submission.[102] The address can include proposals on how to amend the existing regulations or how to improve the community.[103] If the collective address has been duly submitted, the Board of the Riigikogu assigns it to a committee of the parliament, who is then obligated to discuss the address and form an opinion by either agreeing, disagreeing or partially agreeing with the proposal. This means the fate of the proposal depends on the opinion of the parliament. The new instrument is indeed a collective petition right and nothing more. It does not trigger a referendum, nor does it oblige the parliament to fulfil the will of the signatories.

---

100 Liivik, Legitimacy, p. 91ff.; Liivik, Learning, pp. 27, 32–34.

101 See https://www.riigiteataja.ee/en/eli/507042014003/consolide (accessed on 30.06.2014).

102 Art. 7^1, par. 1 CAA.

103 Art. 7^1, par. 2 CAA.

4. The legal assessment of referendums

In connection with direct democracy, there is a particular function that the judicial power has to adopt. The Supreme Court is able to repeal the resolution of the Riigikogu concerning submission of a draft act or other national issue to a referendum.[104] According to article 152 of the Estonian Constitution, 'the Supreme Court shall declare invalid any law or other legislation that is in conflict with the provisions and spirit of the Constitution'. Further, if the president of the republic refuses to proclaim a law passed by the parliament, he or she can return it together with a reasoned resolution to the Riigikogu for a new debate and decision, as is indicated in article 107 CE. If the parliament again passes the returned law unamended, the president shall then promulgate the law or apply to the Supreme Court for a declaration of unconstitutionality with respect to the law in question.

104 Art. 8, par. 1 sec. 1 ERA.

Table 1: Direct Democratic Institutions and their Use in Estonia (1991–2014)

Mechanism of Direct Democracy[7]	Name of DD Institution	Subject matter	Submitted due to	Character	Intention	Pol. Actor / Veto-Player[1]		Formal Restrictions for						Use
						Asking (Framing)	Triggering	Turnout	Approval	Signatures	Collection Time	Collection Place	Range of Issues	q / a / ai[2]
REQUIRED	Mandatory constitutional referendum	to alter the provisions of chapter I and XV of the constitution	law	binding	proactive / reactive	parliament	automatic	no	>50% of voters[3]	–	–	–	yes only for referred issues	1 / 1 / 0
TOP-DOWN	Parliamentary constitutional plebiscite	to amend the constitution in regular cases	parliament	binding	proactive / reactive	>1/5 of the parliament[9] or president	>3/5 of the parliament	no	>50% of voters[3]	–	–	–	yes[8]	3[6] / 2 / 0
	Parliamentary plebiscite for draft acts	to initiate a law	parliament	binding	proactive / reactive	parliamentary member, faction, committee, government	>1/2 of the parliament	no	>50% of voters[4]	–	–	–	yes[8]	0 / 0 / 0
	Parliamentary plebiscite for other national issues	to initiate a national issue	parliament	binding	proactive / reactive	parliamentary member, faction, committee	>1/2 of the parliament	no	>50% of voters	–	–	–	yes[8]	0 / 0 / 0

Mechanism of Direct Democracy[7]	Name of DD Institution	Subject matter	Submitted due to	Character	Intention	Pol. Actor / Veto-Player[1]		Formal Restrictions for						Use
						Asking (Framing)	Triggering	Turnout	Approval	Signatures	Collection Time	Collection Place	Range of Issues	q / a / ai[2]
 BOTTOM-UP[5]	–	–	–	–	–	–	–	–	–	–	–	–	–	–
Total Votes														4 / 3 / 0

Source: Author's characterisation

Remarks

1: The possibility of a referendum introduces the citizens as one additional veto player into the public legislative process. A veto player is an individual or collective actor whose agreement is needed for a change in the legislative status quo. If an existing or latent veto player controls both the framing of the proposal and the triggering of the referendum, other veto players lose their ability to veto outcomes, the number of veto players decreases and potential of policy change increases (Hug/Tsebelis, 2002).

2: q / a / ai = quantity of referendums / approved / approved but invalid due to precise formal restrictions.

3: In case of a negative outcome, the corresponding issue cannot be initiated within one year of its rejection.

4: If a bill submitted to referendum does not receive the majority of the votes in favour, the president shall declare extraordinary elections to the parliament. This legal provision is deemed a further formal restriction.

5: The implementation act of the 1992 constitution provided under art. 8, sec. 2 the right of a popular initiative for constitutional amendments for three years. But, the parliament was not obliged to submit it to a referendum.

6: One of them refers to the referendum on independence (1991).

7: Time limits: there are no referendums allowed during a state of emergency or a state of war. No referendums should be held when less than 90 days remain until parliamentary elections.

8: Issues according to art. 106 CE.

9: The Estonian unicameral parliament has 101 members (art. 60 CE).

B. Estonian direct democracy in practice

Estonia is a weak practitioner of direct democracy. From 1991 to 2014, four referendums have been held in Estonia (see *Table 1, last column* and *Figure 1*). After the approval of the new constitution, only one referendum was held. The other three referendums had been held previous to this. Of these four referendums, three succeeded in full, while one popular vote was rejected.

Figure 1: Referendums held in Estonia

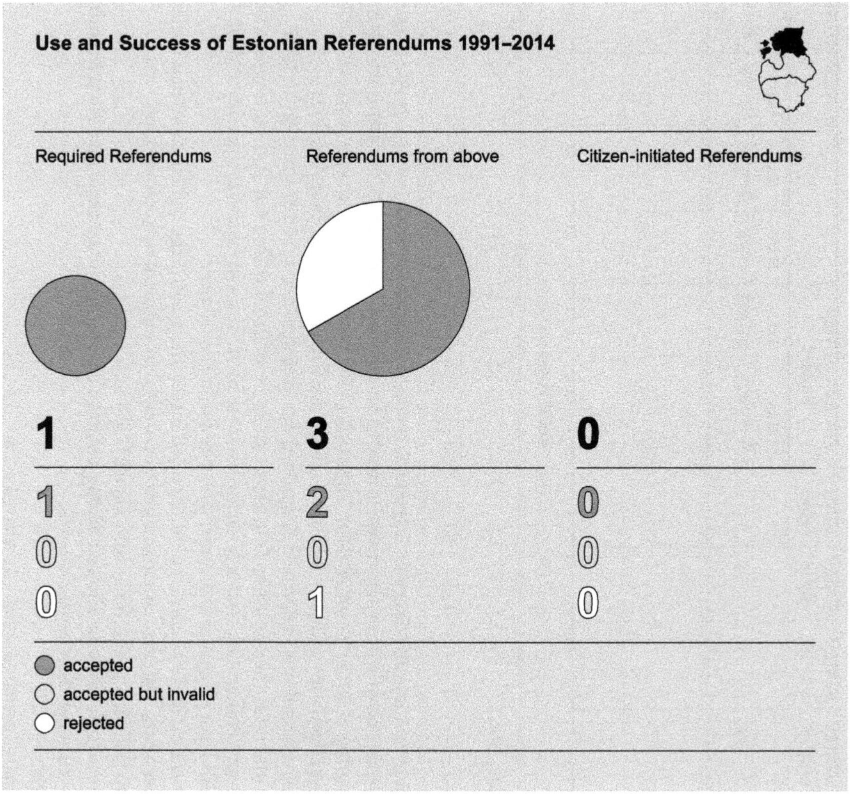

Source: Author's own calculations based on the data from www.c2d.ch and Estonian National Electoral Committee

The referendum on independence and two referendums concerning the constitutional draft during the transition period were parliamentary plebiscites that were framed and submitted to a vote by the parliament. By contrast, the EU accession referendum in 2003 was a mandatory constitutional referendum that had to be submitted automatically to a popular vote, as prescribed by article 162 CE.

The number of referendums that have been held in the last twenty years is obviously very limited and none of them were bottom-up initiated. Issues that the four referendums mainly dealt with refer to the organisation of the state, such as national identity, citizens' rights, and the political system or to foreign policy, namely, European integration. All four referendums are subject to constitutional norms. No proposal below the constitutional normative level has been submitted to a referendum, although according to article 105 CE, the parliament would have the right to put a bill to a popular vote.

1. The referendum of 3 March 1991 on Estonia's independence

The parliamentary plebiscite on independence that was held in a critical and volatile time showed that the Baltic states did not want to be a part of any new Soviet Union. In the beginning of the 1990s, MICHAEL GORBACHEV was increasingly squeezed between democrats, reformers, and independence-oriented republics on the one side and a sceptical and recalcitrant party and 'apparat' on the other side. To obtain the authority he needed to keep the Soviet Union intact, he turned to the public. GORBACHEV tried to exert pressure on the fifteen Soviet Republics[105] to sign a new 'Union Treaty' by holding a referendum on the preservation of the Union of Soviet Socialist Republics on 17 March 1991. However, the parliaments of the Baltic states, Georgia, Armenia and Moldavia boycotted the referendum that was intended to hold the Soviet Union together.[106] Estonia, Latvia, Lithuania, Georgia and Armenia went even further and held referendums on independence in their own way.[107] Moldavia refused to hold GORBACHEV's union referendum too, but, without holding an own referendum on independence.[108] Four other republics took the more moderate but still disruptive step of either changing the question of GORBACHEV's union referendum or adding questions of their own.[109]

---

105 Estonia, Latvia, Lithuania, Georgia, Armenia, Moldavia, Kazakhstan, Kirghizia, Uzbekistan, Ukraine, Russia, Azerbaijan, Belorussia, Tadjikistan and Turkmenistan.

106 However, the regions of Abkhazia and South Ossetia in Georgia, as well as the regions of Transnistria and Gagauzia in Moldova, participated.

107 RUUS, Estonia, p. 51; RUUS in KAUFMANN/WATERS, p. 56; see also BRADY/KAPLAN, p. 186–201.

108 The Referendum Scorecard, The Economist [London, England], 23 March 1991, p. 62.

109 BRADY/KAPLAN, p. 187f.

In Estonia, the question that was put to the referendum was: 'Are you in favour of re-establishing the national independence of the Republic of Estonia?' The required turnout of 50 percent was exceeded, with 82.9 percent of the eligible population participating in the vote. 78.4 percent voted in favour of national independence and a no-vote was cast by 21.6 percent of those answering the question.[110] The percentage of those voting against independence showed the loyal and pro-union forces among the adult population of Estonia.[111] The fact that more than twenty percent of the citizens voted against the independence is too large a minority to be ignored.

2. The referendum of 28 June 1992 on the constitution

After Estonia regained independence, a constitutional assembly, which was composed of 30 members elected by the Estonian Congress[112] and 30 members elected by the Supreme Council, prepared a draft constitution to restore Estonia's statehood of the basis of legal succession. The question was to define what kind of nation-state Estonia should be, what form of government it should have and what policies should be followed. With regard to the form of government, four proposals were discussed. At the end, the general assembly decided for a parliamentary system with a president as a figurehead. The constitution was put to the people on 28 June 1992.[113] To be approved, a minimum of 50 percent participation was required. Around 67 percent of all eligible voters went to the polls and the parliamentary plebiscite was approved by a majority of 92 percent.[114] In Estonia, citizenship was restricted to those who were Estonian citizens in 1940 and their descendants. Only citizens have the right to vote in national elections.[115]

---

110 Detailed results from the c2d database, http://www.c2d.ch/detailed_display.php?lname=votes&table=votes&page=1&parent_id=&sublinkname=results&id=38754 (accessed on 21.05.2013).

111 Ruus, Estonia, p. 52.

112 The congress was an unofficial grassroots parliament that was elected by those who challenged the authority of the Supreme Council, which they held to be a Soviet-created body.

113 Ruus, Estonia, p. 53f.; Ruus in Kaufmann/Waters, p. 57; Mole, p. 96.

114 c2d database, http://c2d.ch/detailed_display.php?lname=votes&table=votes&page=1&parent_id=&sublinkname=results&id=37908 (accessed on 21.05.2013).

115 Duvold, Making Sense, p. 121.

3. The referendum of 28 June 1992 on voting rights for those who did not yet have citizenship status

In addition to the referendum question on the Estonian constitution that was put to the people, eligible Estonian citizens were also asked whether people who had applied for citizenship before 5 June 1992 should obtain the right to participate in the first parliamentary and presidential elections after the ratification of the constitution. The parliamentary plebiscite, however, was defeated by a vote of 53 percent.[116]

Putting the additional question to the vote and the subsequent rejection by the people caused some domestic and foreign policy conflicts. The West interpreted the no-decision of the voters as discrimination against mainly Russian-speaking non Estonians[117] residing in Estonia and as a violation of their human rights.[118] Concerning integration of the minorities, the additional question may not have been a wise step towards fostering a peaceful coexistence. However, at that time, the arguments to include or exclude the minorities from their *demos* were not primarily presented as a question of ethnicity or nationhood. For Estonia as well as Lativia, the arguments for restricting the access to citizenship were rather legalistic in nature. According to the Baltic states as well as to Western Europe, the Soviet incorporation was illegal. Consequently, Estonian and Latvian officials concluded that the immigration that took place during the Soviet period was also to be seen as illegitimate. As such, it was argued that offering these immigrants citizenship in the restored republics would effectively amount to recognition of the Soviet annexation.[119] Therefore, it was decided that the citizenry and their descendants of the pre-Soviet republics would constitute the current citizenry. Cleary, as Kjetil Duvold notes, underneath this reasoning lies a much more profound demographic question. In Estonia and especially Latvia the minority groups (around 40 percent) were proportionally large enough to alter the state's configurations and perhaps also the democratic order itself. Indeed, Estonians and Latvians were not in danger of becoming minorities in their own countries,

---

116 Results from the c2d database, http://www.c2d.ch/detailed_display.php?lname=votes&table=votes&page=1&parent_id=&sublinkname=results&id=38964 (accessed on 22.05.2013).

117 Those who had settled in Estonia from other parts of the USSR since 1940 and their descendants.

118 Ruus, Estonia, p. 55; Leftovers, The Economist [London, England], 18 July 1992, p. 41.

119 Duvold, Making Sense, p. 90, 109f; Rozenvalds, Baltische Staaten, p. 69.

however, the strong presence of Russian-speaking minorities would have had a serious impact on them. Furthermore, Estonian and Latvian officials were anxious that these immigrants were not 'loyal' to their country of residence.[120] As Estonia and Latvia also Lithuania reasoned, immigration from the external homeland to Lithuania was not determined to be internal immigration. However, due to more favourable demographic conditions in Lithuania (fewer immigrants, resulting in a more homogenous population than two other countries and an ethnic majority of 80 percent), it adopted a more generous policy towards Soviet-era immigrants, even before the declaration of the independence on 11 March 1990. By offering citizenship to all inhabitants, Lithuania undoubtedly removed a major issue from the political agenda – and somehow undermined the 'legalistic' arguments employed by the Estonians and Latvians. With this act, Lithuania also eliminated a major obstacle towards building democracy based on *demos* rather than *ethnos*. In Estonia and Latvia, the *demos* is still based on nationality. Citizens from other nations can apply for Estonian and Latvian citizenship, respectively. However, both countries have very restrictive citizenship laws. According to the arguments employed by Estonian and Latvian officials, they are not permanently barred from becoming citizens but they have to make some substantial efforts in terms of learning the official language and actively trying to become full members of the new states.[121] The majority of Estonians as well as Latvians agree that Soviet-era immigrants eventually must be included in the citizenry but question is what sort of threshold should be used.[122]

4. The referendum of 14 September 2003 on the accession to the European Union

Since the constitution came into force, the referendum on Estonia's accession to the European Union had been the only official popular vote. Before Estonia joined the European Union, some parts of the constitution had to be altered.[123] The Estonian parliament submitted one single question and enacted a constitutional law for the accession to the European Union according to articles 105, 162, 163, 164 and 167 of the constitution. The ballot question of the mandatory constitutional referendum that was put to popular vote stated: 'Are you in favour of accession to the European Union and the amendments to the Constitution

120 Duvold, Making Sense, p. 90, 109f., 131.
121 Duvold, Making Sense, p. 90, 93, 96, 110, 119, 248.
122 Duvold, Making Sense, p. 122.
123 Liivik, Legitimacy, p. 89.

of the Republic of Estonia?' Only Estonian citizens had the right to vote and a significant number of Russian-speaking minorities were left out.[124] Affirmative votes were cast by 66.8 percent of voters, with a turnout of 64.1 percent.[125] According to some opinion polls, the Estonian people were initially sceptical about joining the European Union.[126] The final result of 66.8 percent votes in favour of the referendum, however, could be seen as solid approval of European Integration.[127] Liivik's answer to this change of voter opinion is based on the referendum's essential function itself. According to him, the referendum, for one, substantially increased the citizens' factual knowledge about the European Union and their country's real political choices through debates and newly available information sharing. Secondly, the referendum was the instrument that had legitimized the process of decision-making in terms of integration into the European Union. It should also be mentioned that there was a huge pro-accession campaign made possible by the considerable financial resources spent by the Estonian government and the local EU delegation office.[128] Today, compared to other EU citizens, Estonians are still optimistic about the future of the European Union. The necessity for the union is strongly supported by them. Among other EU citizens, Estonians tend to trust the European Union the most.[129]

5. Rejected draft acts in the Estonian parliament

In addition to the referendum on EU accession, the parties of the Riigikogu put forward two other draft acts. However, the majority of the legislature rejected both proposals. One draft act proposed electing the president directly by the people and the other aimed at preventing the privatisation of the Estonian electric power plants by international investors.[130]

Since then, there have been other attempts by different parties to put some issues to a referendum, but these have also been rejected. These failed attempts included policies about developing nuclear energy and holding extraordinary elections of the parliament. The Estonian Green Party managed to get into the Riigikogu in

124 Mikkel/Pridham, p. 729; Probably accounts for about 10 percent of the population living in Estonia.
125 See c2d database, http://www.c2d.ch/detailed_display.php?lname=votes&table=votes&page=1&parent_id=&sublinkname=results&id=37874 (accessed on 22.05.2013).
126 Compare Pettai, p. 997; Vetik, p. 258.
127 Mikkel/Pridham, p. 716.
128 Pettai, p. 997.
129 EB80, p. 9, 10, 13, 67, 75f., 90, 134, 140.
130 Liivik, Legitimacy, p. 92.

2007, and two years later they initiated a draft bill to enact local popular initiatives by both submitting new bills and by vetoing the acts in force. The Estonian Green Party is one of the strongest supporters of direct democracy, aiming to contribute to the people's participation in the local decision-making process, and by doing so, reducing the people's distance from power and the governing processes.[131]

C. Explanations for the Estonian practice

After the overview of the existing practice of direct democracy in Estonia, it can be argued that referendums have only rarely been applied and held within the last two decades. There are two main factors that explain the minimal use of direct democratic instruments in Estonia. From a structural view, the institutional legal framework constrains the citizens' ability to be directly involved in the public decision-making procedure. From an informal approach, the political attitude of the elites is shaped by the given structural context.[132] Those with political influence and governing parties in the parliament have thus far shown little interest in applying and extending direct democracy.

1. Legal constraints

Structural factors, such as formal institutions, are legal rules that shape the public actors' behaviour relating to a procedure in different ways.[133] With regard to direct democratic mechanisms in Estonia, there are four main factors affecting the citizens' participation in legislation. The first shaping factor stems from the type of direct democracy mechanism itself. As previously described, referendums in Estonia are either initiated by constitution or by parliament top down. In Estonia, the majority of the Riigikogu decides if and which issues shall be submitted to a referendum and at what time. The lack of citizen-initiated referendum arrangements in the constitution constricts the use of direct democracy and thus the will of the people. All attempts from opposition parties to modify the constitution in order to legalise the popular initiative nationwide have been rejected by governing majorities in the Riigikogu.

A second constitutional constraint concerns the subject matter of referendums that can be held in Estonia. There are many restrictions on the range of issues. Indeed, referring to article 162 CE, a required referendum occurs if the

131 Liivik, Legitimacy, p. 92f.

132 See Hall/Taylor, New Institutionalism, p. 945.

133 See Hall/Taylor, New Institutionalism, p. 936ff.

chapters of 'General Provisions' and 'Amendment of the Constitution' have to be amended. Estonian legal provisions on referendums not only exclude a certain number of constitutional issues from being brought to a popular vote but also leave out further statutory issues concerning budget, taxation, financial obligations of the states, ratification and termination of international treaties and the declaration or termination of a state of emergency or national defence.[134] Some of these issues would presumably deserve to be part of a direct democratic mechanism as they directly shape the daily life of citizens.

A third limitation of the application of direct democracy concerns the *interaction* of the legal framework and governing elites. Indeed, the Riigikogu can submit a bill or other national issues to a referendum as indicated in article 105, section 1 CE. Yet section 4 of the same article requires the dissolution of the parliament if such a draft put to referendum does not receive a majority of the votes in favour. The analysis of Estonian practice thus leads to the conclusion that 'no parliament would risk holding a referendum if the issue put to it may fail and new parliamentary elections may have to be held'.[135]

The last restriction caused by institutional arrangements refers to time limits. On the one hand, there is a waiting period of one year for the same constitutional issue that has been rejected by the parliament or by a referendum.[136] On the other hand, a popular vote cannot be held on any kind of referendum when less than 90 days remain until parliamentary elections.[137]

Regarding formal restrictions, Estonia can be commended for its turnout and approval requirements. At least these legal provisions do not make citizens' access to direct democracy difficult. Both required referendums and referendums from above do not have to meet high approval requirements in order to be valid and to come into force and a participation quorum must not be met. The status quo can already be overturned if the majority of the voters are in favour of a policy change.

2. Informal constraints

Although the Estonian constitution constrains the use of direct democracy formally, the Estonian political parties in parliament were free to open constitutional provisions towards more direct democracy. After independence, however,

---

134 See art. 106 CE.

135 Liivik, Legitimacy, p. 89.

136 Art. 168 CE.

137 Art. 3, par. 3 ERA.

Baltic elites had established a new political and societal order in which no direct democratic procedures existed to constrain their legal choices. Only the preferences of political actors were crucial for what should be designed at that time.[138] In other words, the Baltic elites were free to engineer these legal frameworks in the ways they wanted to achieve political authority. In Estonia, the political actors went for a representative democracy with relatively limited range of direct democratic instruments. Nowadays, the current institutions have become more useful for the political parties than for the Estonian people.[139]

As Ero Liivik points out, the majority of political elites in Estonian parliament have not yet showed much interest in strengthening direct democracy; instead, they support representative parliamentary democracy. There were some attempts to legalize popular initiatives in the Riigikogu, but within recent years no agreement could be reached between proponents and opponents of bottom-up direct democracy.[140] Moreover, as Liivik notes, the Estonian proportional party system works in a majoritarian decision-making style. There are no productive deliberations between the groups negotiating with the opposition and finding consensus is considered a sign of weakness in Estonian political culture.[141] In addition, most political parties still perceive, in an elitist sense, that more progressive policies would be attained within the framework of representative institutions and that direct democracy is an inadequate method for making decisions. They hold it to be a rather dangerous, demagogic and costly phenomenon.[142] Finally, a major issue impeding direct democracy is a political question: Any enhancement of direct democracy such as legalising citizen-initiated referendums (e.g. citizens' facultative referendums and citizens' initiatives) by the political elite would simultaneously imply a restriction of their own existing authority and thus a destabilization of parliamentary decision-making. Thus, even if there is a stronger civil society than twenty years ago and even if there are some democratic shifts towards a new political culture after the break with the communist past, the current constitution (as it is framed) and the majority of the elite still deny citizens access to more radical direct legislation. It seems that the Latvian institutional constellation will remain frozen as long as the

---

138 See Kaiser, Types, p. 435.

139 Møller, p. 291f.

140 See Liivik, Learning, p. 30, 42.

141 Liivik, Legitimacy, p. 94ff.; Liivik, Learning, p. 42.

142 Ruus, Estonia, p. 60; Liivik, Learning, pp. 30, 37–41.

contextual conditions are stable. A reform of direct democratic institutions in the sense of opening them towards citizens may only succeed if 'the political costs of maintaining current institutional arrangements are higher than the expected transaction costs of change' or when a greater political crises should occur.[143]

143 See KAISER, Types, p. 438.

IV. The legal framework and practice of direct democracy in Latvia

A. Direct democratic instruments in Latvia

The current constitution [Satversme] of the unicameral parliamentary (100 representatives, elected by proportional representation[144]) Republic of Latvia, which was first adopted by the Constitutional Assembly of Latvia on 15 February 1922 (in force until 15 May 1934) and re-adopted with some modifications (but not totally amended) on 6 July 1993, confers Latvian citizens not only the right to participate in parliamentary elections but also to take part in national referendums, as stated in article 80 of the Constitution of Latvia (CLv). Latvian referendum rights were introduced after the collapse of the Soviet Union. But, many of them were already part of the 1922 Constitution that lasted until KARL ULMANIS' coup d'état in 1934. The 1922 Constitution at that time largely replicated the 1919 Weimar Constitution that contained several provisions for direct democracy. The establishment of referendum rights in Latvia in 1922 was further influenced by leading Latvian social democrats who had spent part of their exile from the Russian Empire in Switzerland, a federal state with the most developed direct democratic instruments at all three state levels (federal, cantonal, municipal). Accordingly, the re-adoption of the 1922 Constitution in May 1993 also meant the revitalisation of such referendum rights from a long period of torpor. Compared to Estonia, currently there are not only automatic and top-down referendums but also important arrangements for bottom-up direct democracy mechanisms with which the citizens of Latvia are able to actively stimulate the legislative process.[145] According to article 64 of the Satversme, 'the Saeima [Latvian Parliament] and also the people have the right to legislate, in accordance with the procedures, and to the extent provided for by [the] Constitution'.[146] As the Latvian Constitutional Court concludes, 'the people's will should be the foundation and the source of power [and] the sovereignty of people in Latvia is implemented with the same element of democracy as a national referendum or the electors' legislative initiative'.[147]

144 Art. 5 and 6 Constitution of the Republic of Latvia of 15 February 1922 (CLv).
145 Art. 2 of Law on National Referendums and Legislative Initiatives and European Citizens' Initiative of 31 March 1994, (LoNRILaECI) last amended on 8 November 2012.
146 AUERS, p. 54f.; for 1922 referendum rights see KOMÁROMI, Popular law-making, p. 59; art. 65 and 78 CLv.
147 JLvCC 2013-06-01, point 14.

The constitution comprises the basic rules for realising the citizens' direct democratic rights. All specific techniques and procedures of Latvian direct democracy are regulated and defined by the 'Law on National Referendums, Initiation of Laws and European Citizens' Initiative' (LoNRILaECI), which was adopted by the parliament on 31 March 1994. Since then, this law has been altered several times by the legislature. The last extensive revision with decisive changes (see below), caused inter alia with the introduction of the European Citizens' Initiative, was made on 8 November 2012. Some amendments to the law entered into force on 11 December 2013; others will enter starting on 1 January 2015. Pursuant to article 3 of the LoNRILaECI, the Central Election Commission of Latvia (CECLv) prepares and supervises national referendums. The CECLv is a state institution established by the parliament that acts independently.

According to my theoretical classification, the current Latvian constitution provides a total of eight different direct democratic institutions (see *Table 2*). They are all legally binding. However, as GITA FELDHUNE notes, neither the constitution nor the LoNRILaECI provide any legal obstacles that could prevent the parliament from readopting a law that has been repealed by the citizens.[148] In fact, in Latvia as in Lithuania, an issue triggered by a citizens' initiative and adopted by a referendum can also be amended by the parliament thereafter, as long as it is not subject to a required referendum.[149] However, this should not necessarily be considered negative. Instead, it reflects a vibrant legislative environment that can be corrected every time by both the parliament and citizens.

The eight different direct democratic instruments of Latvia can be categorised into three mechanisms of direct democracy as follows:

1. Referendums required by the constitution

The Latvian constitution contains two types of mandatory referendums: a mandatory referendum for some specific constitutional amendments and another one for the EU membership. Generally, such referendums are framed by the parliament and triggered automatically since the law prescribes its submission to a popular vote for it to become legally binding. However, the framing of a mandatory referendum can also be initiated by Latvian citizens because there is

148 FELDHUNE p. 80.

149 A Lithuanian citizens' initiative that was put on popular vote on 29.06.2014 aimed to alter the constitution so that a decision adopted by referendum could be amended only by a referendum. But, the referendum failed. See explanations for Lithuanian Referendum the chapter V-B-14.

a proactive citizen-initiated mechanism in Latvia. In such cases, we refer rather to citizens' constitutional referendums.

a) The mandatory constitutional referendum

The mandatory constitutional referendum is a popular vote that is automatically called under specific circumstances, which are defined in the Latvian constitution.

In general, any amendment of a constitutional provision requires a qualified majority of two-thirds of the members of parliaments who are present. And for any alteration, three sittings are required, in which at least two-thirds of the total members must participate.[150] A higher qualified majority than these requirements is prescribed for an amendment of such issues that are stated under article 77 CLv. According to this article, 'if the Saeima has amended the first, second, third, fourth, sixth or seventy-seventh article of the Constitution, such amendments, in order to come into force as law, shall be submitted to a national referendum'.[151]

The first chapter of the constitution of Latvia concerns the General Provisions. It constitutes the foundation of the state, such as the form of government (Art. 1 CLv), the people's sovereignty (Art. 2 CLv), domestic territorial borders (Art. 3 CLv), as well as the official language and national symbols of the Republic (Art. 4 CLv). Any amendment concerning those articles requires a national referendum in order to come into force as law (required referendum). This rule also applies to the sixth stated article, which defines the procedure of the parliamentary elections and the pattern of the electoral system. It also applies, of course, to article 77 CLv itself. Any other constitutional provision is excluded from being subject to required referendums.

A mandatory constitutional referendum on such issues has to be held not earlier than one month before and no later than two months after the date when the Saeima adopts any of these articles.[152] According to the first section of article 79 CLv, a constitutional amendment shall be adopted if at least half of the entire electorate has approved it. There are around 1,545,000 eligible voters[153] in Latvia. Without a doubt, this quorum is a very high approval restriction that strongly limits the sense of direct democracy. Indeed, there is no formal participation threshold. Nevertheless, the requirement of approval by 50 percent of the entire electorate

150 Art. 76 CLv.

151 Art. 77 CLv; see also art. 1, par. 1 and art. 4, par. 1 LoNRILaECI.

152 Art. 4, par. 2 LoNRILaECI.

153 See the Central Election Commission of Latvia, http://www.tn2012.cvk.lv/ (accessed on 06.06.2013).

automatically causes a high informal turnout hurdle. Compared to the Estonian approval prescription (which requires a majority of the participants), the Latvian quorum for adopting a constitutional amendment is much stricter in this respect.

b) The mandatory referendum on EU Membership

Until 2003, the constitution did not include any legal provisions for referendums on international matters. With the aim of providing a clearer legal basis for referendums related to joining or changing the terms of participation in the European Union, the parliament had to amend articles 68 and 79 of the constitution according to the corresponding law on 8 May 2003.[154] These amendments had to be made to accommodate EU membership for Latvia, which would formally modify the concepts of independence and sovereignty as they are expressed in articles 1 and 2 (CLv).[155] But these were not the only reasons to amend the constitution. As GATE FELDHUNE states, the government also wanted to avoid risking the accession decision by changing the acceptance quorum.[156] The revised article 68 CLv now stipulates that 'membership of Latvia in the European Union shall be decided by a national referendum, which is proposed by the Saeima'.[157] The new formulation of article 68 CLv is also a legal foundation specifying that withdrawal from the European Union would also be subject to this mandatory referendum.[158]

In order to be accepted, the number of voters must be at least half of the voters who had participated in the previous parliamentary election, and the referendum in favour of membership of Latvia in the European Union must be supported by the majority of voters.[159] Although EU membership formally modifies the sense of independence and popular sovereignty, the turnout and approval quorum for the accession referendum are less strict than the quorum for mandatory constitutional referendums that are required for any alteration of articles 1, 2, 3, 4, 6 and 77 of the constitution.

2. Referendums from above

The Latvian constitution contains three different types of referendums that can be optionally asked by the public authorities. All three referendums are legally

154 IKSTENS, Latvia 2004, p. 1056; MIKKEL/PRIDHAM, p. 730.
155 UŠACKA, p. 96.
156 FELDHUNE, p. 77.
157 Art. 68, sec. 3 CLv; art. 1, par. 5 and art. 11, par. 3 LoNRILaECI.
158 FELDHUNE, p. 82.
159 See art. 79, sec. 2 CLv.

binding, but with different intentions and aims. There is also a variation with regard to the actor who asks and triggers the referendum, and also with regard to further formal restrictions.

a) *The parliamentary plebiscite for substantial changes in EU membership*

The parliamentary plebiscite for substantial changes in EU membership is the first popular vote procedure that is launched from above. It is an authorities' referendum triggered by the parliament to confirm significant legal alterations related to EU membership. In addition to the automatic 'Referendum on EU-Membership' article 68, sec. 4 CLv states that 'substantial changes in the term regarding the membership of Latvia in the European Union shall be decided by a national referendum if such a referendum is requested by at least one-half of the members of the Saeima'.[160] With regard to its intention, this referendum can be both proactive and reactive: it is proactive because it gets popular legitimation for a corresponding policy change launched by the one half of the parliament and reactive in the sense that the plebiscite triggered by the parliamentary opposition must find popular support for a return to the status quo.

To be approved, the constitution states that 'substantial changes in the terms regarding such membership submitted for a national referendum shall be deemed adopted if the number of voters is at least half of the number of electors that participated in the previous Saeima election and if the majority has voted in favour of the draft law, membership of Latvia in the European Union or substantial changes in the terms regarding such membership'.[161] These requirements are the same as stipulated for a mandatory referendum on EU membership. Currently, both the referendum on the EU membership and the referendum for substantial changes related to EU membership are subject to a popular vote. However, they are submitted to popular vote either automatically or by the Saeima. The people cannot trigger a referendum on these two issues on their own.

After Estonia in 2011, Latvia became the 18th EU Member State to use the Euro as its official currency, giving up its national currency, the lat, on 1 January 2014.[162] The arrival of the Euro was accompanied by scepticism in Latvia. Although joining the common currency could be interpreted as a substantial change regarding Latvian membership in the European Union, the parliament did not consider this

160 See art. 68, sec. 4 CLv, art. 1, par. 6 and art. 11, par. 4 LoNRILaECI.

161 Art. 79, sec. 2 CLv.

162 Lithuania will follow, starting from 1 January 2015; see Litauen ist fit für den Euro, *Neue Zürcher Zeitung*, 5 June 2014, p. 23.

a substantial change and had avoided putting the question of joining the monetary union with a single currency to a referendum. For Latvian authorities, membership in the Euro zone meant completing the mission of joining all the main institutions, from the European Union to the North Atlantic Treaty Organization (NATO). On the other hand, considering Russia's growing clout in the former Soviet regions, the decision to not put the question on joining the Euro to a referendum was also politically motivated.[163]

b) The semi-plebiscite on repealing a law

The semi-plebiscite on repealing a law is a direct democratic institution to abolish parliamentary resolutions that are below the constitutional normative level. It is a reactive referendum intending to sustain the status quo. In the language of article 72 CLv, 'the President has the right to suspend the proclamation of a law for a period of two months. The President shall suspend the proclamation of a law if so requested by not less than one-third of the members of the Saeima. This right may be exercised by the President, or by one-third of the members of the Saeima, within ten days of the adoption of the law by the Saeima. The law thus suspended shall be put to a national referendum if so requested by not less than one-tenth of the electorate. If no such request is received during the aforementioned two-month period, the law shall then be proclaimed after the expiration of such period. A national referendum shall not take place, however, if the Saeima again votes on the law and not less than three-quarters of all members of the Saeima vote for the adoption of the law'.[164] In other cases, a national referendum for repealing the suspended law has to be held not earlier than one month before and no later than two months after the day of the announcement of the referendum.[165]

The 'repealing referendum' could either be considered a plebiscite or a citizens' facultative referendum to veto a law, which has been framed by the parliament. However, due to its different triggering actors, it is neither a full plebiscite nor a full citizen-initiated facultative referendum. To some extent there is an overlap of two mechanisms of direct democracy. On the one hand, it has to be triggered either by the president or by one-third of the members of the parliament and, on the other hand, national voting takes place only if requested by no less than

163 See Latvia and the Euro. Lat go, *The Economist* [online], http://www.economist.com/blogs/theworldin2014/2014/01/latvia-and-euro (accessed on 05.06.2014).

164 See also art. 1, par. 3 LoNRILaECI.

165 Art. 10, par. 2 LoNRILaECI.

one-tenth of the electorate.[166] It is, therefore, a joint action of oppositional public authorities and the electorate.[167] However, since triggering the referendum by the citizens can only occur if the authorities have called for the suspension of the proclamation of a law, I rather classify this mixed type of referendum – by naming it a *semi-plebiscite on repealing a law* – to the direct democracy mechanism that is launched from above. The triggering of this instrument depends on the will of parliament or the president himself. Nevertheless, it has an oppositional character, offering parliamentary minorities or the head of the state the possibility to subject the amended law, together with the citizen, to a decision on the popular stage.

In the case of a popular request to repeal a suspended parliamentary law, the Central Election Commission of Latvia (CECLv) has to organise the collection of signatures. A limit of 30 days is set to collect signatures of one-tenth of the electorate.[168] Signatures can be collected at collection stations that are set up in each city and municipality. Legally, at least one station per 10,000 voters must be available.[169] However, 30 days for collecting ten percent of the electorate's signatures is a relatively short time.

After 30 days have passed, the CECLv counts signatures, records results and notifies the president of the results. If more than one-tenth of the eligible citizens have signed the signatures sheets, the CECLv then announces a national referendum within three days.[170]

Concerning the definitive abolition of such a suspended law, article 74 CLv states that, 'a law adopted by the Saeima and suspended pursuant to the procedures specified in article seventy-two [of the constitution] shall be repealed by the national referendum if the number of voters is at least half of the number of electors that participated in the previous Saeima election and if the majority has voted for a repeal of the law.'

With regard to the policy area of 'repealing referendum', there are some issue restrictions, as required by article 73 CLv. Namely, 'the Budget and laws concerning loans, taxes, customs duties, railroad tariffs, military conscription, declaration and commencement of war, peace treaties, declaration of a state of emergency and its termination, mobilisation and demobilisation, as well as agreements with other

166 Art. 72, sec. 2 CLv; art. 1, par. 3 LoNRILaECI.

167 FELDHUNE, p. 80.

168 Art. 7, par. 1 LoNRILaECI; in contrast to citizens' initiatives there will be no changes with regard to requirements pertaining to number of signatures needed and timeframe after the revision of the LoNRILaECI beginning on 1 January 2015.

169 Art. 7, par. 2 LoNRILaECI.

170 Art. 10, par. 1 LoNRILaECI.

nations may not be submitted to national referendum'. Furthermore, urgent laws according to article 75 CLv may not be submitted to a national referendum.

c) *The presidential plebiscite on recalling parliament*

The presidential plebiscite on the recall of the parliament is the last tool of a top-down initiated mechanism of Latvian direct democracy. With regard to subject matter, it is a proactive referendum, but it results in neither an amendment of a law nor does it create or veto a legal norm. Instead, its outcome has wide political consequences for authorities of the state, namely for either the parliament or the president himself. According to article 48 CLv, the president is enabled to 'propose the dissolution of the Saeima. Following this proposal a national referendum [not earlier than one month before and not later than two months after presidents notification] shall be held.[171] If in the referendum [independently of the number of participants] more than half of the votes are cast in favour of dissolution, the Saeima shall be considered dissolved, new elections called, and such elections held no later than two months after the date of the dissolution of the Saeima'. It should be noted that the recall is asked and triggered by the same actor, which means that the referendum is fully controlled by the president. But, at least it takes place on a single issue, such as the dissolution of the parliament. It could otherwise lead to an abuse of power.

Although the president is the single actor with full control over the referendum regarding the dissolution of the parliament, there exists a specific formal restriction on the constitutional level that would forestall the president's attempt to launch the dissolution of the parliament. This becomes much clearer if we consider article 50 CLv, which stipulates that 'if in the referendum more than half of the votes are cast against the dissolution of the Saeima, then the President shall be deemed to be removed from office, and the Saeima shall elect a new President to serve for the remaining term of office of the President so removed'. Due to the uncertainty about the outcome of a plebiscite on recalling the parliament, it is to be assumed that the president will hesitate to avail himself of this institution. Until 2011, not a single president had used his or her right to recall the Saeima. However, on 28 May 2011, for the first time in Latvian history, the former president Valdis Zatlers, acted according to his constitutionally given right and called for the dissolution of the Saeima before his term had ended (see chapter IV-B-9).

---

171 See also art. 1 par. 2, art. 5, par. 1 and par. 2 LoNRILaECI.

3. Citizen-initiated referendums

In comparison to Estonian direct democracy, there is a major difference in Latvia, namely the right of the Latvian people to initiate legislation from the bottom up.[172] Indeed, bottom-up mechanisms already existed from 1923 to 1934. It took more than fifty years until they were re-established at the end of the communist period in 1989.

Thanks to the citizens' initiative, which is a proactive direct democratic instrument, the people not only become an additional veto player in the decision-making process, but also an innovative actor with the ability to change public policy by proposing a law or an amendment to the constitution.[173] An amendment not only includes the enactment of new provisions but also the alteration and repealing of existing laws and constitutional provisions. In addition to the citizens' initiatives that create and change legal norms, there is also the popular initiative to recall the parliament.[174] In addition to national initiatives, since 2012 Latvian citizens (like other EU citizens) also have the opportunity to participate in signatures collection drives organized to support European citizen's initiatives within the framework of the European Union. It is regulated by the LoNRILaECI as far as not otherwise provided in the EU Regulation No 211/2011 of the European Parliament and of the Council of 16 February 2011.[175] However, within this work the focus lies on initiatives regarding national issues.

In the theoretical part of this book (chapter II-B-1-c), it was stated that the 'citizens' facultative referendum' to veto laws is the second instrument of citizen-initiated direct democratic mechanisms. Indeed, as shown under 'Chapter IV-A-2, Referendums from above', in Latvia, such a reactive instrument (the semi-plebiscite on repealing a law) exists. However, due to its specific triggering feature, this direct democratic mechanism is based on joint action of both public authorities and the citizens (multiple actors); the latter cannot start collecting signatures unless the authorities have requested the suspension of the law ante. For this reason, I have classified this veto instrument instead as a top-down mechanism of direct democracy. Therefore, the Latvian direct democracy from below is only partially completed.

A total of two different citizens' initiatives to alter the state's legal settings – the citizens' constitutional initiative and the citizens' legislative initiative – and one

172 Art. 64 CLv and art. 22 LoNRILaECI.

173 See also art. 1, par. 4, art. 11, par. 1 LoNRILaECI.

174 Art. 14 CLv; art. 1, par. 7 and art. 11, par. 5 LoNRILaECI.

175 See art. 1^1 and art. 25^{1-4} LoNRILaECI; http://ec.europa.eu/citizens-initiative/public/welcome?lg=en (accessed on 24.05.2014).

initiative on the right to recall the parliament are available to Latvians. They are legally binding and proceed according to the same rules and procedures, with the exception of the turnout-approval quorum and temporal conditions.

Indeed, in all three cases, citizens are in complete control of the referendum, both with regard to framing the proposal (e.g. enactment, alteration and repeal of laws and constitutional provisions / recall of parliament) and triggering the relevant referendum. Nevertheless, there are still numerous constraints preventing Latvians from exercising their sovereignty to the fullest. Due to some formal procedural rules, such as collection provisions and quorums, their ability to control the vote is restricted. This limitation also stems from the fact that citizens' initiatives cannot be framed (asked) on matters of policy, as stated in article 73 CLv.[176] These policy issues are excluded from the initiative process.[177]

With regard to the citizens' initiatives on creating a legal norm, the law states that only a fully elaborated draft law or a draft amendment to the constitution can be subject to a popular vote.[178] This means that general suggestions cannot be issued for referendums. However, in order to better democratically integrate citizens into the law-making process, it would also be appropriate to extend the right to launch initiatives for general suggestions. This is due to two important reasons: (1) a citizens' initiative could also be requested by those who do not have any legal knowledge on formulating a elaborated draft; and (2) a general suggestion would bring direct democracy closer to representative democracy, since such proposals have to be elaborated into formulated drafts by the parliament.

a) The citizens' constitutional initiative

According to article 78 CLv, 'electors, in numbers comprising not less than one tenth of the electorate, have the right to submit [within 30 days[179]] a fully elaborated draft of an amendment to the Constitution [...] to the President, who shall

176 'The Budget and laws concerning loans, customs duties, railroad tariffs, military conscription, declaration and commencement of war, peace treaties, declaration of a state of emergency and is termination, mobilisation and demobilisation, as well as agreements with other nations may not be submitted to a national referendum'.

177 Art. 73 CLv; see also Auers, p. 56.

178 Art. 22 LoNRILaECI.

179 Art. 7, par. 1 LoNRILaECI, however, starting from 1 January 2015 signature collection of no less than one-tenth of eligible citizens will last for 12 months; see art. 2 Transitional Provisions of LoNRILaECI and art. 22, par. 1 of the LoNRILaECI-2015.

present it to the Saeima'.[180] The Saeima is obliged to consider the constitutional amendment, and if the parliament does not adopt it without changing its content, the original proposal shall then be submitted to a national referendum.[181] In other words, the parliament either adopts the citizens' initiative without making any change to its content or there is a referendum to be held if the parliament changes or rejects the citizens' initiative. The referendum on the 'draft amendment to constitution has to be held not earlier than one month before and not later than two months after the day [...] the draft amendment to the constitution has been rejected or has been adopted with changes in its content'.[182]

For an approval, at least half of the entire electoral votes in favour is needed.[183] As for mandatory constitutional referendums, there is no formal turnout quorum requested to validate the ballot. At least 50 percent of all eligible citizens who are in favour of the citizens' initiative have to participate for the proposal to be adopted; as long as there are some voters who reject the draft, the actual turnout quorum to validate the yes votes has to be much higher than 50 percent of the entire electorate.[184]

b) The citizens' legislative initiative

In addition to the constitutional initiative, Latvians can also frame and trigger legislative initiatives to change statutory provisions. Pursuant to article 78, not less than one tenth of the electorate has the right to submit their formulated draft to the president (within 30 days[185]), who then forwards it for parliament's consideration.[186] An identical provision is also contained under article 65 of the constitution, 'Draft laws may be submitted to the Saeima by the President, the Cabinet or committees of the Saeima by not less than five members of the Saeima or, in accordance with the procedures and in the cases provided for in [the] Constitution, by one tenth of the electorate'.[187] Similar to the citizens' constitutional initiatives, the referendum on the relevant draft law takes place only if the parliament

180 See also art. 1, par. 4 LoNRILaECI.

181 Art. 78 CLv; art. 11, par. 1, art. 25, par. 2 LoNRILaECI.

182 Art. 11, par. 2 LoNRILaECI.

183 Art. 79, sec. 1 CLv.

184 See also UŠACKA, p. 96.

185 Art. 7, par. 1 LoNRILaECI, however, starting from 1 January 2015 signature collection of no less than one-tenth of eligible citizens will last for 12 months; see clause 2 of the Transitional Provisions of LoNRILaECI and art. 22, par. 1 of the LoNRILaECI-2015.

186 See also art. 1, par. 4 LoNRILaECI.

187 See also art. 78 CLv.

rejects the citizens' draft law or approves it with changes to its content.[188] The referendum on the draft law has to be held no earlier than one month and no later than two months after parliaments' decision on the initiative.[189]

Unlike constitutional initiatives, a draft law shall be adopted if 'the number of voters is at least half of the number of electors as participated in the previous parliamentary election and if the majority has voted in favour of [it]'.[190]

(a) A two-stage signature collection (until 2015)

Up to now, it has been stated that not less than one-tenth of the electorate who was eligible to vote in the previous parliamentary elections is needed to submit within one month a formulated draft law or a fully elaborated draft amendment to the constitution to the president, who then presents it to the parliament for its consideration.[191] Here, the matter is the triggering of the popular vote. It has not explicitly been stated who formulates the question (asking) and how the framing of the elaborated draft proceeds.

It should be noted that Latvian citizen-initiated direct democracy to change the status quo is based on a *double stage signatures collecting process*. Submitting a popular draft to the president by at least one tenth of the electorate is, in fact, the second stage of triggering a referendum. Before the second stage is reached, however, the formulated draft first must be submitted over a course of 12 months by no less than 30,000 eligible citizens to the Central Election Commission (CECLv).[192] Until the end of 2012, this number was limited to 10,000 signatures.[193] However, on 8 November 2012 the parliament decided to raise the hurdle for initiating a citizens' initiative to 30,000 signatures during the first round within 12 months from the day when the draft law or draft amendment to the constitution was registered with the CECLv.

With regard to registration, until recently the LoNRILaECI did not mention who precisely forms the group of the citizens' initiative for framing and registering the issue. Nor did it say if there is a preliminary examination of the proponent's proposal as to its form and content. After the last amendment of LoNRILaECI on 8 November 2012, the law has finally clarified the rules of application for popular initiatives. According to the new law, an initiative group can either be a political

---

188 Art. 1, par. 4 and art. 11, par. 1 LoNRILaECI.
189 Art. 11, par. 2 LoNRILaECI.
190 Art. 79, sec. 2 CLv.
191 Art. 78 CLv; art. 25, par. 1 LoNRILaECI.
192 See clause 4 of the Transitional Provisions of the LoNRILaECI.
193 See art. 22 LoNRILaECI.

party, an association of political parties or an association of at least 10 electors.[194] Before beginning with the first collection stage, the initiative group has to submit its application to the CECLv along with the draft law or draft amendments to the constitution for which it plans to collect signatures.[195] The CECLv is then responsible for the registration of the elaborated draft in question as well as for the evaluation of the proposal. It has to make a decision thereon within 45 days.[196] The commission has the right to refuse to register the draft law or draft amendments to the constitution if the drafts at stake are not completely developed in terms of form or content.[197] In other cases, if the groups' application conforms to the legal requirements, then the registration takes place and the first stage of signature collection in support of the initiated draft can begin. Within 12 months from the registration day, all 30,000 collected signatures must be collected and certified by a notary public or an orphans' court that performs notarial functions before being submitted to the CECLv.[198] The second stage entails the official collection of signatures of one-tenth of the electorate and can only start if the initiative group has been able to collect 30,000 valid signatures in favour of its proposal at the initial stage. The second collection period is limited to 30 days, as article 7, par. 1 of the LoNRILaECI prescribes. During the second round, the signature sheets for voters to sign are to be made available at the places designated by city or municipal councils.[199] In order to gather signatures from one-tenth of the electorate, each city and municipality must set up a collection station (at least one per 10,000 citizens).[200] Voters located abroad can also sign the signature sheets that are placed in the embassies or other diplomatic or consular missions of Latvia.[201] Signatures of 30,000 citizens who have signed the submitted formulated draft at the first collection stage are included in the total number of supporters who have participated in the second round.[202] After the 30 days have passed, the CECLv counts the signatures and records the results. Within three days, the commission notifies the president

194 Art. 23, par. 2 sec. 1 and 2 LoNRILaECI.
195 Art. 23, par. 3 LoNRILaECI.
196 Art. 23, par. 4 LoNRILaECI.
197 Art. 23, par. 4, sec. 3 and par. 5, sec. 1 and 2 LoNRILaECI; for validation of initiatives see chapter IV-A-4.
198 See clause 4 of the Transitional Provisions of the LoNRILaECI.
199 Art. 7, par. 1 LoNRILaECI.
200 Art. 7, par. 2 LoNRILaECI.
201 Art. 7, par. 6 LoNRILaECI.
202 Art. 24, par. 2 LoNRILaECI.

about the results.[203] Further, article 25 para. 1 elaborates that 'if the draft law or the draft amendment to the constitution has been signed by not less than one-tenth of Latvian citizens who were eligible to vote in the previous Saeima elections, the President of Latvia shall submit to the Saeima the draft law or the draft amendment to the Constitution'.[204] The parliament must consider the draft in question during the session in which the draft was submitted.[205]

With regard to the first signature collection stage, DAUNIS AUERS states that collecting [3]0,000 signatures within 12 months would be quite a modest figure.[206] However, it should be noted that this is a large number of signatures needed to formally activate an initiative process. As such, an additional 30 days for signatures from one-tenth of the electorate in the second collection stage is far from modest. Nevertheless, at this stage a large part of the logistical burden of collecting signatures is borne by the state, in that it prescribes that there must be at least one signing station per 10,000 voters.[207] Still, it remains ambiguous: on the one hand, it is beneficial for the initiative group to save financial and personnel resources but on the other hand, they are not free to collect signatures at just any public place. It has to be done at prescribed polling stations set up by city and municipal councils or abroad in embassies and consulates. Thus, proponents first have to get people to turn up to these signing locations. This might not be so easy, especially if the level of political participation is low within civil society or if the initiative group does not have enough money to finance public campaigns. In addition to the logistical and temporal constraints at the second stage, financial challenges may also arise at the first collection stage because certifying a signature by a sworn notary or a custody court costs around 3€, amounting to some 90,000€ total.[208] This places a considerable financial burden on either the citizen signing the initiative or for the committee of the initiative, particularly for poorer social segments or minorities.[209] The second round of signature collection, however, is funded by the state.

(b) A one round signature collection (in force as of 2015)

As already mentioned the procedure for collecting signatures was been amended on 8 November 2012 and will come into force starting on 1 January 2015. The

---

203 Art. 24, par. 3 LoNRILaECI.
204 See art. 25, par. 1 LoNRILaECI.
205 Art. 25, par. 2 LoNRILaECI.
206 See AUERS, p. 56.
207 See art. 7, par. 2 LoNRILaECI.
208 See clause 4 of the Transitional Provisions of the LoNRILaECI.
209 At that time, 10,000 signatures were required for the first round; see AUERS, p. 56f.

difference is that there will only be only one round of signature collection for triggering an initiative, which will last for 12 months instead of 30 days. Indeed, this is a considerable improvement. During the new collection period, no fewer than one tenth of Latvian citizens who were eligible to vote in the previous parliamentary elections must be collected.[210] According to the altered law, signature collection should also be possible online via the single state and local government services if identification of signatories and protection of natural persons' data are ensured.[211] For online signature collection, the procedure will follow what has been described for the two-stage collection procedure above. At the end of 12 months, the signature sheets will have to be submitted CECLv. The CECLv must then count the signatures and verify whether the signatories are indeed eligible voters. If the draft law or the draft amendment to the constitution is signed by a total of less than one tenth of the eligible electorate, the CECLv will have to notify the president within three days and send him the citizens' draft.[212] The president will have to submit it to the parliament for its consideration.[213] There after, the parliament can adopt the citizens' draft or if it rejects or adopts the draft by changing its content, a referendum has to be held.[214]

(c) A quasi-indirect initiative procedure

If an initiative group manages to overcome all these structural hurdles within the signature collection process, then the citizens' initiative is in the hands of public authorities.[215] If the parliament passes the popular proposal, the president proclaims its adoption and the draft in question comes into force 14 days after its proclamation, as stated in article 69 of the constitution. The term may differ from 14 days if it is stipulated otherwise.[216]

And as previously mentioned if the parliament does not adopt the draft in question without changing its content or if it rejects the draft, it is then submitted to a national referendum.[217] The referendum must be held no earlier than one month before and no later than two months after parliament's decision on the

210 Art. 22, par. 1 LoNRILaECI-2015.
211 Art. 22, par. 4 and 5 LoNRILaECI-2015.
212 Art. 24 LoNRILaECI-2015.
213 Art. 25, par. 1 and 2 LoNRILaECI-2015.
214 Art. 11, par. 1 LoNRILaECI-2015.
215 Art. 25, par. 1 and 2 LoNRILaECI.
216 Art. 69 CLv.
217 Art. 11, par. 1 LoNRILaECI; art. 78 CLv.

citizens' initiative.[218] It is important to note that a legislative gap can arise if, at the same time, the parliament adopts the citizens' initiative with changes to its content and the popular draft is approved in the referendum. In this scenario, neither the constitution nor the LoNRILaECI contain a specific provision to determine which proposal would then come into force as law. One can assume that the citizens' proposal rather than its parliamentary version would come into force.

Whether a citizens' initiative has been directly approved or not, it has to be taken into account that its formal efficacy can vary. No legal success is achieved if an initiative has been rejected both by the parliament and by the voters of the referendum. In contrast, partial success is achieved by the proponents of the initiative if their proposal has been rejected in the referendum but is nevertheless adopted by the parliament with changes to its original content. In this respect, the referendum never corresponds to the original content its proponents suggested or initially intended, but at least it partially succeeds. And finally, a complete success is achieved if the corresponding draft on an amendment to the law or to the constitution has been adopted without any changes to its content by parliament, or if the citizens' draft was rejected by the parliament but accepted by popular vote.

The fact that an initiative can submitted to a national referendum without bypassing the parliament is indeed a central characteristic of an indirect initiative procedure.[219] Generally within such a process the parliament has the possibility to deliberate on the citizens' draft before submitting it to the popular vote. With an indirect initiative procedure, the parliament is free to give its approval to the citizens' proposal. It can further propose a counter-proposal as an alternative draft to the citizens' initiative and submit it at the same time as the initiative to a popular decision. The counter-proposal, however, should not materially differ from the content of the citizens' initiative. It has to pursue the same aim as far as possible; only the means to realize the goal may differ. Such a parliamentary alternative usually leads the initiative group to withdraw their initiative in favour of the parliamentary alternative draft.

In the Latvian case, the option of a counter-proposal or of a withdrawal provision is mentioned neither in the constitution nor in the LoNRILaECI. The parliament can instead adopt, reject or even revise and adopt the corresponding draft formulated by the citizens.[220] The Latvian mechanism is indeed well thought out but still too static and narrow. It quickly leads to an exclusion of the initiative

218 Art. 11, par. 2 LoNRILaECI.

219 See Somer, Initiativverfahren, p. 359ff.

220 Art. 1, par. 4 and art. 11, par. 1 LoNRILaECI.

group from the procedure and leaves no room for negotiations between the parliament and the initiative group, in which the latter may withdraw its initiative in favour of a parliamentary concession. Furthermore, in Latvia it is not possible that both an initiative and an initiative with changes in its content (namely the quasi-counter-proposal) are simultaneously submitted to popular decision in which the voter could choose from either both alternatives or only one of them.[221] Additionally, initiatives have to be submitted as a fully elaborated draft. There is no option for general suggestions that could be put in concrete terms by the parliament.

Nevertheless, a full indirect initiative procedure that includes a counter-proposal and withdrawal option would lead to many advantages due to the following reasons. First of all, the procedure plays a significant role in linking representative democracy with direct democracy, in which a mutual give and take between the authorities and initiative group arises. A counter-proposal that may come out from these negotiations is indeed an alternative proposal that does not meet popular claims in full, however, due to its framing by the parliamentary majority, it also likely represents a wider spectrum of opinions than the proposal originally put forth by the supporters of the initiative. A counter-proposal generally corrects and improves the initiative both formally and materially, which means that as a result, the legal norm can generally be better put into practice. In addition, for the voters it offers an additional legislative choice, which lies between the status quo and the citizens' draft. A positive effect is also the win-win situation for both sides following the withdrawal of the initiative in favour of a parliamentary concession. As such, both the initiative group and the authorities can avoid a costly and tricky referendum campaign. Finally, in case the counter-proposal comes into force, the initiative will still formally succeed even without being submitted to the referendum, which carries with it an uncertain outcome. In order that the indirect procedure could be put to full use, a maximum of at least one year should be allotted for parliamentary consideration. Only with adequate time can well-reasoned proposals that present a serious alternative to the citizens' initiative be framed by the authorities.[222]

---

221 To avoid a possible privileged treatment of the counter-proposal and hence a violation of citizens' will, ballot voters should be able to accept both proposals (double-yes). In case of an approval of both the citizens' initiative and counter-proposal, a third ballot question is necessary. In response to the third question, voters can indicate the proposal that they prefer if both are accepted (double-yes with third question; the so-called 'System Haab'); see HAAB, Verfahren, p. 518ff.

222 See WERDER, Bedeutung, p. 152, 157f.; AUER/MALINVERNI/HOTTELIER, Volume I; p. 288f.; VON ARX, Ähnlich, pp. 67–71, 143, 195–199; HOFER, Verhandlungspfand,

c) *The citizens' initiative on recalling parliament*

The citizens' initiative on recalling parliament is the third citizen-initiated direct democratic mechanism in Latvia. However, instead of creating a legislative norm, it aims instead to remove the entire parliament from office if one-tenth of the electorate proposes the dissolution of the parliament.[223] Citizens do not have the right to recall an individual member of the parliament, as stated in the second section of article 14 CLv.

Until 2009 a referendum on recalling the parliament could be asked and triggered solely from top down by the president[224], as outlined above (see chapter IV-A-2-c). Since 2009, the Latvian people also have the right to initiate the dissolution of the parliament and call for new elections. In this procedure, the citizenry is the sole actor in full control of the referendum.

According to Jānis Ikstens, in 2009 the free fall of the Latvian economy continued and within the European Union, Latvia suffered most from the global recession. The disaffection of Latvians over the Saeima's politics resulted in strong and some violent protests, unlike anything seen in Latvia during the previous two last decades. Consequently, the former state president Valdis Zatlers, 'in an extraordinary move, formulated an ultimatum to parliament and the government requiring a number of institutional changes: giving citizens a direct right to vote on the calling of extraordinary parliamentary elections; limiting the number of electoral districts in which a person can run for Parliament; setting up a council supervising the use of the international rescue loan; immediately drafting a plan of reorganisation of the system of public administrations; recruiting able ministers or broadening the coalition; and choosing the new head of the Anti-corruption Bureau'.[225] Although the Saeima did not comply with the presidential ultimatum in full, in 2009 it decided to fulfil a part of those presidential proposals under heavy pressure from the public and the president. The parliament amended the parliamentary election law to allow each eligible citizen to run for the Saeima in only one of five electoral districts, as desired. Furthermore, it revised the constitution to enable a direct popular vote through calling extraordinary parliamentary elections from bottom up (see also chapter IV-B-7).[226]

---

p. 207, 215, 220, 226; Papadoupolos, Matter, p. 37; 43f; 56; Somer, Initiativerfahren p. 363f., 374; Möckli, Gliedstaaten, p. 25.

223 Art. 14, sec. 1 CLv; art. 1, par. 7 and art. 11, par. 5 LoNRILaECI.

224 See, art. 48 CLv.

225 Ikstens, Latvia 2010, p. 1054f.

226 Ikstens, Latvia 2010, p. 1054f.

According to the new wording of article 14 of the constitution, the first section now establishes that 'Not less than one tenth of electors have the right to initiate a national referendum regarding a recall of the Saeima'.[227] Rules for gathering signatures in favour of parliament's dissolution are in accordance with the procedures set out for citizens' initiative as described above. Until the end of 2014, a double-stage collection process is also required here. But at the first stage, no fewer than 10,000 (instead of 30,000 signatures) have to be collected within 12 months. For the second round, 30 days are given to collect signatures from no less than one-tenth of the electorate. Signatures of 10,000 voters from the first round are to be regarded as a part of the number of signatures that are collected at second stage.[228] To be adopted, a majority of voters and at least two thirds of the number of voters who participated in previous parliamentary elections are required. There are no turnout requirements.[229]

As with the initiation of citizens' constitutional and legislative initiatives, the collection procedure for recalling the parliament has also been changed and specified by the amendments to the LoNRILaECI on 8 November 2012. Beginning on 1 January 2015, only one collection round will be set to gather signatures of not less than ten percent of the entire electorate. The initiative to hold a national referendum on recalling of the parliament will have to be submitted within a period of 12 months after the day when the CECLv has registered the initiative group. Signatures can be collected at designated places or via online systems.[230] An initiative group may be a political party, an alliance of political parties or an association of at least ten electors.[231] Within the collection period, each signature has to be certified by notaries and local government institutions.[232] Thereafter, the CECLv has to count the certified signatures and decide to hold a national referendum on recalling of the parliament if not less than ten percent of eligible citizens have signed the initiative.[233] The referendum must be held no earlier than one month and no later than two months from the day when the decision of the

227 See also art. 1 par. 7 LoNRILaECI.

228 See clause 11 and 12 of the Transitional Provisions of the LoNRILaECI.

229 Art. 14 CLv.

230 See art. 25^5, par. 1 and 5, art. 7 LoNRILaECI-2015.

231 See art. 23, par. 2 sec. 1 and 2 LonRILaECI and LoNRILaECI-2015 (no changes), as well as art. 25^6, par. 1 LoNRILaECI-2015.

232 See art. 25^5, par. 2 LoNRILaECI-2015.

233 See art. 25^7, par. 1 and 2 LoNRILaECI-2015; in contrast to citizens' constitutional and legislative initiatives, the authority to decide on the referendum on recalling parliament is vested in the central election commission and not the parliament.

CECLv to hold a national referendum on recalling the parliament is announced in the official publication *Latvijas Vestnēsis.*[234] The requirements for approval of the initiative on the ballot are the same; they have not been changed. The majority of the voters and at least two thirds of electors who participated in previous parliamentary elections are required for the dissolution of the parliament.[235]

In contrast to citizens' constitutional and legislative initiatives, there are some temporal hurdles for an initiative on recalling the parliament. The right to initiate a recall of the parliament cannot be exercised under the following circumstances: (1) within one year after the Saeima first convenes; (2) or one year before the end of legislative period of the parliament; (3) during the last six months of the term of office of the President; (4) or less than six months after the previous national referendum regarding the recall of the Saeima.[236] Despite these restrictions, it is important to note that today, Latvia is the first EU country in which a popular recall mechanism to dissolve the parliament and call new elections exists. In 2013, it was used for the first time by the association 'Par latu, pret eiro' [For the Lats, against the Euro]. On 28 May 2013, the group submitted its application to collect signatures on an initiative to organize a national referendum to dissolve the 11th Saeima to the Central Election Commission.[237] It remains to be seen just how practical and effective this new direct democratic tool will be.

To sum up, according to article 1 of LoNRILaECI, in Latvia 'a national referendum shall be held if: (1) the Saeima has amended the first, second, third, fourth, sixth or seventy-seventh articles of the Constitution [mandatory constitutional referendum]; (2) the President of Latvia has proposed the dissolution of the Saeima [presidential plebiscite on recalling parliament]; (3) the President of Latvia has suspended the proclamation of a law for two months, and during this period a petition by not fewer than one-tenth of the electorate has been received to put the suspended law to a national referendum [semi-plebiscite on repealing a law]; (4) the parliament has not adopted without changes as to its content a draft law or a draft amendment to the Constitution submitted by not less than one-tenth of the electorate [Citizens' constitutional and legislative initiative]; (5) membership of Latvia in the European Union must be decided [mandatory referendum on the EU-Membership]; (6) substantial changes in the terms regarding the membership of Latvia in the European Union must be decided, and at least one-half of the members of the Saeima have requested a national referendum on this matter'

---

234 See art. 25^8, par. 2 LoNRILaECI-2015.

235 Art. 14 CLv.

236 Art. 14 CLv.

237 See http://cvk.lv/pub/public/30688.html (accessed on 24.05.2014).

[parliamentary plebiscite for changes in EU-Membership]. After the amendment of the constitution in 2009, in which the parliament had decided to grant citizens the right to propose the dissolution of the parliament, a seventh paragraph was added to the LoNRILaECI in November 2012 which states that a popular initiated national referendum [citizens' initiative on recalling parliament] shall also be held if 'at least one tenth of the electorate has proposed the dissolution of the Saeima'.[238]

4. The legal assessment of citizens' initiatives

Citizens' initiatives have to comply with requirements of legal techniques as well as fundamental values of a democratic and judicial state in order to be advanced to a national referendum. According to the Latvian Constitutional Court, since the adoption of the constitution in 1922 the Central Election Commission has been entrusted with the jurisdiction to verify the compliance of popular drafts with legal requirements. The court also takes the view that at that time it had been 'self-evident within the state order of Latvia that the respective decision by CEC[Lv] could be appealed against before the Senate'[239] of the Supreme Court, meaning that there was a mechanism for assessing the legality of the decisions adopted by the Central Election Commission.[240] Presumably due to the lack of large direct democratic practices, however, until recently the rules for verifying the legal assessment of citizens' initiatives, guidelines for requirements for being legally valid, and the mechanisms for appealing the inadmissibility decision by the CECLv had not been fully established in Latvian law.

After the amendments to the LoNRILaECI on 8 November 2012 and according to recent guidelines provided by the Constitutional Court's decisions in cases No. 2012-03-01 and No. 2013-06-01, currently the procedure for assessing the legality of a citizens' initiative and the procedure for appealing against the CECLv decisions to refuse to register a popular initiative has been specified.[241] The elaboration of the law and thus clarification of the rules within this framework once again stress the importance of the jurisdiction of the courts in developing the legal order.

As described under chapter IV-A-3-b, the Central Election Commission is responsible for registering citizens' initiatives and must make a decision within 45 days.[242] The procedure of the signature collection can only start if the registration

238 Art. 1, par. 1–7 LoNRILaECI.

239 JLvCC 2013-06-01, point 4.

240 JLvCC 2013-06-01, point 4, 13, 15.

241 See JLvCC 2012-03-01; JLvCC 2013-06-01.

242 Art. 23, par. 3 and 4 LoNRILaECI.

succeeds. Within the framework of the registration procedure, the CECLv has also to perform a legal assessment of the citizens' draft law or the draft amendment to the constitution. The legal assessment must be set apart from the political assessment, which can be performed by the parliament or the people.[243] As such, initiatives in Latvia are already reviewed with regard to their legal form and content at the beginning of the initiative process, namely before the signature collection starts. The CECLv is authorized to reject the application of the proponent's draft if the initiative group does not comply with the requirements for an initiative group as prescribed in article 23 par. 2 LoNRILaECI, or if the draft law or draft amendment to the constitution is incomplete in form or content.[244] While the decision to form an initiative group can be made without any difficulties, the commission may face some challenges when it comes to deciding whether a draft law or draft amendment to the constitution is fully developed in its form and content. Here, in order to make a legally sound and well-reasoned decision, the CECLv can request additional information, explanations and opinions from state and local government institutions. It can also consult with (legal) experts.[245] Depending on the conclusions of experts, the CECLv may stop the submitted draft from moving forwarding by rejecting its registration, if the draft submitted by the citizens' is not fully elaborated in its form or content. In such cases, the initiative group can appeal the decision made by CECLv before the Department of Administrative Cases of the Senate of the Supreme Court, which examines complaints regarding decisions adopted by CECLv as a court of first instance.[246] The court has to consider the case and make a decision within one month of the day of receiving the application.[247] The court's decision upon examining the application is final and cannot be subject to appeal.[248]

Latvian law states that the electors have the right to submit a 'fully elaborated draft' of an amendment to the constitution or of a law.[249] Thus, while performing the legal assessment, the CECLv must also to verify whether a draft law submitted by the electorate can be considered fully elaborated or not. Article 23 par. 5 sec. 2 of LoNRILaECI provides some specific indications with respect to

243 JLvCC 2013-06-01, point 14.3.
244 Art. 23, par. 4, sec. 3 and par. 5, sec. 1 and 2 LoNRILaECI.
245 Art. 23, par. 6 LoNRILaECI.
246 Art. 23^1, par. 1 and 2 LoNRILaECI.
247 Art. 23^1, par. 3 LoNRILaECI.
248 Art. 23^1, par. 6 LoNRILaECI; JLvCC 2013-06-01, point 15.1.
249 Art. 78 CLv; clause 4 of the Transitional Provisions of the LoNRILaECI; Art. 22 LoNRILaECI.

this requirement, stating that a draft law or draft amendment to the constitution should be complete in form and content.[250] A draft law is fully elaborated in its form when its wording is unalterable, meaning that it can be directly integrated into positive law. This means general proposals that would otherwise need to be put into concrete norms cannot be submitted for popular decision. To comply, draft laws should also be fully elaborated in terms of content. In its decision, the Latvian Constitutional Court declares that 'a draft law cannot be considered to be fully elaborated as to its content, if (1) it envisages deciding on issues, which are not be regulated by law at all; (2) in case of adoptions, would be incompatible with the norms, principles and values included in the constitution; (3) in case of adoption would be incompatible with Latvia's international commitments'.[251]

In its decision, the Constitutional Court also explains that 'since the text of the draft law submitted by the initiative group cannot be amended in the further procedure, it must be ensured that a draft, which is incompatible with the fundamental values of a democratic and judicial state, is not forwarded for a national referendum'.[252] Here, the court makes further specification to its conclusion by adding that '...CEC may refuse to register a draft law submitted by electors, only if it as to its content *obviously* incompatible with the guidelines provided by the Constitutional Court in Decision in Case No. 2012-03-01'.[253] This would mean that citizens' initiatives, which are *not obviously* incompatible with the guidlines provided by the court, should be advanced further and registered by the CECLv. In other words: *in dubio pro populo*. As previously mentioned, to get a clear answer to the question of the compatibility of draft laws with material requirements, the CECLv is entitled to request different experts or public institutions.[254] As Inese Nikulceva rightly observes, however, in her statement in the Court's decision in Case 2013-06-01, it cannot be ruled out that the opinions of these experts and public administration will be opposite and equally split. According to her, the commission should then decide in favour of registering the initiative (*in dubio pro populo*), thus allowing the electorate and the parliament to decide on the submitted popular proposal.[255]

---

250 Art. 23, par. 5 sec. 2 LoNRILaECI.
251 JLvCC 2013-06-01, point 13.2.
252 JLvCC 2013-06-01, point 13.2.
253 JLvCC 2013-06-01, point 14.3.
254 Art. 23, par. 6 LoNRILaECI.
255 JLCC 2013, point 8.

Table 2: Direct democratic institutions and their use in Latvia (1991–2014)

Mechanism of Direct Democracy	Name of DD Institution	Subject Matter	Submitted due to	Character	Intention	Pol. Actor / Veto-Player[1]		Formal Restrictions for						Use
						Asking (Framing)	Triggering	Turnout	Approval	Signatures	Collection Time	Collection Place	Range of Issues	q / a / ai[2]
 REQUIRED	Mandatory constitutional referendum	to alter articles 1, 2, 3, 4, 6 and 77 of the constitution	law	binding	proactive or reactive	parliament (citizens)	automatic	formally no, factually yes[3]	>50% of total electorate	–	–	–	yes, referred issues	0 / 0 / 0
	Mandatory Referendum on EU-Membership	to join or leave the EU	law	binding	proactive or reactive	parliament / EU	automatic	>1/2 of electors who participated in previous parl. Elections	>50% of the voters according to turnout restriction	–	–	–	yes only EU membership	1 / 1 / 0
	Parliamentary plebiscite for substantial changes in EU-Membership	a draft law or decision regarding substantial changes in the terms regarding EU membership	parliament	binding	proactive or reactive	parliament / EU	>1/2 of the parliament	>1/2 of electors who participated in previous parl. Elections	>50% of the voters according to turnout restriction	–	–	–	EU members: related provisions	1[10] / 1 / 0

Mechanism of Direct Democracy	Name of DD Institution	Subject Matter	Submitted due to	Character	Intention	Pol. Actor / Veto-Player[1]		Formal Restrictions for						Use
						Asking (Framing)	Triggering	Turnout	Approval	Signatures	Collection Time	Collection Place	Range of Issues	q / a / ai[2]
	Semi-plebiscite on repealing a law	to veto (refuse or repeal) a law	president or parliament and citizens	binding	reactive	parliament	president or >1/3 of the parliament[4] and >10% of total electorate[4]	>1/2 of electors who participated in previous parl. Elections	>50% of the voters according to turnout restriction	>10% of electorate	1 month[14]	designated collection stations	yes[6]	4 / 0 / 3
TOP-DOWN	Presidential plebiscite on recalling the parliament	to recall (dissolve) the parliament and to set new parl. elections	president	binding	proactive	president	president	no	>50% of the voters[5]	–	–	–	only to recall the parliament	1 / 1 / 0
	Citizens' constitutional initiative[7]	to initiate an elaborated draft to amend the constitution	citizens	binding	proactive	political party, association of pol. parties or >10 electors	1st stage: >30'000 citizens (1.94%) 2nd stage: >10% of total electorate[11]	formally no, factually yes[3]	>50% of total electorate	1st stage: 30'000 = >1.94% 2nd stage: >10% of total electorate[11]	1st stage: 12 months 2nd stage: 1 month[12]	designated collection stations[15]	yes[8]	2 / 0 / 1

Mechanism of Direct Democracy	Name of DD Institution	Subject Matter	Submitted due to	Character	Intention	Pol. Actor / Veto-Player[1]		Formal Restrictions for						Use
						Asking (Framing)	Triggering	Turnout	Approval	Signatures	Collection Time	Collection Place	Range of Issues	q / a / ai[2]
BOTTOM-UP	Citizens' legislative initiative[7]	to initiate an elaborated draft to amend a law	citizens	binding	proactive	political party, association of pol. parties or >10 electors	1st stage: >30'000 citizens (1.94%) 2nd stage: >10% of total electorate[11]	>1/2 of electors who participated in previous parl. elections	>50% of the voters according to turnout restriction	1st stage: 30'000 = >1.94% 2nd stage: >10% of total electorate[11]	1st stage: 12 months 2nd stage: 1 month[12]	designated collection stations[15]	yes[8]	1 / 0 / 1
	Citizens' initiative to recall parliament	to dissolve or recall the parliament and set new elections	citizens	binding	proactive	political party, association of pol. parties or >10 electors[9]	1st stage: >10'000 citizens (0.65%) 2nd stage: >10% of total electorate[13]	no	>2/3 of electors who participated in previous parl. elections	1st stage 10'000 = >0.65% 2nd stage: >10% of total electorate[13]	1st stage: 12 months 2nd stage: 1 month[13]	designated collection stations[15]	only to recall the parliament	0 / 0 / 0
Total Votes														10 / 3 / 5

Source: Author's characterisation

Remarks

1: The possibility of a referendum introduces the citizens as one additional veto player into public legislative process. A veto player is an individual or collective actor whose agreement is needed to change the legislative status quo. If an existing or latent veto player controls both the framing of the proposal and the triggering of the referendum, other veto players lose their ability to veto outcomes. Thus, the number of veto players decreases and the potential for policy change increases (HUG/TSEBELIS, 2002).

2: q / a / ai = quantity of referendums / approved / approved but invalid due to precise formal restrictions.

3: Depending on the approval quorum, it can range from 50 percent to 100 percent.

4: The Latvian unicameral parliament is composed of 100 members (Art. 5 CLv) and there are around 1,545,000 eligible citizens (2012).

5: If 50 percent of votes are cast against the dissolution of the parliament, then the president shall be deemed removed from office and the parliament elects a new president.

6: Issues according to art. 73 CLv and also urgent laws (art. 75 CLv) and no referendum shall be held if there is a second reading and a majority of 3/4 of all parliamentary members votes for the adoption of the law (art. 72 CLv).

7: It is an indirect initiative procedure. A referendum on the citizens' initiative only happens if the parliament rejects or adopts a citizens' proposal with changes to its content.

8: Policy areas according to art. 73 CLv are excluded from the popular initiative process.

9: There are some time restrictions during which the right to recall the parliament cannot be exercised (art. 14 CLv).

10: This popular vote refers to the referendum on independence of 3 March 1991. Indeed, at that time it was framed and triggered by the parliament. In the recent constitution, a similar top-down direct democratic provision is only possible for issues related to the EU.

11. In November 2012, the minimum number of signatures for the first stage had been raised by the Latvian parliament from 10,000 to 30,000. As of 1 January 2015, there will only beone signature collection round in which signatures from no less than one tenth of the eligible citizens must be collected within 12 months.

12: In November 2012, the collection procedure of signatures (for citizens' constitutional and legislative initiatives) had been changed. As of 1 January 2015, there will only be one signature collection round in which signatures from no less than one tenth of the eligible citizens have to be collected within 12 months.

13: As of 1 January 2015, there will be only one round, and signatures from no less than one tenth of the electorate will have to be collected within a period of 12 months.

14: No changes regarding time limit.

15. As of 1 January 2015 online collection via the Latvian Single State and Local Government Service Portal www.latvija.lv or via other online system chosen by the initiative group should be possible in addition to ordinary signature collection stations (art. 22 par. 4 and art. 7 LoNRILaECI.

B. Latvian direct democracy in practice

Since re-independence from Soviet occupation until the end of 2014, ten national referendums[256] have been held in Latvia (see Table 2, last column and Figure 2). The last referendum took place on 18 February 2012.[257] Only three of these referendums have been adopted and seven referendums have failed, which does not mean that they were rejected by the people. Much to the contrary, five of these seven were clearly accepted by the voters who had participated in the polls. But due to the missed turnout quorum that is formally (or factually) required, the ballot result had to be declared invalid. An invalidation of an approved referendum is often a result of the opponents' tactical call to their supporters that they should not participate in a corresponding popular vote.

As presented under part A of this chapter, eight different direct democratic tools, divided into three direct democratic mechanisms, exist in Latvia. Until recent times, though, not every tool has been used with the same frequency (*see Figure 2*).

Top-down referendums are the leading mechanism of Latvian direct democracy. Six referendums were triggered by the authorities or by joint action with the people. The first referendum from above (the referendum on independence) was triggered by the parliament. In four other cases, they resulted from a joint action of the authorities and the citizens to veto a law that the majority of the parliament had drafted (4 semi-plebiscites on repealing a law). The sixth plebiscite was brought forward by the president (presidential plebiscite on recalling parliament). Within two decades, only one required referendum (mandatory constitutional referendum) and three popular votes, which had been initiated by the citizens from below (2 citizens' constitutional initiatives, 1 citizens' legislative initiative), were carried out. The low number of citizen-initiated referendums does not automatically imply weak popular interest in bottom-up legislative procedures. Due to indirect initiative procedures, some popular drafts have been adopted without any changes to the content by the parliament itself and, thus completely succeeded as well (see chapters IV-B-11 and IV-B-12). Furthermore, there are around twenty other citizen-initiated referendums that either failed to collect the required number of signatures or are still being processed.

---

256 Including the referendum on re-independence that was approved on 3 March 1991.

257 See database c2d, http://www.c2d.ch/votes.php?level=1&country=196&yearr=time periods&fromyear=1992&toyear=2012&speyear[]=2013&result=0&terms=&table =votes&sub=Submit_Query (accessed on 03.02.2013).

Figure 2: Referendums held in Latvia

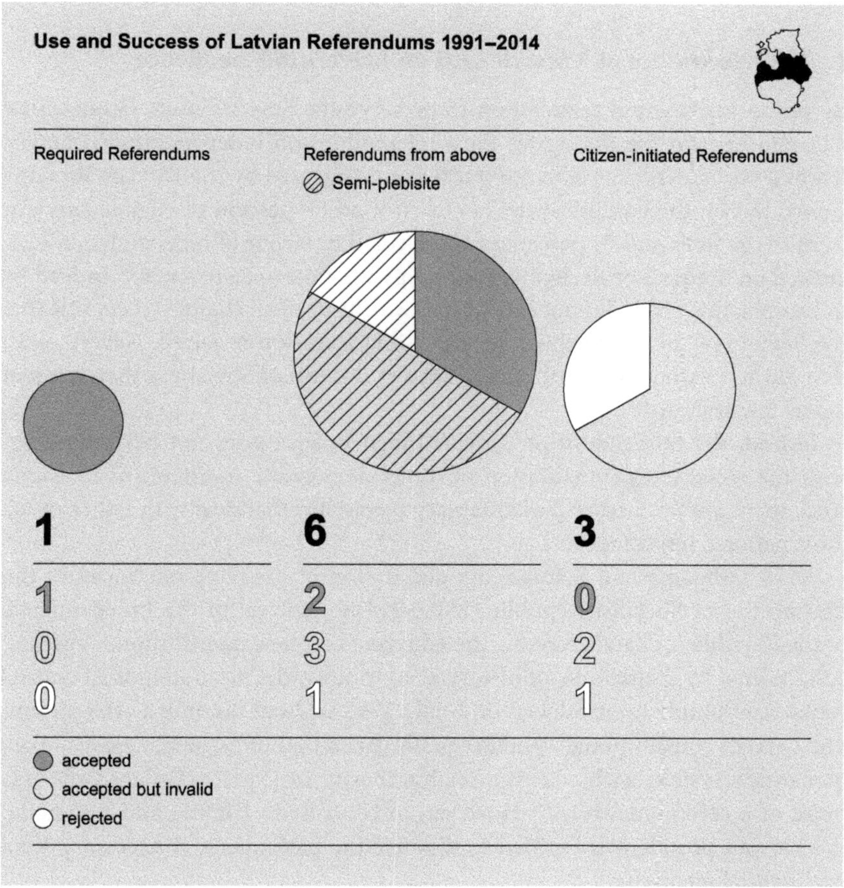

Source: Author's own calculations based on the data from www.c2d.ch and Latvian Central Election Commission

With regard to their political content, these ten referendums that have been held can be categorized in the following different policy areas: The main political issue which has been dealt with concerns state organisation and national identity, and legal and political systems as well as fundamental rights. There were five referendums on this topic. Two other referendums concerned social policy, specifically, the social security system. In two other cases, Latvian citizens had to come to a decision on security issues, namely on public security. In one case, the referendum referred to foreign policy, namely the accession to the EU.[258] The popular proposal that was adopted by the parliament directly dealt with energy issues.

1. The referendum of 3 March 1991 on Latvia's independence

By proposing a union referendum to preserve the Soviet Union, GORBACHEV had also opened the floodgates for a referendum on independence in Latvia. It was a parliamentary plebiscite framed and triggered by the Latvian Supreme Court, but on the base of Soviet law.[259] Around 88 percent of eligible Latvians went to the polls and 74 percent of them voted in favour of independence. Calculated on the basis of all eligible voters, this amounts to 65 percent.[260] Indeed, as in Estonia, this result did not exceed the two-thirds of all eligible voters rule that the Soviet law for its republics on a possible secession required. Nevertheless, that did not worry the Baltic states, since at the end of Soviet era they rejected Soviet law anyway.[261]

Indeed, the referendum on Latvia's independence does not perfectly align with the recent conceptualisation of direct democratic mechanisms in Latvia since there are no further parliamentary plebiscites that deal with issues of utmost national importance.

As in Lithuania and Estonia, the declaration of the Supreme Soviet of the Latvian Soviet Socialist Republic (SSR) on the Renewal of the Independence of the Republic of Latvia foresaw the adoption of a new constitution. However, conditioned by a discourse of historical continuity, the pre-communist constitution was simply reintroduced on 6 July 1993 without holding a referendum. The Latvian constitutional structure is similar to that of Estonia, namely a parliamentary system with constitutional authority over the president, who has more of a ceremonial role.[262] However, in contrast to Estonia and Lithuania, the Latvian president is entitled to dissolve the parliament, if necessary, by a presidential plebiscite.

---

258 Results available from http://www.c2d.ch/votes.php?table=votes (accessed on 30.05.2013).

259 BRADY/KAPLAN, p. 192f.; Loser Gorbachev, *The Economist* [London, England], 9 March 1991, p. 16.

260 See c2d database, http://www.c2d.ch/detailed_display.php?lname=votes&table=votes&page=1&parent_id=&sublinkname=results&id=39084 (accessed on 10.07.2013).

261 The Referendum Scorecard, *The Economist* [London, England], 23 March 1991, p. 62.

262 MOLE, p. 97.

2. The referendum of 3 October 1998 on the repeal of the facilitated naturalisation amendment

Six years after the restoration of independence, the first official referendum that was submitted to popular vote concerned the liberalisation of the regulations on naturalisation. The parliamentary reform aimed to facilitate citizenship for stateless children born after independence and to abolish the limitation on naturalisations per year (framing the question). The relevant new law was passed in part due to pressure from the Organisation for Security and Cooperation in Europe (OSCE). However, because of opposition from the Fatherland Party, the reformed law had to be taken to a referendum for approval.[263] As stated in article 72 CLv, the proclamation of a law adopted by the parliament can be suspended for a period of two months if there is such a request by the president or by one-third of the members of the parliament. The Fatherland Party, holding 38 seats, availed itself of this article and within the given time frame, they gathered the required signatures from one-tenth of all eligible citizens in order to submit the issue to a national referendum (semi-plebiscite on repealing a law based on a joint action). For the referendum, which had been held on the same day as the parliamentary elections, a participation quorum of at least 50 percent of the electors who participated in the previous Saeima elections was necessary.[264] As the referendum vote took place on the same day as the parliamentary elections, the obstructive tactic towards referendum supporters was prevented and the turnout was 19 percent higher than the formally requested quorum. Nevertheless, the repealed issue put to a popular vote did not get enough support by the participants. Only 46 percent of Latvian citizens voted in favour of the referendum to abolish facilitated naturalisation.[265] Due to this negative outcome, the reformed naturalisation law could not be repealed as the Fatherland Party had intended. In contrast, we can argue that the majority of Latvians voted in the same sense as the rest of the parliament, which reformed the law to facilitate naturalisation.

263 See c2d database, http://www.c2d.ch/detailed_display.php?lname=votes&table=votes&page=1&parent_id=&sublinkname=results&id=39221 (accessed on 13.08.2013); Ušacka, p. 106f.

264 See art. 74 CLv.

265 See c2d database, http://www.c2d.ch/detailed_display.php?lname=votes&table=-votes&page=1&parent_id=&sublinkname=results&id=39221 (accessed on 13.08.2013).

3. The referendum of 13 November 1999 on the repeal of the pension system reform amendment

On 5 August 1999, the parliament approved a new pension law, which would increase the retirement age for both men and women to 62 and to modify wage regulations for working pensioners (asking the question). The wage regulation aspect of the law aimed to limit pension benefits to persons who continued to work after retirement age.[266] Once more, in accordance with article 72 of CLv, three parties from the opposition moved to suspend the promulgation of the amendments on the retirement law for two months. During the given collection period of 30 days signatures from almost 14 percent of the electorate were collected (joint action on triggering the referendum) and the referendum (semi-plebiscite on repealing a law) was held on 13 November 1999. In spite of yes-votes from almost 95 percent of the voters who cast ballots, the referendum failed because the necessary participation threshold of 50 percent of the voters who participated in the previous parliamentary elections had not been reached.[267] Hence, the amendments to the pension system law were not repealed and the new law, as requested by the majority of parliament, entered into force.

4. The referendum of 21 September 2003 on accession to the European Union

The only mandatory referendum that has been held in Latvia is related to European integration. For Latvia, the referendum on joining the EU held on 21 September 2003 was the single most important political event in that year.[268] As mentioned previously, the Latvian Constitution had not contained any authorisation for referendums on such issues before. After the necessary supplementation of articles 68 and 79 of the Satversme, a formally accurate procedure in the sense of automatic triggering had been opened for holding a referendum on EU accession. On the ballot, the required turnout of at least 50 percent of the electors voting at the last elections to the parliament was cast by around 73 percent. Latvian electors voted 67 percent in favour of accession to the European Union.[269]

---

266 UŠACKA, p. 101ff.

267 See art. 74 CLv; c2d database, http://www.c2d.ch/detailed_display.php?lname=-votes&table=votes&page=1&parent_id=&sublinkname=results&id=39220 (accessed on 13.08.2013).

268 IKSTENS, Latvia 2004, p. 1056.

269 See c2d databae, http://www.c2d.ch/detailed_display.php?lname=votes&table=votes&page=1&parent_id=&sublinkname=results&id=39219 (accessed on 14.08.2013).

5. The referendum of 7 July 2007 on the repeal of amendments to the law on state security services

The Law on State Security Services and State Security Authorities (see next chapter IV-B-6), which had been enacted based on the emergency clause of the constitution[270] by the governing parties, aimed at enabling the government to access data from the intelligence services office, the security police and the military secret service (asking the question). However, the former Latvian President VAIRA VĪĶE-FREIBERGA voiced clear resistance to the amendments and submitted her veto according to article 72 of the constitution. Hence, the promulgation of the law was suspended for a period of two months. VĪĶE-FREIBERGA did not want to give political actors extensive access to secret services, which she believed could endanger Latvia's alliance with NATO. Consequently, a popular referendum was launched (joint action on triggering the referendum).

The president's move put the coalition on the defensive. As a consequence of this political pressure and to avoid a potentially major public embarrassment, the two corresponding amendments were withdrawn by the parliament in March 2007. Nevertheless, the initiated procedure of the presidential popular veto could not be stopped anymore and the referendums still went ahead.[271] The necessary ten percent of signatures to repeal the designed laws had been collected within the given period of 30 days and on 7 July 2007, the national ballot to repeal the amendments took place. The first referendum abolishing the amendment to the Law on State Security Services had been accepted by 97 percent of the voters. But, the requested turnout of half the number of those who had participated in the previous national parliamentary elections had not been reached and, thus, the final result did not count.[272] Nevertheless, the availability of the semi-plebiscitary referendum had demonstrated its efficacy ante, namely by forcing the parliament to withdraw its two amendments.

6. The referendum of 7 July 2007 on the repeal of amendments to the law on state security authorities

The second referendum repealing the amendment to the Law on State Security Authorities also followed according the same circumstances as described above

270 Art. 81 CLv. On May 3, 2007 the emergency clause was repealed by the parliament by a margin of 90 to 0 votes.

271 IKSTENS, Latvia 2008, p. 1043; AUERS, p. 64.

272 See c2d database, http://www.c2d.ch/detailed_display.php?lname=votes&table=votes&page=1&parent_id=&sublinkname=results&id=57318 (accessed on 14.08.2013).

(chapter IV-B-5). It was also accepted by 97 percent of the voters and failed to receive the qualified turnout quorum. However, it did not fail to show its full effect by forcing the parliament to withdraw its initial draft on the issue.[273]

7. The referendum of 2 August 2008 on the dissolution of parliament by popular vote

The first citizens' constitutional initiative that went to referendum was submitted by the Trade Union Confederation in November 2007. It was prompted by growing dissatisfaction with the performance of the parliament, an overheating economy and a growing trade deficit. The initiative claimed the amendment of articles 78 and 79 of the Satversme, enabling citizens to directly demand the dissolution of the parliament and thus to call extraordinary elections to it. Until this time, only the president was entitled to trigger a popular vote on recalling the parliament and to set preterm national elections, as stipulated in article 48 of the constitution.[274]

To launch the initiative on recalling the parliament by popular vote (triggering the referendum), initially no fewer than 10,000 signatures by eligible citizens were necessary. After gathering these signatures at a first collection stage, the initiative group submitted their corresponding constitutional draft amendment to the Central Election Commission.[275] After the CECLv had confirmed that 11,095 of the signatures collected were valid, the official collection of signatures (second stage) in support of the initiated draft began. The required 151,521 signatures (ten percent of the total electorate 2008) to submit the proposal to the Saeima for its mandatory consideration and eventual adoption were easily collected from 12 March to 10 April. In total, 217,567 voters had signed the proposal. According to procedures stated in articles 76 and 78 CLv, the president must submit the elaborated draft to the parliament.[276] For the initiated amendment to the constitution to be approved without the Saeima making any change to its content, it had to be passed by a majority of no less than two-thirds of the members of parliament. However, the citizens' proposal failed to reach this margin (with 44 to 37 votes and 17 abstentions). Consequently, a national referendum on this constitutional initiative was held on 2 August 2008. Around 97 percent of the 629,064 voters

273 See c2d database, http://www.c2d.ch/detailed_display.php?lname=votes&table=votes&page=1&parent_id=&sublinkname=results&id=57767 (accessed on 14.08.2013).

274 Ikstens, Latvia 2009, p. 1016f.

275 See art. 22 LoNRILaECI.

276 See also art. 25 LoNRILaECI.

who participated voted in favour of the proposal, but due to the low number of participants – 41.5 percent of the total 1,515,213 electors – the referendum fell short of the formally required approval quorum of 50 percent of the total electorate. Consequently, the adoption of the proposed constitutional amendment failed and the positive result had to be deemed void.[277]

This outcome was mainly caused by the political establishment's strong opposition. The majority of the parliament's parties called the citizens to boycott the vote in order to prevent the necessary threshold from being reached.[278] On the other side, the proponents of the amendment complained about the contest being rigged. In their view, setting the ballot date to the beginning of August undermined the required minimum of 50 percent threshold because many people were on holiday at that time.[279]

Surprisingly, only one year after the citizens' initiative on recalling the parliament by popular vote, an important institutional change to this matter took place, namely the amendment of article 14 of the constitution. Due to the growing economic crisis in the country and the pressure from the population as well as from the former President Valdis Zatlers, the Latvian parliament felt obliged to amend the constitution, thereby giving the citizens the right to ask and trigger a national referendum regarding the recall of parliament. Although the referendum on the dissolution of the parliament by popular vote had initially failed to be effective, we can certainly say that it had still achieved its purpose, namely by both bringing the issue into the political agenda and by putting public pressure on the parliament.[280]

8. The referendum of 23 August 2008 on a limited increase of public pensions

In the same month as the referendum on the dissolution of the parliament by popular vote, Latvian voters also had to vote on a second bottom-up initiated referendum, which was submitted to the Central Elections Commission by the association 'Society for Different Politics and Law-Governed State' together with

277 See c2d database, http://www.c2d.ch/detailed_display.php?lname=votes&table=votes&page=1&parent_id=&sublinkname=results&id=57768 (accessed on 14.08.2013); Ikstens, Latvia 2009, p. 1017f.

278 Auers, p. 64.

279 Ikstens, Latvia 2009, p. 1017.

280 See also the explanations in chapter IV-A-3-c 'The citizens' initiative on recalling parliament'.

the Pensioners and Seniors Party. It is the one legislative initiative that has been successfully submitted to a referendum. The draft law provided to amend article 34 of the transitional provisions of the Law 'On State Pensions' for establishing a minimum amount for pension payments.[281]

The proposal to increase public pensions was supported by 11,989 voters (quorum 10,000) at the initial signature drive. The following collection of signatures of no less than one-tenth of the electorate in a second step could be successfully accomplished with 170,342 instead of the necessary 151,610 signatures. The proposed draft law to the parliament was rejected with 6 to 44 votes and 46 abstentions. Therefore a national referendum on the proposed legislative initiative had to be held. Although the proposal had been supported by 96 percent of the voters, the law draft could not be adopted since the required turnout of at least 50 percent of the participants in the last parliamentary elections was not reached[282]; only 38 percent of the voters who voted in the 2006 parliamentary elections participated in this referendum. Thus, the referendum was declared to be not legally binding. The low turnout quorum was once again a result of a tactical campaign of non-participation, which was used by the opponents of the proposal, namely by government coalition parties and the liberal media.[283]

9. The referendum of 23 July 2011 on the early dissolution of the Saeima

On 28 May 2011, approximately one month before president VALDIS ZATLERS' four-year term was due to end, he called a referendum on recalling the parliament. This was the first dissolution referendum that a state president had triggered since a majority of parliamentary deputies had blocked a corruption inquest by the country's anti-corruption agency (KNAB) into one of the country's most notorious oligarchs and member of parliament, AINĀRS ŠLESERS.[284] According to president ZATLERS, the parliament had 'showed disrespect and mistrust of the competency of the judicial authorities'. But Zatlers' decision to dismiss the session of the parliament and invoke extraordinary elections was also caused by flagging support for his forthcoming re-election for a second term. In the negotiations

281 See http://cvk.lv/pub/public/29083.html (accessed on 23.05.2014).

282 Art. 79 CLv; see also the comments and results in the c2d database, http://www.c2d.ch/detailed_display.php?lname=votes&table=votes&page=1&parent_id=&sublinkname=results&id=57769 (accessed on 14.08.2013); IKSTENS, Latvia 2009, p. 1018.

283 IKSTENS, Latvia 2009, p. 1018; AUERS, p. 61.

284 A Long Hot Summer, *The Economist* [online], http://www.economist.com/blogs/easternapproaches/2011/06/latvian-politics/ (accessed on 15.08.2013).

with high-level party representatives, he failed to secure the necessary support for his re-election. As such, the decision for calling a referendum on extraordinary elections was also a decision motivated by retaliation.[285]

A few days after VALDIS ZATLERS's dissolution decision on 2 June 2011, there were presidential elections in the parliament and as expected ANDRIS BĒRZIŅŠ rather than VALDIS ZATLERS was elected the new president of Latvia. ZATLERS' defeat in the parliament was greeted with dismay by some anti-corruption protestors and the previous president VAIRA VĪĶE-FREIBERGA.

Indeed, ZATLERS had been ruled out for a second presidential term, but his political career was not yet finished. A few days after he had left office, he announced the establishment of his new centrist party: the 'Zatlers' Reform Party' (ZPR, in 2013, the party changed its name to 'Reform Party' by removing the name of its founding father ZATLERS). And according to the polls, his ZRP could expect enough support from the citizens for the extraordinary parliamentary election in September 2011.[286]

Two months after ZATLERS' dissolution decision, the presidential plebiscite on recalling the parliament was upheld on 23 July 2011. Approximately 45 percent of 1.5 million registered voters cast ballots and an overwhelming majority of these voters (95 percent) pursued ZATLERS' decision and voted in favour of dissolving the Saeima.[287] Consequently, as there is formally no minimum turnout quorum required for presidential plebiscites on recalling the parliament,[288] the parliament was dissolved. And almost one year after the last Saeima elections in October 2010 (the 10th Saeima Elections), new elections to the parliament were set for 17 September 2011. Although ZATLERS' request for the dissolution of the parliament led to retribution on part of the Saeima by refusing to grant him a second term, it was now the parliament that had been punished. Latvian citizens did not accept parliament's refusal to deal with state corruption. It can be argued that direct democracy from above has helped the people to protest against the lack of transparency and to act as a corrective. Furthermore, it was a tool to caution against corrupt developments in the establishment and to combat the power of the oligarchs. Thus, it should also be noted that this presidential plebiscite was not used to secure special legitimacy for the president's position, but rather to oblige the parliament to do its job correctly with respect to transparency.

---

285 IKSTENS, Latvia 2012, p. 179f., 183.

286 Valdis Zatlers plant Comeback, *Neue Zürcher Zeitung*, 23 July 2011, p. 7; see IKSTENS, Latvia 2013, p. 138.

287 Die Letten für baldige Wahlen, *Neue Zürcher Zeitung*, 25 July 2011, p. 2.

288 Art. 48 CLv.

On the extraordinary elections to the 11th Saeima on 17 September 2011, around 60 percent of the eligible voters went to the polls. Zatlers' party won 22 of 100 seats straight away and became the second largest political party in the Saeima after the winning party 'Harmony Centre' (HC, with 31 mandates), which is mainly supported by the Russian-friendly electorate. Until autumn 2014 'Zatlers' Reform Party', the 'Unity' party of the Prime Minister VALDIS DOMBROVSKIS, the right nationalist 'National Alliance' and a group of six independents who split away from the ZRP formed the Latvian government coalition, without the 'Harmony Centre', the winner of the parliamentary elections in 2011.[289] The 11th Saeima lasted for three years and the 12th Saeima elections were held on 4 October 2014. Once again the Russian friendly 'Harmony' party was the winner of the 2014 elections. Despite some losses (–7 mandates) it remained with 24 of 100 possible mandates the largest faction in parliament followed by the three governing parties, the 'Unity', the National Alliance 'All For Latvia' and the Union of Greens and Farmers.[290]

10. The referendum of 18 February 2012 on Russian as the second official language

Around 33 percent of Latvians are ethnically Russian or Belarusian and about 38 percent of the population declare Russian their native language.[291] There are also plenty of mixed marriages and bilinguals among the population. However, language as a symbol of nationality is more than a statistical matter in Latvia. It has more historical and political relevance for Latvians because during the Soviet occupation of over fifty years, Latvian was systematically supressed.[292] As a result of this traumatic experience, after re-independence the Latvian constituency recognized only Latvian as the official language of the country.[293] In recent times, some Latvian nationalists wanted to go much further and launched

289 See Die Linksopposition siegreich in Lettland, *Neue Zürcher Zeitung*, 19 September 2011, p. 3; Dombrovskis bleibt im Amt, *Neue Zürcher Zeitung*, 12 October 2011, p. 7; IKSTENS, Latvia 2012, p. 178, 181f.

290 See http://cvk.lv/pub/public/30868.html (accessed on 18.10.2014); Keine politische Experimente in Lettland, *Neue Zürcher Zeitung*, 6 October 2014, p. 5; The Reform Party dissapeared from the party landscape and its' members candidated for the Unity party.

291 See also DUVOLD, *Making Sense*, p. 96.

292 Lativia's Failed Referendum, *The Economist* [online], http://www.economist.com/blogs/easternapproaches/2012/02/more-questions-please (accessed on 20.11.2013).

293 Art. 4 CLv.

a citizens' constitutional initiative to amend article 112 of the constitution. The formulated draft claimed that Latvian should become the only official language at public schools as well. But in May 2011, this initiative failed to collect one tenth of the electors' signatures required at the second collection stage.[294]

As a counter reaction to this failed constitutional initiative, the association 'Native Language' (consisting of predominantly Russian-speaking Latvians) triggered its own constitutional initiative, intending to make Russian the second official language of Latvia.[295] According to their elaborated draft, articles 4, 18, 21, 101 and 104 of the constitution required alterations. In contrast to the nationalists' initiative, the proposal did not fail the second signature collection stage and succeeded in obtaining 187,378 signatures (10 percent quorum: 154,379). The success of the second citizens' constitutional initiative that had been submitted to a popular vote stemmed in part from the disappointment of the 'Harmony Centre' electors in the new government. As outlined under chapter IV-B-9, after the pre-term parliamentary elections in September 2011, the 'Harmony Centre' had been excluded from being part of the coalition despite the fact that it was the winner of the extraordinary elections. Officially, the 'Harmony Centre' itself did not support the initiative. However, this did not prevent its disillusioned supporters from signing the initiative 'Russian as second official language'.[296]

After successfully collecting the number of required valid signatures, the proposed constitutional amendment was submitted to the President ANDRIS BĒRZIŅŠ to present it to the parliament.[297] During the session, the government parties rejected the proposal by a margin of 0 to 60 and they also attempted to have the provision declared unconstitutional. However, the Constitutional Court did not stop the ballot. Even if the parliament had given its approval to the proposal, a popular vote would have been inevitable, since the formulated draft also included an alteration of article 4 of the constitution. And any amendment of article 4 requires a mandatory referendum, as article 77 CLv states.[298]

On the voting day, 71.10 percent of the total electorate cast ballots, which was the second highest referendum turnout since the March 1991 poll on Latvia's independence from the Soviet Union. The highly charged atmosphere mobilised

---

294 See chapter IV-B-12.

295 See IKSTENS, Latvia 2013, p. 136.

296 «Es gibt kein stärkeres Mittel, um uns wütend zu machen», *Neue Zürcher Zeitung*, 18 February 2012, p. 7; Russisch wird nicht zweite Amtssprache in Lettland, *Neue Zürcher Zeitung*, 20 February 2012, p. 3.

297 Art. 25, par. 1 and 2 LoNRILaECI.

298 See also art. 1, par. 1 LoNRILaECI.

many citizens both at home and abroad.[299] To come into force, a constitutional initiative had to be approved by at least half of the electorate[300] but the popular initiative was clearly rejected by around 75 percent of the voters.[301] As in other referendums, opposition to the initiative could have voided the referendum result by staying away from the polls. Nevertheless, the mobilisation was very high and many Latvians followed the former President Vaira Vīķe-Freiberga's and other top politicians' appeal to go cast their ballots and show the international community that the question of language does not matter exclusively to an ethnic minority, but to the whole population of the country.

Despite the high turnout and high rejection quota of 'Russian as second official language', the referendum still illustrates the existing ethnic cleavage between the pro- and anti-Russian groups after re-independence.[302] Latvian as well as Estonian policies regarding citizenship from the past have allowed ethnic divisions of society to emerge, which may entail potential for conflict.[303] The issue submitted to referendum once again had pushed up the political agenda and entrenched Latvian fears of assimilation and intimidation by their big eastern neighbour. Latvian citizens still fear that Russia and ethnic Russians in Latvia, many of whom regard Latvia's independence as a temporary situation.[304] Furthermore, in reaction to the referendum, the Latvian parliament raised the minimum number of signatures necessary for the first collection step to launch an initiative in 2013 from 10,000 to 30,000, a requirement which will be valid until 31 December 2014.[305]

11. Proposed and adopted initiatives without holding referendums

In April 2000, trade unions mobilised over 12,000 Latvian citizens (the required number at that time was 10,000) to submit a draft law to the Central Election Commission. The relevant amendment to the 'Law on Electric Power Industry' aimed at prohibiting the privatisation of Latvian electricity monopolist 'Latvenergo'. After the validation of these signatures, the second collection

299 See Ikstens, Latvia 2013, p. 137.

300 Art. 79, sec. 1 CLv.

301 See c2d database, http://c2d.ch/detailed_display.php?lname=votes&table=votes&page=1&parent_id=&sublinkname=results&id=132497 (accessed on 06.12.2013).

302 See Auers, p. 62.

303 Duvold, Making Sense, p. 94; Kneuer, Transformationsstaaten, p. 84, p. 88.

304 Latvia's Failed Referendum, *The Economist* [online], http://www.economist.com/blogs/easternapproaches/2012/02/more-questions-please (accessed on 20.11.2013).

305 Ikstens, Latvia 2013, p. 136.

stage started. Within 30 days, a total of 307,330 signatures of the electorate (23%) were collected and the draft law was submitted to the parliament for consideration. Due to huge popular support, the Saeima did not dare to reject the popular proposal and adopted the proposed law without making substantial changes to its content, preventing the need for a referendum. The popular initiative on the energy law succeeded fully and forced the government to backtrack on its proposal concerning the privatisation of the national electrical utility provider.[306]

12. Initiatives without sufficient signatures

In addition to the implemented initiatives described in the preceding sections, there have also been other attempts in Latvia to initiate some referendums from above between 1991 and 2014. There were six proposals for amending the constitution, two legislative initiatives and one launch for initiation a national referendum on three suspended laws. Most of them failed since the necessary number of signatures was not collected either at the first or at the second collection stage within the given time frame.

In one case in September 2012, the Central Election Commission took the view that the legislative initiative on amending the citizenship law had not been submitted as an elaborated draft as to its content and hence could not be forwarded for the second collection stage.

In 1995, the Farmer's Union of Latvia for instance aimed to reform the constitution and formulated a new draft amendment to the Satversme which contained several proposals, including directly electing the president, extending the parliament's term to four years, guaranteeing provisions for the dismissal of deputies and even a chapter devoted to local governments. In order to submit the draft to the CECLv, 10,000 signatures were necessary at that time. However, this number was not reached. Although the necessary amount failed to start the second stage of signature collection, in the following years the Latvian parliament adopted the aforementioned amendments, except the amendment stipulating direct election of the president by the Latvian citizens.[307] Hence, the popular initiative had a long-term effect.

In 1995, another popular initiative sought to recall single members of the parliament. Although over 10,000 (at that time) notarised signatures were collected

306 Ušacka, p. 108; Auers, p. 60.
307 Ušacka, p. 100, p. 105.

in favour of this proposal, this draft amendment to the constitution was never submitted to the CECLv. In 1996, a citizens' legislative initiative to make the citizenship law more stringent failed the second signature collection stage.[308]

Attempts after 2001 to reform the constitution and provide for a popularly elected state president, especially those by the Latvian Social Democrats, failed to gather the necessary support of 10,000 voters to initiate a referendum. The second attempt in 2009 at instituting a popularly elected head of state by 'All for Latvia!' also failed to gather the required 10,000 signatures.[309] Nevertheless, the later adoption of some other stated amendments by the Saeima shows that even if such referendum attempts fail to have a direct effect on the legislative process in the beginning, they boost the reform will in the legislation in the desired direction. In 2005, 'All for Latvia!' also launched a citizens' initiative that sought to put all amendments on the naturalization law to a referendum. However, it failed to collect the 10,000 notarised signatures required at that time.[310]

In June 2011 the '13 January' movement tried to collect signatures for a constitutional initiative to elevate the status of Russian by making it the second official language, but it failed at the first collecting stage to gather the 10,000 signatures required at that time.[311] However, as mentioned previously (see chapter IV-B-10), the second attempt by the association 'Native Language' to make Russian the second official language was more successful. Although it was successful in the first and second phase of the collecting process, it failed to win an absolute majority in the voting on February 2012.

In contrast, another initiative from the political opposition, namely the nationalist parties (National Alliance), aimed at making Latvian the sole language used at public schools by amending the article 112 of the Constitution. According to their draft law 'the state should provide an opportunity to acquire elementary education and secondary education in the state language (Latvian) free of charge' and from 1 September 2012 education, should be in the state language used from the first class on in all state and self-governing educational institutions.[312] As already outlined, the constitutional initiative failed to gather sufficient signatures from 10 percent of the electorate at the second collecting stage in May 2011. A total of 113,704 were gathered, far short of the 153,232 signatures required to

308 Feldhune, p. 82.
309 Ikstens, Latvia 2003, p. 1008f.; Auers, p. 63, p. 65.
310 See Auers, p. 63.
311 See explanations under chapter IV-B-10.
312 See http://cvk.lv/pub/public/29952.html (accessed on 23.05.2014).

support the constitutional proposal.[313] Once again, such attempts by nationalist parties illustrate that initiatives are mainly used to preserve the importance of the Latvian culture and language.[314]

In 2011, the parliament had amended the following laws: on state benefits in the time period from 2009 until 2012, on maternity and sickness insurance and on insurance in case of unemployment. Thereafter, the proclamation of these three laws was suspended by the president, since 37 members of the parliament had requested it.[315] To see whether the people supported the parliamentary decision for initiation, the process of holding a national referendum was started and signatures were collected from 18 May through 16 June 2011. A minimum number of no less than one-tenth of the electorate was required to put the suspended laws to a national referendum. However, for each suspended law only around 62,000 instead of 153,000 signatures were gathered, which did not result in a referendum being held.[316]

Another citizens' initiative that has recently failed to proceed refers to the draft law 'Amendments to the Citizenship Law'. After the first collection stage in September 2012, the draft law intending to introduce a facilitated naturalisation was submitted to the Central Election Commission for verification of the signatures. Indeed, after the initial stage it had received 12,686 valid signatures. However, the Central Election Commission had raised doubts as to whether the draft law could be considered a fully elaborated draft as prescribed by article 78 of the constitution. To decide that matter, the CECLv consulted various institutions and legal experts for their input on the citizens' initiative. In light of their conclusions, the commission decided that the initiative could not be considered a fully elaborated draft in terms of its content and thus could not be advanced to the second collection stage.[317] However, when considering the opinions of various experts consulted on the draft law, it becomes clear that the decision was also motivated by the fear of the loss of Latvian identity and possible gradual

313 c2d database, http://c2d.ch/detailed_display.php?lname=votes&table=votes&page=1&parent_id=&sublinkname=results&id=132497 (accessed on 07.12.2013); «Es gibt kein stärkeres Mittel, um uns wütend zu machen», *Neue Zürcher Zeitung*, 18.02.2012, p. 7; http://web.cvk.lv/pub/public/29982.html (accessed on 23.05.2014).

314 See Auers, p. 63.

315 See art. 72 CLv.

316 See http://cvk.lv/pub/public/29954.html and http://web.cvk.lv/pub/public/29993.html (accessed on 23.05.2014).

317 See http://cvk.lv/pub/public/30436.html (accessed on 24.05.2014).

Russification.[318] While excluding sizable minorities was justified in the immediate post-independence period on the grounds of 'nation-building', in more recent years, the concept of 'nation keeping' has been invoked to justify such exclusions. Today, 14 percent of the Latvian population are still 'non-citizens'.[319]

In addition to these initiatives that did not reach the required number of signatures, there were also some other signature-gathering drives held in 2008 and 2009 that would influence the policy agenda. Some associations tactically gathered non-notarised signatures to increase pressure on the political elite.[320]

13. Pending Initiatives

In addition to these failed initiatives, there are also some initiative launches that are still pending: there is an initiative (recall) on organizing a national referendum on dissolving the 11th Saiema, which has been submitted by the association 'Par latu, pret eiro' [For the Lats, against the Euro] to the Central Election Commission on 28 May 2013.[321]

In May 2013, the same association also submitted an application and a draft amendment to the constitution (citizens' constitutional initiative) as well as a draft law (citizens' legislative initiative) to amend the law 'on National Referendums, Legislative Initiatives and European Citizens' Initiative' to the Central Election Commission. According to the initiatives, no fewer than one tenth of voters should be allowed to propose a national referendum on Latvia's membership in the European Union and on substantial changes to its terms of membership.[322] The procedure is still open.

Another legislative initiative to amend the law 'on Protection of the rights of the Child' (articles 47 and 50^1) was submitted to the Central Election Commission by the association 'Sargāsim mūsu bērnus!' [Let's Protect Our Children] in October 2013.[323] The homophobic draft law states that 'sexual education in institutions of child education and care must be based on the provision of article 110 of the Constitution of the Republic of Latvia, popularisation and advertising of sexual and marriage relationship of homosexual persons must be prohibited in

318 See explanations and opinions of various experts at http://web.cvk.lv/pub/public/30422.html (accessed on 24.05.2014).

319 Die Ukraine-Krise wirft ihren Schatten auf Lettland, *Neue Zürcher Zeitung*, 26 September 2014, p. 5.

320 For more information see Auers, p. 61f.

321 See http://cvk.lv/pub/public/30688.html (accessed on 24.05.2014).

322 See http://cvk.lv/pub/public/30687.html (accessed on 24.05.2014).

323 See http://cvk.lv/pub/public/30686.html (accessed on 24.05.2014).

institutions of child education and care; it must be prohibited to involve a child as a participant or spectator in undertakings aimed to raise popularity and advertise sexual and marriage relationship of homosexual persons, as well'. Required signatures for the controversial initiative have not yet been collected; however, it appears that the initiative will trigger discussions both in Latvia and in the European Union, should it lead to a popular decision.

C. Explanations for the Latvian practice

Ten referendums – six more than in the case of Estonia – have been held in Latvia since re-independence and many others have failed to collect the mandatory number of signatures. Again, a structural and informal approach has to be used to explain the factors driving the differences in the use and successes of referendums in these countries. In Latvia, the success and variation in the number of referendums result largely from the formal institutional arrangements that are provided for direct democracy. The political elites and the citizens act within a framework of constitutional institutions that circumscribe and define their behaviour. According to ELLEN IMMERGUT, the different policy outcomes are a result of different institutional designs of a country – not exclusively a result of the actors' decisions. Specific institutional configurations create strategic contexts that determine the interest and actions of the political actors.[324] In addition to the formal settings in Latvia, the informal arrangements also have to be considered. Within the framework given by the constitution, political parties and actors tend to use direct democratic instruments in different strategic ways and with different degrees of success. Insofar, it is the interaction between the formal arrangements and political players that define to what extent direct democracy is used in Latvia.

1. Legal constraints

The most important difference in Latvian direct democracy concerns the degree of direct democratic institutions that are constitutionally given to the Latvian people. Indeed, there are eight different direct democratic tools that can either be started automatically, like mandatory referendums, or top down by the authorities. Most importantly, a citizen-initiated direct democratic mechanism to create new laws is also available to Latvians. Recently, Latvians got an additional bottom-up instrument that entitles them to initiate a national referendum regarding

324 IMMERGUT, Policy-making, p. 58, p. 85; IMMERGUT, Health Politics, p. 5; KAISER, Types, p. 422.

the recall of the parliament. All types of referendums produce a legally binding result for all state institutions.

Due to a wide range of these direct democratic tools, one might expect they are frequently used. However, there are several formal obstacles that prevent Latvians from using these tools more frequently. Therefore, it is not only important to have different mechanisms of direct democracy, but also to ensure that it works in practice. Any formal obstacle that favours the public elites over the people would lead to a lack of interest and disappointment in the direct democratic political process. Citizens will remain unconvinced about the performance of democracy and they will harbour negative feelings and attitudes towards the current elites and the institutions they represent.

The first legal constraint concerns policy areas of a referendum. Some political issues cannot be submitted to a national referendum. According to article 73 of the Latvian constitution, for instance, 'loans, taxes, custom duties, railroad tariffs, military conscription, declaration and commencement of war, peace treaties, declaration of a state of emergency and its termination, mobilisation and demobilisation, as well as agreements with other nations', along with urgent laws pursuant to article 75 CLv are excluded from the referendum process.

A second constraint concerns signature collection, which is based on two collection stages (only, however, until the end of 2014). In Latvia, there are around 1.5 million registered voters. Article 78 in conjunction with article 65 of the Satversme enables the people to 'submit a fully elaborated draft of an amendment to the Constitution or of a law to the President, who shall present it to the Saeima'. But such a submission requires valid signatures from at least 10 percent of the entire electorate, which are to be gathered at a second stage. Compared to signature collection in Swiss direct democracy for instance, in which around 2 percent of the registered voters – within a period of 18 months – are needed to propose a total or partial revision of the Federal Constitution, the Latvian threshold seems to be rather high. This requirement can hamper the collection of required signatures, especially if the collection time is limited to 30 days and signatures can only be collected at designated collection places.[325] At least within the framework of provisions of LoNRILaECI on 8 November 2012, the collection period was extended to 12 months and it will come into force starting on 1 January 2015 (see remarks in Table 2). Moreover, according to article 22 par. 4 LoNRILaECI from then on, in addition to signature collection at designated stations, signatures could also be collected via online systems.

---

325 Art. 7, par. 1 LoNRILaECI.

In order to trigger a referendum, the same high number of signatures (within one month, unchanged) is also required for a semi-plebiscite on repealing a law, as indicated in article 72 CLv, or for the citizens' initiative on recalling the Saeima, as established in article 14 CLv. One should also be aware of the fact that the referendum on repealing a law can only be triggered if the authorities suspend the proclamation of a law for period of two months in advance. Hence, in order to veto parliamentary laws, a joint action of the authorities and citizens is needed.

The third obstacle for Latvian referendums is both the turnout and approval quorums required by the constitution. To be declared legally binding in a mandatory constitutional referendum, at least half of the eligible electorate has to vote in favour. The same criterion is also required for the adoption of a citizens' constitutional initiative.[326] Indeed, there is no formal turnout quorum required but to effectively reach such a high approval quorum, many citizens have to participate in the ballot. In a semi-plebiscite on repealing a law or in a citizens' legislative initiative, at least half of the number of electors that participated in the previous parliamentary election has to participate, and the majority of them have to vote in favour of the referendum. Another quorum pursuant to article 14 CLv is required when Latvian citizens initiate a referendum on recalling the parliament. To dissolve the parliament and set new elections, at least a majority of two thirds of the number of the voters who participated in the last parliamentary elections is necessary.

Turnout quorums, whether formal or factual, may be the most significant factor that impacts the adoption of a referendum. As mentioned above, in Latvia there were three referendums on repealing a law; one citizens' constitutional and one citizens' legislative initiative had been declared legally non-binding, despite the fact that they had all been accepted by the majority of the voters. An exception among these referendums is the presidential plebiscite on recalling the parliament; in this case, neither a formal nor a factual turnout quorum is required.

2. Informal constraints

The five referendums that have been accepted by the majority of the voters but have been declared legally non-binding due to low turnouts illustrate how the interaction between institutions and political actors matters. Knowing that there is both formally and factually a minimum turnout required, opposition to the referendum can act tactically to block it from getting approved. They do not only

326 Art. 79 CLv.

oppose such proposals but they also urge citizens to ignore them and not participate in the corresponding polls, so that the decision will be void. An exception was the last referendum on Russian as the second official language in February 2012, and this because of its cultural and historical significance for all Latvians. It is less advisable to introduce such quorums because it does not only strongly decrease the potential of an approval, but also the potential of having constructive political discourse on the issue subject to referendum. The opponents of a reform should instead seek to convince the majority of the citizens with arguments rather than simply working to boycott the ballot. Such a mentality does not help to the development of a critical civil society within a country, nor does it contribute to direct democracy.

A second informal aspect that influences the outcome of direct democracy in Latvia is caused by the party system. In Latvia, the parliament is elected based on a system of proportional representation. The formal rule of a proportional electoral system results in an informal multi-party system, which, according LUISE P. MØLLER, creates different incentives for political parties to use referendums.[327] She states that the Latvian party system is a fragmented system that has been characterized by large coalition governments.[328] In Latvia as in Estonia and Lithuania, voter volatility is two or three times higher than the average score for Central and Eastern Europe.[329] Considering the developments in the Latvian party system since 2002 and the emergence of new parties and fractions, as has been described by JĀNIS IKTENS in his annual Latvian reports,[330] we can confirm that the Latvian party landscape, shaped by ethnic cleavages (Latvian vs. Russian), is still quite volatile and unstable. The former president VALDIS ZATLERS' new political party, ZRP, which was established after his defeat in parliament 2011 and its disappearance from the party landscape in 2014, does not promise any stabilisation in the party system at all. In such a fragmented and loose constellation, new parties and their electorate are less equipped to organise and win a popular vote, either by collecting signatures to initiate a referendum or by mobilising the supporters to achieve the requested minimum turnout on the polling day.[331] Indeed, most attempts in this sense of triggering citizens' initiatives have

---

327 MØLLER, p. 281f.

328 MØLLER, p. 285.

329 DUVOLD, Making Sense, p. 192f., 197f.; SIKK, How Unstable, p. 396; KREUZE/PETTAI, Instablility, p. 83f; KNEUER, Transformationsstaaten, p. 87.

330 IKSTENS, Latvia 2003, p. 1001; IKSTENS, Latvia 2004, p. 1055; IKSTENS, Latvia 2005, p. 1077; IKSTENS, Latvia 2009, p. 1019; IKSTENS, Latvia 2012, p. 183f.

331 Similar to MØLLER, p. 290.

been done to attract political publicity for the parties and to increase popular support, especially in the lead-up to an election.[332]

Another informal constraining aspect results from the political culture itself. As far as the constitution is concerned, there is no lack of bottom-up direct democratic mechanisms in Latvia. However, it still lacks a strong participatory culture 24 years after independence.

At least recent developments within last two years display a trend toward increased popular activity. This may become much stronger after 2015 when the collection period of signatures from no less than one-tenth of electorate is extended to 12 months. But still, as mentioned above, turnout or approval quorums are the most effective hurdles. They are not conducive to strengthening a participatory culture, which is why they might be altered within another revision to the provisions of referendums. Furthermore, civil society may become stronger when there are also some arrangements for civic participation at local level. Given the communist legacy, though, it takes considerable time to build independent associations, particularly when there are still fewer informal ties between minority and native groups and little fertile ground for 'segmented-style democracy'.[333]

332 See Auers, p. 59.

333 Duvold, Making Sense, p. 256f.

V. The legal framework and practice of direct democracy in Lithuania

A. Direct democratic instruments in Lithuania

Lithuania is a unitary state with a parliamentary system. The unicameral parliament is composed of 141[334] deputies, who are elected to a four-year term. The Lithuanian electoral system is a combination of majoritarian and proportional representation. Half of the parliament's members are elected in each of 71 districts according to majoritarian rule, the other half according to proportional representation.[335] The president of the state is also elected through a popular vote, but for a term of five years.[336] Direct election ensures the president a great degree of legitimacy as the head of state. This is also apparent in the presidential functions, which are more than representative ones. In particular, the president's strong position becomes especially clear in foreign policy,[337] which is why some scholars characterize Lithuania as a parliamentary-presidential system.[338] However, the president's decision-making competencies are dependent on the consensus of the government and on a strong parliament (Seimas).[339] Therefore, Lithuania could also be referred to as a semi-presidential system dominated by the parliament.[340]

In addition to the government and parliament, there is an additional important political body that can be involved in the legislative process, namely the Lithuanian people. As article 4 of the constitution[341] states, 'the nation shall execute its supreme power either directly or through its democratically elected representatives'.[342] The Lithuanian representative democracy is completed by a system of decision-making on public issues in which citizens over 18 years can

334 Art. 55, sec. 1, Constitution of the Republic of Lithuania of 25 November 1992 (CLt).

335 See TAUBER, Litauen, p. 194.

336 A second term is possible.

337 Art. 84, sec. 1 CLt.

338 KRUPAVICIUS/ZVALIAUSKAS, p. 120.

339 TAUBER, Litauen, p. 176f., 179.

340 For more information on the competences of the institutions of the parliament and the president see SAULIUS, Sovereignty, pp. 99–109.

341 Adopted by the citizens of the Republic of Lithuania in the referendum of 25 October 1992.

342 See art. 3, art. 9, art. 33 CLt and also JLtCC 1994-07-22, point 1.

directly get involved.[343] Implementing the people's sovereignty into the legislative process can occur in three ways. According to the theoretical classification of the mechanisms of direct democracy set forth in the beginning, it can be implemented by a referendum that is either called automatically, from above or from below. There are around 2,538,400 eligible voters in Lithuania.[344] The current 'Law on Referendum' (LoR) distinguishes between referendums that are mandatory in terms of being decisive and those that are consultative.[345] As in Estonia and Latvia, decisive referendums enable Lithuanians to become a veto player within the decision-making process. Mandatory referendums are binding and are designed to deal primarily with constitutional issues,[346] including Lithuania's membership in international organisations in certain respects and amendments the constitutional act of 8 June 1992.[347] Legally it is also possible to hold a mandatory referendum on issues that might refer to other national issues or to legal norms below the constitutional level.[348] Any issue below the constitutional normative level that has not been deliberated in a mandatory referendum is considered consultative. Although such referendums are non-decisive, the parliament is obliged to hold a debate on the issue and to submit it to a popular decision. Regardless of the citizens' approval the final say is vested in the parliament.[349] Unlike in Estonia and Latvia, in Lithuania there is no restriction on the range of issues for top-down and bottom-up referendums. Any issue falling within the jurisdiction of parliament can be subject of a referendum. In accordance with Lithuanian jurisprudence and constitutional tradition, a referendum must be understood 'as the popular vote on the issues concerning the adoption of the

343 Art. 2, par. 2, Law on Referendums (LoR) passed by the Lithuanian Parliament on 4 June 2002.

344 See the Central Electoral Commission of the Republic of Lithuania (CECLt), http://www.2013.vrk.lt/2014_referendumas/output_en/referendumas/referendumas.html (accessed on 30.06.2014).

345 Art. 3 LoR in conjunction with art. 5, art. 6, par. 2, art. 12, par. 1 LoR.

346 According to art. 168 of Seimas, statute laws provided in art. 150 of the constitution, constitutional amendments, laws which are directly specified in the constitution, as well as other laws which give specific expression to constitutional norms and are set forth in the Law on the List of Constitutional Laws can be deemed to be constitutional laws.

347 Krupavicius, Lithuania 2003, p. 1017.

348 The constitution does not make any clear specifications. Advice for such a distinction can be derived from art. 4, par. 2 and art. 7, par. 4 of the LoR. See also Krupavicius, Citizens' Initiatives, p. 136.

349 Krupavicius, Citizens' Initiatives, p. 136.

Constitution, laws or provisions of laws, as well as home and foreign policy'. According to the constitutional court, any restriction on these issues would contradict articles 3, 4, 9 and 33 of the constitution.[350] Despite that openness a serious weakness of Lithuanian referendum rights arises from other legal obstacles. The constitution prescribes a short time period for the collection of a large number of signatures, and requires a very high threshold for participation and approval.

All specific rules and procedures are established by the 'Law on Referendum'[351] (LoR-1989), which was first passed by the Supreme Soviet of the Soviet Socialist Republic of Lithuania in 1989. Even at that time, article 3 of the LoR guaranteed Lithuanian citizens, political parties, and other political and public organisations the right to campaign without any restrictions on proposing to call a referendum, adopting legal provisions, or settling issues of the utmost significance. In the following years, the 'Law on Referendum' was amended by the Seimas several times because some amendments had been found to be inconsistent with the constitution by the constitutional court.[352] Real discussion on new proposals to the law started in 1999, evidently brought about by the forthcoming referendum on EU accession.[353] Finally, on 4 June 2002, the LoR was substituted by a totally new law. The last modification to the 'Law on Referendum' (LoR) was made on 6 May 2014.[354]

Today, depending on the categorisation made in this book, nine different direct democratic tools can be applied in Lithuania (for an overview see Table 3). The form and complexity of their procedure is determined by three mechanisms of direct democracy that were characterised in the beginning, although the complexity also results from numerous and often controversial changes that were made to Lithuanian legislation.[355] Referendums are organised and carried out by the Central Electoral Committee (CECLt).

---

350 JLtCC 1994-07-22, point 1 and 4. For instance, art. 3 CLt states 'No one may restrict or limit the sovereignty of the Nation or make to the Sovereign powers belonging to the entire Nation. The Nation and each citizen shall have the right to resist anyone who encroaches on the independence, territorial integrity, and constitutional order of the State of Lithuania by force'.

351 See also art. 9, sec. 2 CLt.

352 Krupavicius/Zvaliauskas, p. 113.

353 Mazylis/Unikaite, p. 1.

354 See http://www3.lrs.lt/pls/inter3/dokpaieska.showdoc_l?p_id=470578&p_tr2=2 (accessed on 04.06.2014).

355 Mazylis/Unikaite, p. 2.

1. Referendums required by constitution

According to article 9 CLt, 'the most significant issues concerning the existence of the state and the nation shall be decided by a referendum'. An issue can be deemed as important if the constitution or law explicitly demands its decision by a referendum. In the case of Lithuania, there are three different mandatory referendums automatically required by the constitution or the law: mandatory constitutional referendums, mandatory referendums on amendments to the Constitutional Act, and mandatory referendums on participation in international organisations.[356] All three instruments have a delaying effect, regardless of whether the proposal is accepted or rejected. In most cases, these referendums are framed by the parliament and triggering follows automatically, as required by the constitution. Framing of referred issues can also be brought about from the bottom up if citizens propose a policy change on the issue individually.[357] Another framing actor can also appear if the proposal submitted to vote deals with international treaties. Here the framing is mostly a result of a joint action of the national parliament and the other state or international organisation.

a) The mandatory constitutional referendum

In general, amendments of the majority part of constitutional provisions must be considered and voted on twice in the parliament. To be deemed adopted, a draft law on the alteration of the constitution has to be approved in both sessions by a qualified majority of no less than two-thirds of all members of the parliament and no referendum is required.[358] However, in case of an alteration of the provisions of chapter I and chapter XIV of the constitution, a popular vote is mandatory. Otherwise, these provisions cannot be changed.[359] Chapter I, 'The State of Lithuania', covers the first 17 articles of the constitution that determine the form and governing rules of the Lithuanian political system, including other fundamentals, such as referendum rights, territorial integrity, citizenship, official language, the state flag and the capital. Chapter XIV, consisting of articles 147–154 CLt, refers to these legal provisions that concern the 'Alteration of the Constitution'. It is forbidden to amend the constitution during a state of emergency or martial law.[360]

356 Art. 4, par. 1, sec. 1, 2, 3, 4 and 5 LoR.

357 See chapter V-A-3 Citizen-initiated referendums.

358 Art. 148, sec. 3 CLt.

359 Art. 148, sec. 1 and 2 CLt; art. 4, par. 1, sec. 1–3 LoR.

360 Art. 147, sec. 2 CLt.

b) *The mandatory referendum on the Constitutional Act*

The mandatory referendum on the Constitutional Act is another direct democratic tool, which is automatically triggered if there is any alteration to the Constitutional Act of 8 June 1992 'on the Non-Alignment of the Republic of Lithuania to Post-Soviet-Eastern Alliances'.[361]

c) *The mandatory referendum on participation in an International Organisation*

Any decision concerning Lithuanian membership in international organisations that requires a 'partial transfer of the scope of competence of government bodies to the institutions of international organisations or jurisdictions thereof' has to be submitted to a popular vote as well.[362]

d) *The procedure of referendums required by the constitution*

All three 'automatic referendums' are binding and conducted by almost the same procedures. Any referendum on the amendment of chapters I and XIV of the constitution, on the Constitutional Act of 8 June 1992, as well as on participation in international organisations in certain respects, as previously indicated, require both a high turnout and approval quorum. According to article 7, par. 1 LoR 'a mandatory referendum shall be deemed to have taken place if over one half of the citizens, who have the right to vote and have been registered in electoral rolls, participated in it'. If a participation quorum fails to reach 50 percent of the total electorate, an automatic referendum is deemed void, even if approved.

For an approval of a 'mandatory constitutional referendum' the support of more than half of registered electorate is required.[363] One deviation from this approval provision concerns the alteration of the first article of the constitution, which states that 'the state of Lithuania shall be an independent, democratic republic'. The first provision of the constitution can 'only be altered by referendum if not less than three-fourths of the citizens of Lithuania with electoral rights vote in favour thereof'.[364]

The same wide approval quorum is also required for an amendment to the Constitutional Act of 8 June 1992, as described under 'mandatory referendum

361 Art. 4, par. 1, sec. 4 LoR.

362 Art. 4, par. 1, sec. 5 LoR.

363 Art. 7, par. 3 LoR.

364 Art. 148, sec. 1 CLt and art. 7, par. 2 LoR.

on constitutional act'.[365] Finally, the third compulsory referendum, the 'mandatory referendum on participation in international organizations', will be deemed approved if more than one half of the voters who participated in the referendum has accepted it.[366] Given the required turnout threshold of no less than one half of all enfranchised citizens, this means that no less than one-quarter of total electorate is needed for a legally binding decision.

The Central Electoral Committee is entitled to establish and officially announce the final results of the referendum on its website within four days of the referendum vote.[367] In case of an approval, the CECLt also has to present the text of the resolution adopted by referendum to the president no later than the next day following the official publication of the final referendum results.[368] The decision of the Central Electoral Committee on the final results can be appealed to the Supreme Administrative Court of Lithuania by a group, party or representatives no later than within two days of its official publication.[369] If there are no complaints, the president must sign and officially proclaim the resolution passed by referendum within five days of the official publication of the results. Should the president fail to sign and proclaim such a law, the chairman of the parliament must then sign and proclaim it.[370] A law passed by referendum on an amendment to the constitution enters into force no earlier than one month from the date of its approval by the referendum vote.[371] Other laws that pass an automatic referendum 'shall enter into force on the next day following their official publication in the Register of Legal Acts, unless a later date of the entry into force is stipulated in them'.[372]

2. Referendums from above

In addition to Estonia and Latvia, the right to trigger a referendum from above is also given to the Lithuanian authorities. The Lithuanian top-down direct democratic mechanism is composed of two instruments: the 'parliamentary constitutional plebiscite' and the 'parliamentary plebiscite on other issues, laws and provisions'. Considering the wording of article 9, par. 3 LoR, 'a group comprising

365 Art. 7, par. 2 LoR.
366 Art. 7, par. 5 in conjunction with art. 4, par. 5 LoR.
367 Art. 71 and 73, par. 1 LoR.
368 Art. 73, par. 2 LoR.
369 Art. 74, par. 1 LoR.
370 Art. 78, par. 2 and 3 LoR.
371 Art. 78, par. 4 LoR.
372 Art. 78, par. 5 LoR.

of at least one-fourth of the Seimas members may submit to the Seimas a proposal to call a referendum', it suggests that a parliamentary plebiscite, whether constitutional or not, can either be proactive or reactive.

A *proactive* policy change supporting parliamentary plebiscite may occur if a reform wing in the parliament is afraid that it may not receive the support of the required parliamentary majority and thus wants to get the needed approval of the people (framing and asking by the same actor). A *reactive* status quo supporting parliamentary plebiscite may be held if some of the parliamentary members trigger a referendum on a resolution that has been framed and passed by the majority part of the parliament (different actors for framing and triggering). In both cases, the necessary threshold for triggering a referendum requires at least one-quarter of all members of parliament.[373] Therefore, it is a parliamentary minority referendum. However, this does not prevent the parliamentary majority from also calling a referendum.

The threshold for calling a parliamentary referendum has been decreased two times since 1992. In the beginning, more than half of the parliamentary members and after 1996, one-third of the deputies, were asked to initiate the calling of a referendum.[374] As such, the right to initiate a plebiscitary referendum has become somewhat more of an instrument of parliamentary minorities. That said, it is still a significant obstacle for small parties in the parliament.

a) The parliamentary constitutional plebiscite

According to article 9, par. 1 LoR, the right to initiate the calling of a referendum is given not only to the citizens, but also to the Lithuanian parliament.[375] As mentioned previously, such referendums can either be proactive or reactive. The procedures for submitting the issue to popular vote are the same. The proposal of the parliamentary group to call a referendum must indicate the type of referendum (mandatory or consultative; it should be noted that resolutions on constitutional issues are mandatory) and the text of the resolution that should be adopted by a referendum.[376] The resolution can either concern a motion to alter or supplement the constitution, which has been submitted by a parliamentary minority consisting of a group of no less than one-fourth of all members of the

---

373 Art. 9, par. 3 LoR.

374 Krupavicius, Citizens' Initiatives, p. 136f.

375 See also art. 4, par. 2 LoR; art. 147 CLt.

376 Art. 12, par. 1 LoR.

parliament,[377] or an issue framed by the legislative majority that should be vetoed by popular decision. For both the proactive and reactive types of constitutional plebiscites, a group comprising at least one-fourth of the members of parliament is needed to submit a proposal to parliament calling for a referendum.[378]

It is important to note that no policy area is excluded from the referendum process. The parliamentary group can propose resolutions for any constitutional issue within the competence of parliament that it deems significant to the existence of the state and the nation.[379] The parliament's decision on the proposal to call a referendum must be made in accordance with the procedure set forth by the Seimas statute[380] and the referendum must be held 'no later than in three months and no sooner than in two months from the day of passing the Seimas Resolution on the date of calling the referendum'.[381]

As with other referendums, parliamentary plebiscites also require a turnout quorum of 50 percent of the total electorate.[382] A constitutional plebiscite fails if less than 50 percent of the electorate take part in it. Depending on the issue submitted to referendum, the procedure on approval can vary. If it refers to the provisions of chapters I and XIV of the constitution, which are subject to required referendums, then the approval quorum ranges from at least one-half to three-fourths of the entire electorate.[383] If it refers to constitutional provisions other than those in chapters I and XIV, then the parliamentary constitutional plebiscite shall be deemed adopted if it has been approved by at least one-third of the electorate.[384] Before the total revision of the LoR in 2002, the minimum approval quorum for such referendums was at least 50 percent of all enfranchised voters. With the new law, which partially lowered some approval quorums, direct democracy became a bit more citizen-friendly, but the procedure of direct legislation still poses a significant obstacle. If the law passes a referendum on an amendment to the constitution, it must enter into force no later than one month from the day the referendum was passed.[385]

---

377 Art. 147, sec. 1 CLt.

378 Art. 9, par. 3 LoR.

379 Consider art. 4, par. 2; art. 9, par. 3 LoR.

380 Art. 9, par. 3 and art. 12, par. 1 LoR, see chapters XIX–XXVI of *Seimas of the Republic of Lithuania Statute of 17 February 1994.*

381 Art. 15, par. 1 and 2 LoR.

382 Art. 7, par. 1 LoR.

383 Art. 7, par. 1–3 LoR.

384 Art. 7, par. 4 LoR.

385 Art. 78, par. 4 LoR.

b) The parliamentary plebiscite on other issues, laws and provisions

As paragraph 3 of article 9 LoR states, the right to calling a referendum belongs not only to the citizens, but also to any parliamentary group comprised of no less than one-fourth (>141:4) of the members of parliament.[386] Here, the article does not make any distinction as to whether such a referendum is applicable to constitutional or other issues. In conjunction with article 3; article 4, par. 2; article 5; article 6; article 7, par. 4; article 12, par. 1 LoR, as well as with article 67, par. 3 and article 69, sec. 4[387] CLt, we can state that a parliamentary plebiscite is also possible for other issues and laws than were provided by the constitution. Once the parliamentary minority considers an issue fundamental to the state and the nation, it can become subject to a referendum.[388] As with parliamentary constitutional plebiscites, there are no formal restrictions on potential policy areas. Such authorities' referendums can be held on any issues and laws that are within the jurisdiction of parliament.[389] Also here, both intensions of the referendum are possible: a proactive parliamentary plebiscite to make an alteration of laws possible and a reactive parliamentary plebiscite to veto a parliamentary resolution. As with constitutional plebiscites, the parliamentary minority proposal on other issues must also be deliberated by the parliament.

One distinction with constitutional plebiscites is the character of the referendum vote. Insofar as the proposal does not deal with constitutional matters, it can either be consultative or binding. As article 12, par. 1 in conjunction with article 3, article 5 and article 6, par. 2 LoR states the parliamentary group must indicate the type of referendum, and according to the procedure set forth in the 'Seimas Statute', the parliament adopts a decision on it. For the validation of the results, a turnout quorum of 50 percent of the total electorate is also required here.[390] To be adopted, a consultative parliamentary minority plebiscite has to be approved by at least one half of the voters who participate – i.e. no less than 25 percent of the entire electorate, considering the participation threshold that is needed.[391] Even if approved by the citizens, the final decision on consultative parliamentary plebiscites depends on the volition of the entire parliament. It is

386 Art. 9, par. 1 and 3 LoR.
387 Provisions of laws of Lithuania may also be adopted by referendum, see art. 69, sec. 4 CLt.
388 Art. 9, sec. 1 CLt.
389 Consider art. 4, par. 2, art. 7, par. 4 and art. 9, par. 3 LoR.
390 Art. 7, par. 1 and art. 8, par. 1 LoR.
391 Art. 8, par. 1 and 2 LoR.

up to the parliament to decide whether or not to consider the voters' decision.[392] By contrast, a parliamentary minority plebiscite regarding laws and other issues that has been framed as a binding referendum can be deemed as approved and becomes legally binding for all state authorities if at least one-third of the electorate favours it.[393] In such cases, it enters into force on the next day following its official publication in the register of legal acts.[394]

3. Citizen-initiated referendums

Citizen-initiated referendums belong to the bottom-up mechanism of direct democracy. It can either be a 'citizens' facultative referendum' to refuse an amendment to a specific law or public issue that has been adopted by the public authorities, or a 'citizens' initiative' to change the status quo by creating a law from below. In both cases, collecting a certain number of signatures from eligible citizens is required. However, due to its popular framing and triggering features, the second type of citizen-initiated referendum – the citizens' initiative – is much closer to the sense of direct democracy.

Currently, the Lithuanian constitution does not distinguish very clearly between citizens' facultative referendums and citizens' initiatives. Following the wording of article 9 of the constitution, which states that 'a referendum shall be announced if not fewer than 300,000 citizens with electoral rights so request', one cannot conclude directly if this legal proposition refers to both instruments. Following the systematic interpretation of further provisions regarding popular rights in the Lithuanian constitution, as well as in the law on referendums (LoR), we can state that citizen-initiated referendums can be either reactive, in that they refuse parliamentary decisions (citizens' facultative referendum), or proactive, in that they enact new provisions or amend existing ones.[395] Policy changing citizens' initiatives can be sub classified as 'citizens' constitutional initiatives', 'citizens' initiatives on laws and other issues' and 'citizens' consultative initiatives'.[396] All three instruments are proactive because they create new laws. Additionally,

392 Art. 8, par. 3 LoR.

393 Art. 7, par. 4 LoR.

394 Art. 78, par. 5 LoR.

395 See art. 1 in conjunction with art. 4, par. 2, art, 6, art. 9, par. 1 and 2 and art. 10 LoR; art. 33, art. 147 CLt and also JLtCC 1994-07-22, point 1 and 4.

396 Art. 9, sec. 2, art. 147, sec. 1 CLt and art. 4, par. 2, art. 5 and 6 in conjunction with art. 3 LoR.

all are framed and triggered by the citizens. However, citizens only fully control the first and second popular initiatives, since the outcome of the third instrument is consultative and not binding, unlike the first and second instruments. Therefore, due to the third instrument's non-binding character, the people cannot be introduced into the decision-making process as an additional veto player since they do not have the final say. For all citizen-initiated referendums, a time period of three months is given to gather at least 300,000 signatures in one collection round.[397]

In Lithuania, another instrument called the 'citizens' agenda initiative' exists,[398] but it is not considered a direct democratic instrument since it works rather like a petition. It contains a proposal addressed directly to the parliament. Parliament is obliged to consider the petition, but does not have to follow the proposal.

a) *The citizens' facultative referendum*

The Lithuanian constitution does not clearly state whether the people are entitled to veto parliamentary decisions. Nevertheless, following article 9, sec. 2 CLt 'a referendum shall also be announced if not less than 300,000 citizens with the electoral right so request' it can be argued that the citizens are also empowered to trigger a binding or consultative referendum on any kind of parliamentary decision.[399] As for citizens' initiatives, three months are given to collect the minimum number of signatures.[400] For an approval of the referendum, in the sense of abrogating the parliamentary resolution, at least half of the electorate has to participate and the necessary quorum for approval varies depending on the issue and the type of referendum. To reject a parliamentary resolution regarding constitutional provisions (others than those under chapter I and XIV) or regarding laws and other issues, at least one-third of all enfranchised voters is required. For Seimas' resolutions regarding laws and other issues that have been deliberated in a consultative referendum, an approval quorum more than half of voters or no less than one-quarter of the entire electorate is needed.[401]

397 Art. 11, par. 5 LoR.
398 Art. 68, sec. 2 CLt.
399 See also art. 9, par. 2 LoR.
400 Art. 11, par. 5 LoR.
401 Art. 7, par. 1 and art. 8, par. 1 LoR.

b) The citizens' constitutional initiative

In addition to the most significant issues that are automatically put to a referendum (mandatory referendums) as required by the constitution,[402] there are other additional subjects of importance concerning core state and national issues that can be decided by a mandatory referendum if no fewer than 300,000 citizens so request.[403] This instrument refers to changes to the constitution, which is supposed to contain the most significant principles and procedures of the state and the nation. There is no restriction on subject matter: any issue, whether political, economic or societal, can be adopted, altered or supplemented by such a tool if it is considered essential by the people.[404]

c) The citizens' initiative on laws and other issues

Although most significant issues are framed in the constitution, it is not legally prohibited to use the citizens' initiative to create new statutory laws.[405] The possibility of referendums on laws is also evident if we consider article 6 LoR and section 4 of article 69 CLt. The latter emphasises that 'provisions for laws of the Republic of Lithuania may also be adopted by referendum'.[406] A referendum might also be called for the adoption of a specific public issue, such as the question of Lithuania's membership in international organisations, if over 300,000 citizens deem it to be important. Here, there is also no legal restriction on subject matter.[407]

d) The citizens' consultative initiative

Consultative referendums can be held with respect to other issues of the utmost importance to the state and the people. However, at least 300,000 signatures are also needed here to trigger a consultative initiative.[408] According to the provisions of the constitution and LoR, it is not always possible to clearly distinguish the kinds of issues that can be subject to such an initiative. If we follow Algis

402 Provisions of chapters I and XIV of the constitution, participation in international organisations and amendment to the Constitutional Act of 8 June 1992.

403 Art. 9, sec. 2 CLt, art. 147, sec. 1 CLt and art. 4, par. 2 LoR.

404 See art. 9, sec. 1 and 3 CLt.

405 See art. 9 CLt and also Krupavicius, Citizens' Initiatives, p. 136.

406 Art. 69, sec. 4 CLt.

407 See art. 9 CLt; art. 4, par. 2, art. 9, par. 2 LoR in conjunction with art. 6, par. 2 LoR.

408 Art. 5 and art. 6, par. 2, sec. 1, art. 10, par. 2 in conjunction with art. 3 LoR.

Krupavicius' argumentation, we can say that no consultative referendum can be held on constitutional issues.[409]

e) Procedures of citizens' initiatives

The LoR establishes and specifies the procedures of initiation, the announcement, organisation and the execution of referendums. The procedures of the 'citizens' constitutional initiative', 'citizens' initiative on laws and other issues' and 'citizens' consultative initiative' are subject to almost the same legal requirements.[410] Unfortunately, in many cases the LoR does not always make a clear distinction between the different types of citizen-initiated referendums.

To launch (framing) an initiative from below, at least 15 eligible citizens have to form an initiative group.[411] The proponents must file their application with the Central Electoral Commission of Lithuania (CECLt). The initiative group has to indicate the referendum type (mandatory or consultative) and if their resolution for adoption by referendum consists of a preliminary or final text.[412] The formal distinction between the preliminary and final text illustrates that Lithuanians are entitled to frame their proposal in both legal forms of an initiative. It can either be proposed as a general suggestion (preliminary text) or as a formulated draft (final text). If the proposed text is preliminary, the Seimas office has to provide assistance in drafting the final text of the resolution by enlisting legal experts, if so requested by the representatives of the initiative group.[413] Once all the members of the initiative group have signed the text of the resolution, it shall be deemed final and any alteration of the text is prohibited.[414] Thereafter, the collection of citizens' signatures for the initiative to call a citizens' referendum begins. A three-month time limit (two months before 1996) is set to collect no fewer than 300,000 signatures.[415] This high signature quota to trigger a popular initiative, which already existed in the LoR of 1989, has remained unchanged to present. The last attempt aimed at lowering the hurdle to 100,000 signatures failed in the referendum held on 29 June 2014.

---

409 Krupavicius, Citizens' Initiatives, p. 136f.

410 It is assumed that the citizens' facultative referendum follows the same procedural steps.

411 Art. 10, par. 1 LoR.

412 Art. 10, par. 2 LoR.

413 Art. 6, par. 2 and 3, art. 10, par. 4 LoR.

414 Art. 10, par. 4 and 6 LoR.

415 Art. 11, par. 5 LoR.

In Lithuania, there is no restriction on collection locations. Signatures can be collected in any public places and residences.[416] As the articles 1 and 6 of the law on electronic signature (LoES) state it is also possible to collect signatures electronically. In such cases, the initiative group has to choose that e-services company that complies with legislative requirements. After the time limit, all signature collection lists have to first be verified by the CECLt within 15 days.[417] The committee, having determined that the documents meet the requirements of the LoR, gives the final act to the parliament, along with the citizens' petitions and its own conclusions.[418] One exception is made if up to 0.5 percent of the required signatures are lacking. In such cases, the CECLt informs the initiative group and sets an additional 15-day time limit to make up for the shortfall.[419] In case of a violation of the time limit or of other principles of the collection set forth in the law (e.g. falsified signatures, violations of the principle of voluntariness in collecting signatures), the CECLt can refuse the proponents' initiative to call a referendum. The initiative group has the right to appeal the committee's decision to the Superior Administrative Court of Lithuania within one month.[420]

If there is no violation of the collecting principles, the CECLt submits the final act of the citizens' group along with citizens' valid signatures and the committee's conclusions to the parliament for deliberation (see 'legal assessment of citizens' initiatives' in chapter V-A-4). The parliament has to pass the resolution on the date of calling the referendum within one month.[421] The parliament's resolution on the referendum has to indicate the type of referendum (binding or consultative), date of conducting and the text of the decision set forth for a referendum.[422] As in Latvia, there is no formal provision allowing the parliament to draft a counter-proposal to a citizens' initiative. Regardless of whether mandatory or consultative, the referendum has to be announced[423] and must be held 'no later than three months and no sooner than two months from the day of passing the [parliament's] resolution on the date of calling the referendum'.[424]

416 Art. 11, par. 4, 5, 6, 9 LoR.
417 Art. 13, par. 1 and art. 20 par. 1 sec. 3 LoR.
418 Art. 13, par. 1 LoR.
419 Art. 13, par. 2 LoR.
420 Art. 13, par. 3 LoR.
421 Art. 14, par. 1 LoR.
422 Art. 15, par. 1 LoR.
423 Art. 9, sec. 3 CLt.
424 Art. 15, par. 1 and 2 LoR.

In all three citizen-initiated referendums, at least one half of the registered electorate has to take part to be deemed as having taken place.[425] After the end of the referendum vote, all counting records are to be delivered to the CECLt. This committee is responsible for officially establishing and announcing the final results.[426]

The main difference among the 'citizens' constitutional initiative', 'citizens' initiative on laws and other issues' and 'citizens' consultative initiative' concerns the approval quorum and to their legal character. The approval quorum for a 'citizens' constitutional initiative' depends on the constitutional issue that is submitted to a vote. If it refers to the same issues for which a mandatory referendum is required by law, the approval quorum can vary. At least three-fourth yes-votes of the registered electorate are asked for an amendment to the provision of article one of the constitution.[427] For an amendment to a provision of chapter I[428] and XIV of the constitution, support from more than 50 percent of the entire registered electorate is required.[429] Other constitutional issues (most parts of it) can be deemed approved if more than one half of the voters in the referendum, but at least one-third of the total registered electorate voted in favour of it.[430] The same approval quota of one-third of the total electorate is also required for adoption of a 'citizens' initiative on laws and other issues'.[431] However, it could be lower (one-quarter of the entire electorate) if the initiative refers to the question of Lithuania's membership in international organisations. Until 2002, the LoR required a very high approval quorum (50 percent of the electorate) to pass citizen-initiated laws; the new LoR, however, has lowered this quorum.[432]

A 'citizens' constitutional initiative' passed by referendum is binding and thus must enter into force 'no earlier than after one month from the day it was passed by referendum'.[433] An approved 'citizens' initiative on laws and other issues' enters into force on the next day following its official publication in the

425 Art. 7, par. 1 and art. 8, par. 1 LoR.
426 Art. 70, art. 71 par. 1, art. 73, par. 1 LoR.
427 Art. 7, par. 2 LoR and art. 148, sec. 1 CLt.
428 With the exception of art. 1 of the constitution.
429 Art. 7, par. 3 LoR.
430 Art. 7, par. 4 LoR.
431 Art. 7, par. 4 LoR.
432 Krupavicius, Citizens' Initiatives, p. 137.
433 Art. 78, par. 4 LoR.

register of legal acts, unless a later date of the entry into force has been previously stipulated.[434]

For a 'citizens' consultative initiative', over one half of the voters (at least 25 percent of the registered electorate) is needed to approve the resolution.[435] However, due to its advisory character, the decision on the referendum is not binding. But since the issue has to be deliberated in a parliamentary session, according to the procedure established by the Seimas Statute, it may come into force if the parliament votes accordingly within one month of the announcement of its results.[436]

f) The citizens' agenda initiative: something between a referendum and petition

In addition to the institutions of the referendum[437] and the right of petition[438], there is another democratic instrument in Lithuania, namely the 'citizens' agenda initiative'.[439] It is somewhere between the two popular rights of referendum and petition. It allows a certain number of enfranchised citizens to place a particular issue on the parliament's agenda; however, it does not have the legal force to bring it to a popular vote. There is also no issue that is prohibited from being presented with this instrument. It does not belong to the direct democratic rights because it does not necessarily trigger a referendum, nor does it entirely have the same characteristics as a petition.[440] In contrast to a petition, it can only be forwarded to the parliament simply in order to propose new legislation to be voted on. Only Lithuanian citizens over 18 years of age and eligible to vote are entitled to apply this instrument,[441] whereas initiating a petition is available to everybody who has reached the age of 16 years. Furthermore, a petition can be forwarded to all public authorities.[442]

---

434 Art. 78, par. 5 LoR.

435 Art. 8, par. 2 and 3 LoR.

436 Art. 8, par. 2 and 3 LoR.

437 See art. 4 and art. 5 LoR.

438 Art. 33 CLt.

439 Art. 68, sec. 2 CLt.

440 According to KAUFMANN/BÜCHI/BRAUN, a petition is a written submission with no particular form that any person may send to an authority. It can contain a proposal, a criticism or a request, and the subject matter may be any state activity, KAUFMANN/BÜCHI/BRAUN, p. 238.

441 Art. 2 of the Law on Citizens' Legislatives of the Republic of Lithuania of 22 December 1998 (LoCLt); there are also procedural differences.

442 Art. 2, par. 2 of the Law on Petitions of the Republic of Lithuania of 7 July 1999 (LoP).

The right to legislate initiatives also differs from a procedural point of view. At least ten citizens with the right of vote are requested to form the steering group to explore the idea in question.[443] They have to submit their proposal to the CECLt for consideration.[444] Thereafter, at least 50,000 signatures are needed within two months to propose a draft law and at least 300,000 signatures are required within four months to suggest a constitutional proposal (adoption, amendment, supplementation) to the parliament.[445] The nature of the Lithuanian agenda initiative is a proposing and not an abrogative one, which means that it is not possible to repeal an existing law.[446] After the collection drive, signature collection sheets have to be submitted to the CECLt for verification[447] and the commission then submits the signatures and citizens' proposal to the parliament for its consideration.[448] The majority of the parliamentarians present is needed to decide whether a citizens' agenda initiative should be accepted.[449] Due to its non-binding character, the Seimas is free to refuse or accept the entire proposal or only some parts of it. In case of an acceptance, the proposed law or alteration to the constitution must be adopted according to the procedure established by the Seimas Statute.[450]

It is reasonable to exclude a citizens' agenda initiative from the realm of direct democracy because it does not provide for a referendum process with a binding result. A referendum may occur if the agenda initiative refers to a constitutional issue that has to be automatically submitted to a referendum or if the parliamentary majority is willing to further consider the citizens' motion during its session. Nevertheless, it is very unlikely that group of citizens would be able to collect 300,000 signatures to start an advisory procedure to amend such constitutional provisions. As such, it makes more sense to trigger the direct procedure for amending the constitution with the 'citizens' constitutional referendum' instead. It might be that a 'citizens' agenda initiative' places strong public and political pressure on the parliament to pursue the intended policy. Nevertheless, in addition to the referendum and petition rights, this kind of

---

443 Art. 5, par. 1 LoCLt.
444 Art. 6, par. 1 LoCLt.
445 Art. 2, par. 1 and 2, art. 9, par. 1 and 2 (LoCLt); see also art. 68, sec. 2 CLt.
446 Krupavicius, Citizens' Initiatives, p. 138.
447 Art. 11 and art. 12 LoCLt.
448 Art. 13, par. 1, art. 17 and art. 19 LoCLt.
449 Art. 19 LoCLt.
450 Art. 20 LoCLt.

political instrument seems – at least compared to referendums – a little superfluous, given its relatively restrictive legal barriers and the fact that it is not legally binding. The right to petition remains a blunt political right. This might also become obvious if we consider the use and success of this democratic instrument. From 2000 to 2014, around twenty attempts have been made. In only eight cases the proponents were successful in collecting the required signature number and in two cases did the parliament pass the proposed changes to the law.[451]

4. The legal assessment of citizens' initiatives

In order to be forewarded to a popular vote citizens' initiatives have to meet some legal requirements also in Lithuania. In contrast to Latvia, the admissibility check of a citizens' initiative takes place after the signature collection process. There is also a variation from Latvia with regard to the authority that is charged to assess the citizens' initiative legality. In Lithuania it is the parliament, and not the Central Electoral Commission, that examines the admissibility of initiatives. The Lithuanian Central Electoral Commission's jurisdiction comprises only the preliminary examination of citizens' initiatives. As mentioned in chapter V-A-3-e, the committee has to verify that the necessary number of signatures has been collected within the given time frame and that no violations were made during the collection procedure. The CECLt further determines if the submitted documents correspond to the requirements of the LoR and gives the final act along with the citizens' initiative and its own conclusion to the parliament.[452] Thereafter, the parliament deliberates the final act. At this point, a group of experts from the Department of Law of Office of the Lithuanian Parliament is formed to assess the draft law in terms of its content. As article 14, par. 2 LoR states, the resolution text supplied in the citizens' initiative has to comply with the constitutional provisions and according to article 6, par. 1 LoR 'a draft law which is being proposed for a referendum must conform to the requirements set forth by the Law on Procedure on Drafting of Republic of Lithuania Laws and other Regulatory Enactments'. The group of legal experts may arrive at the conclusion that the initiative text is in conflict with other legal provisions. The parliament considers and publishes the conclusions of

451 See http://www.vrk.lt/documents/10180/432567/2341_istatymuleidybosiniciatyvos 2012-06.pdf/a5b387c6-5d57-41c8-afaa-3cdfdaf8552e and http://www.vrk.lt/ankstesnes2 (accessed on 13.10.2014).

452 Art. 13, par. 1–4, art. 14 par. 1 LoR.

the consulted experts before passing resolution regarding the date of calling the referendum. However, despite a possible unconformity with legal norms of higher legal force, the parliament is not obliged to follow the experts' conclusion. As the law states, the 'experts' conclusion cannot be the basis for not calling the referendum'.[453] Parliament is the only authority that interprets the law. Following the constitutional courts' decision, parliament, as legislator, can state the contradiction of the draft of the provisions of law to the constitution. It is entitled to 'voice its opinion on the compliance of a draft law or a draft of the provisions of law, submitted for referendum, with the Constitution'.[454]

Constitutionally, there is no prerogative that the constitutional court itself must decide on the compliance of draft laws or other draft legal acts ante.[455] It only takes action in the case of a complaint. Then, it decides whether the laws and other legal acts adopted by parliament conform with the constitution.[456] The court's ruling is final and is not subject to appeal.

Considering the Lithuanian validation procedure of citizens' initiatives it becomes apparent that the validity check by the parliament is basically limited to material aspects. In regard to formal requirements such as the principle of unity of subject matter the law does not specify further conditions. Accordingly, in practice it is still possible that popular initiatives are launched on several issues without a logical material link to each other simultaneously. This regulation is not without difficulties[457]: compiling different matters into one initiative and submitting it as one piece to referendum after does not only increase the likelihood that signatures are collected more easily for several unrelated issues at once, but it also eliminates voters' ability to make different choices for different parts of the initiative. In fact, to give citizens the freedom of choice for both signing and answering unambiguously, initiatives without material link should divided into several parts already before the signature collection starts.

453 Art. 14, par. 1 and 2 LoR.
454 See JLtCC 1994-07-22, point 6.
455 See JLtCC 1994-07-22, point 6.
456 Art. 7 and 102 CLt.
457 See the problematic case under chapter V-B-14.

Table 3: Direct Democratic Institutions and their Use in Lithuania (1991–2014)

Mechanism of Direct Democracy	Name of DD Insitution	Subject Matter	Submitted due to	Character	Intetsion	Pol. Actor / Veto-Player[1]		Formal Restrictions for						Use
						Asking (Framing)	Triggering	Turnout	Approval	Signatures	Collection Time	Collection Place	Range of Issues	q / a / ai[2]
 REQUIRED	Mandatory constitutional referendum	to alter the provisions of chapter I and XIV of the constitution	law	binding	proactive / reactive	parliament (citizens)	automatic	>50% of total electorate[3]	>1/2 of total electorate, exception for first article: >3/4 of total electorate	–	–	–	yes referred issues	1 / 1 / 0
	Mandatory referendum on a constitutional act	to alter the provisions of the Constitutional Act of 8 June 1992	law	binding	proactive / reactive	parliament (citizens)	automatic	>50% of total electorate	>3/4 of total electorate	–	–	–	yes only for referred act	0 / 0 / 0
	Mandatory referendum on participation in international organizations	to access int. org. that involves partial transfer of state competencies	law	binding	proactive / reactive	parliament / int. org. (citizens)	automatic	>50% of total electorate	>1/2 of voters (>25% of total electorate)	–	–	–	yes only for accession to Int. Org.	1 / 1 / 0

Mechanism of Direct Democracy	Name of DD Insitution	Subject Matter	Submitted due to	Character	Intetsion	Pol. Actor / Veto-Player[1]		Formal Restrictions for						Use
						Asking (Framing)	Triggering	Turnout	Approval	Signatures	Collection Time	Collection Place	Range of Issues	q / a / ai[2]
 TOP-DOWN	Parliamentary constitutional plebiscite	to alter and supplement the constitution or to veto a resolution	parliament	binding	proactive / reactive	>1/4 of the parliament[4] in case of proactive otherwise parliament	>1/4 of the parliament	>50% of total electorate	either >1/3 or >1/2 or >3/4 of total electorate	–	–	–	no	5 / 0 / 4
	Parliamentary plebiscite on other issues, laws, provisions	to adopt or amend a national issue or a law or to veto a resolution	parliament	binding or consultative	proactive / reactive	>1/4 of the parliament in case of proactive otherwise parliament	>1/4 of the parliament	>50% of total electorate	if binding >1/3 of total electorate if consultative >1/2 of voters (>25% of total electorate)	–	–	–	no	4[6] / 2 / 1
 BOTTOM-UP	Citizens' facultative referendum	to veto parliamentary decisions, resolutions	citizens	binding or consultative	reactive	parliament	>300'000 = 11.8% of total electorate	>50% of total electorate	if binding >1/3 of total electorate if consultative >1/2 of voters (>25% of total elector.)	>300'000 = 11.8% of total electorate	3 months[5]	public places	no	0 / 0 / 0

Mechanism of Direct Democracy	Name of DD Insitution	Subject Matter	Submitted due to	Character	Intetsion	Pol. Actor / Veto-Player[1]		Formal Restrictions for						Use
						Asking (Framing)	Triggering	Turnout	Approval	Signatures	Collection Time	Collection Place	Range of Issues	q / a / ai[2]
	Citizens' constitutional initiative	to initiate a general suggestion or a formulated draft to alter the constitution	citizens	binding	proactive	>15 eligible citizens	>300'000 = 11.8% of total electorate	>50% of total electorate	either >1/3 or >1/2 or >3/4 of total electorate	>300'000 = 11.8% of total electorate	3 months[5]	public places	no	1 / 0 / 1
	Citizens' initiative on laws and other issues	to initiate a general suggestion or a formulated draft to adopt a law or another issue	citizens	binding	proactive	>15 eligible citizens	>300'000 = 11.8% of total electorate	>50% of total electorate	>1/3 of total electorate or >1/2 of voters[7] (>25% of total electorate)	>300'000 = 11.8% of total electorate	3 months[5]	public places	no	9 / 0 / 9

Mechanism of Direct Democracy	Name of DD Insi-tution	Subject Matter	Sub-mitted due to	Charac-ter	Intet-sion	Pol. Actor / Veto-Player[1]		Formal Restrictions for						Use
						Asking (Fram-ing)	Trigger-ing	Turnout	Approval	Signa-tures	Col-lection Time	Col-lection Place	Range of Is-sues	q / a / ai[2]
	Citizens' consul-tative initiative	to initiate a general sugges-tion or a formu-lated draft to adopt a law or another issue	citizens	consulta-tive	proac-tive	>15 eligible citizens	>300'000 = 11.8% of total electorate	>50% of total electorate	>1/2 of voters (>25% of total electorate)	>300'000 = 11.8% of total elector-ate	3 months[5]	public places	no	0 / 0 / 0
Total Votes														21 / 4 / 15

Source: Author's characterisation

Remarks

1: The possibility of a referendum introduces the citizens as one additional veto player into the public legislative process. A veto player is an individual or collective actor whose agreement is needed to bring about a change in the legislative status quo. If an existing or latent veto player controls both the framing of the proposal and the triggering of the referendum, other veto players lose their ability to veto outcomes. Thus, the number of veto players decreases and potential of policy change increases (Hug/Tsebelis, 2002).

2: q / a / ai = quantity of referendums / approved / approved but invalid due to precise formal restrictions.

3: There are around 2,538,400 eligible voters in Lithuania (2014).

4: The Lithuanian unicameral parliament consists of 141 deputies (art. 55 CLt).

5. If up to 0.5% of the signatures are lacking, an additional 15-day time limit is set to provide the option to collect the missing signatures (art. 13 par. 2 LoR).

6. One of them refers to the approved referendum on independence, which was held on 9 February 1991.

7. In cases where the initiative refers to Lithuania's membership in international organisations (with transfer of the scope of competence of government bodies to the institutions of international organisations).

B. Lithuanian direct democracy in practice

With regard to the frequency of use of direct democratic tools in national politics, Lithuania is the leading country among the Baltic states. Between 1991 and 2014, 21 referendums have been held, including the referendum on independence (see Table 3, last column and Figure 3). However, of these 21 referendums, only four have succeeded in full and come into force. Others have either been rejected (2) or did not become legally binding due to lack of turnout and qualified approval (15).[458]

According to the theoretical framework laid out in this book, we can distinguish between nine different direct democratic tools divided into three direct democratic mechanisms in Lithuania. With regard to these three mechanisms of direct democracy, there were only two required referendums (1 mandatory constitutional referendum and 1 mandatory referendum on participation in international organisations) in 24 years. They were both approved by the people and became legally binding. A significant number (9) of the referendums that have been held in Lithuania belong to the category of referendums from above (five parliamentary constitutional plebiscites and four parliamentary plebiscites on other issues and laws). They have been framed and triggered by public authorities. Indeed, seven of nine top-down referendums have been approved. But due to formal restrictions, such as turnout or approval quorum, five did not become legally binding. Only two referendums from above were able to overcome these two obstacles and succeeded in full. Other two referendums were rejected by the people.

In addition to required and top-down referendums, there were ten citizen-initiated referendums. Except for the last constitutional initiative that was held in June 2014, nine other proposals were citizens' initiatives on laws and other issues. However, the launching was rather by political parties than by the people. A citizens' facultative referendum to refuse parliamentary decisions has not yet been carried out. Indeed, there were attempts, but they all fell short of the necessary minimum number of signatures. As one can see, all ten referendums from below have been adopted by the citizens participating in the ballot, but due to the high turnout or approval quorum they failed to come into force.

---

458 See c2d database, http://c2d.ch/votes.php?level=1&country=202&yearr=timeperiods&fromyear=1990&toyear=2013&speyear[]=2013&result=0&terms=&table=votes&sub=Submit_Query (accessed on 12.12.2013); and CECLt, http://www.vrk.lt/documents/10180/432567/2340_referendumai2012-06.pdf/84adb4dc-41c4-44c3-896d-2aff437125d3 and http://www.vrk.lt/ankstesni (accessed on 10.10.2014).

Figure 3: Referendums held in Lithuania

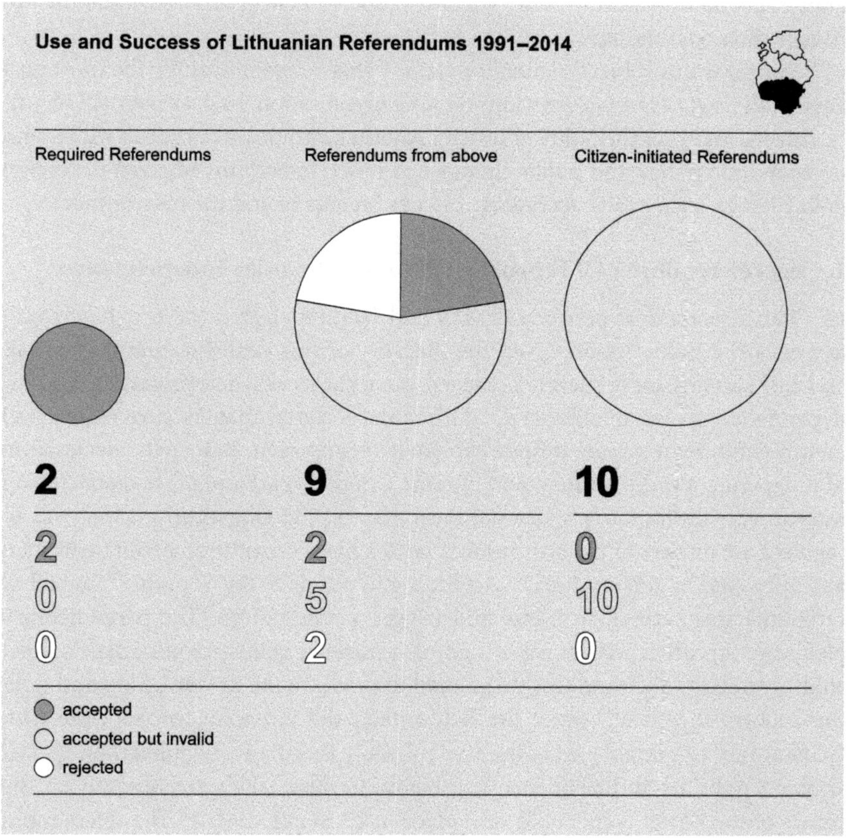

Source: Author's own calculations based on the data from www.c2d.ch and Lithuanian Central Electoral Commission

Beyond these direct democratic tools that have been used in practise, it should be noted that some instruments have not been applied yet. This is not surprising given that there was no mandatory referendum on the constitutional act, as foreseen by article 4, par. 1, sec. 4 of LoR.[459] It is also not surprising that there has been no citizens' consultative initiative, but one may expect that there were some citizens' facultative referendums to veto parliamentary resolutions or popular

459 Art. 4, par. 1, sec. 4 LoR.

constitutional initiatives intending to alter the constitution. However, due to the high collection obstacles, many citizens failed to collect enough signatures to trigger such referendums.

With regard to subject matter, we can say that referendums for the most part have been used to resolve questions on state organisation, such as national identity, citizens' rights or the political system. Another significant part dealt with issues on economic policy and public finances. A few referendums referred to foreign policy issues, such as EU accession or issues on energy and the environment.

1. The referendum of 9 February 1991 on Lithuania's independence

In 1940, a secret deal between STALIN and HITLER cleared the way for STALIN to annex the Baltic states. Given the illegality of this deal, Estonians, Latvians, and Lithuanians subsequently achieved the right to self-determination and independence on reasonable terms. Lithuania declared that its sovereignty had continued to exist *de jure* despite the Soviet occupation. Before the declaration of independence, the Lithuanian Supreme Council (parliament) had enacted an interim constitution, a 'provisional Basic Law' (1938 Constitution) that was to regulate the powers of the government until a new constitution could be written and approved by referendum.[460] According to article 3, the Supreme Council of Lithuania was entitled to frame and trigger a referendum. The parliamentary plebiscite (on other issues) was a sign of resistance against GORBACHEV's initiated sovereignty referendums that aimed to preserve the Soviet Union and hold the country together.[461] Since the Baltic states did not want to cooperate with GORBACHEV or remain part of the Soviet Union, they had scheduled their special 'opinion polls' on independence just before GORBACHEV's referendum on the future of the Soviet State could take place in 17 March 1991.[462] The referendum on Lithuanian independence was not a real decision on independence since the Act of the Re-establishment of the State of Lithuania had already been passed by the Lithuanian Supreme Council on 11 March 1990.[463]

Around 85 percent of the citizens participated in the 'opinion poll' and around 93 percent of the voters (76 percent of total electorate) were in favour

460 The Grip on Lithuania, *The Economist* [London, England], 21 April 1990, p. 13; MOLE, p. 93; EWERT, Potentiale, p. 50.

461 BRADY/KAPLAN pp. 186–201.

462 Backdown, *The Economist* [London, England], 2 February 1991, p. 50; Thunderballot, *The Economist* [London, England], 16 February 1991, p. 54.

463 KRUPAVICIUS, Citizens' Initiatives, p. 135.

of Lithuania becoming an independent democratic republic.[464] Although the Lithuanian opinion poll on Lithuanian independence had no legal consequences per the existing formal rules, its positive outcome left GORBACHEV with even more problems than reforming the Soviet Union politically and economically. After the failed Moscow coup in August 1991, the outcome of the referendum was confirmed not only in Lithuania, but also in Estonia and Latvia.[465] Thus, the outcome of the referendum enabled Lithuanian authorities to enhance the republic's legal sovereignty. To secure its position against the Soviet Union, the Lithuanian parliament added a further clause to its draft constitution that stated that independence can only be overturned by another referendum, not by the parliament.[466]

2. The referendum of 23 May 1992 on the restoration of the presidential institution

After Lithuania broke free from the Soviet Union, its fledgling democratic institutions became paralysed by growing divisions and infighting between the right-wing conservative Sajudis (the former Lithuanian Restructuring Movement) and the opposition block of the formerly communist Lithuanian Democratic Labour Party (LDDP) in the parliament, as well as between the parliament and the government. Both political groups had agreed that a new constitution was needed, but disagreed on the type of political structure the system should take.[467] To break the political gridlock, the Sajudis initiated a parliamentary constitutional plebiscite to establish a strong presidential system. The movement's leader VYTAUSTAS LANDSBERGIS, who was the chairman of the Supreme Council, was at the same time *de facto* the head of state. This was formally possible since the 'Provisional Basic Law' had retained such an institutional structure from the Soviet era. LANDSBERGIS had hoped that the plebiscite would expand and legitimise his own authority by giving the chairman of the parliament new sweeping powers as the republic's first chief executive. Creating a strong, American-style presidency with the powers to act independently of the parliament was the aim

---

464 See c2d database, http://c2d.ch/detailed_display.php?lname=votes&table=votes&page=1&parent_id=&sublinkname=results&id=37911 (accessed on 12.12.2013).

465 The Ex-Communists Ahead in Lithuanian Elections, *The New York Times*, 27 October 1992, p. 10.

466 Thunderballot, *The Economist* [London, England], 16 February 1991, p. 55; Art. 2 of the Constitutional Law of the Republic of Lithuania on the State of Lithuania of 11 February 1991.

467 MOLE, p. 93f.

of empowering the president with the right to dissolve the government and with the right of veto.[468]

According to the Referendum Law of 1989, at least 50 percent of the eligible voters needed to participate in order to amend the constitution. Nearly 70 percent of the voters (41 percent of the whole electorate) who had cast ballots voted yes. However, the referendum failed since not enough voters had turned out (59 percent of total electorate), which meant that the approval quorum of 50 percent of the total electorate was not reached.[469] The low turnout was not the result of chance, but rather an outcome of the tactical behaviour of the rest of the Lithuanian parliamentarians, who were against a strong presidential system. Knowing that the other parliamentary plebiscite – a referendum on the withdrawal of Soviet troops (see next chapter V-B-3) – would be supported by a large share of Lithuanian citizens, they avoided submitting the referendum on the presidential system on the same date as the referendum on withdrawal of Soviet troops. The tactics of lowering the first referendum's turnout succeeded, with many voters avoiding the polls.[470]

3. The referendum of 14 June 1992 on the withdrawal of Soviet troops

Only one month after the referendum on the restoration of the presidential institution, Lithuanian voters faced another referendum. This time Lithuanians were asked to vote on whether they wanted Russian troops to pull out of Lithuania by the end of 1992. All three Baltic states had wrested back their independence after the collapse of the coup in Moscow. But this independence was precarious so long as more than 100,000 Russian troops remained on their soil, with 30,000 in Lithuania alone. Lithuanians endorsed the referendum to have Soviet troops withdraw from the country[471] and by early March 1992, Russian troops slowly began to leave Lithuania. Despite this positive development, VYTAUSTAS LANDSBERGIS and his government were still anxious that Russia would delay the withdrawal of its troops if ALGIRDAS BRAZAUSKAS' Lithuanian Democratic Labour Party (LDDP) would come to power in the coming general elections

---

468 MØLLER, p. 284.

469 Leader Fails to Win Vote, *The New York Times*, 25 May 1992, p. 5; The Ex-Communists Ahead in Lithuanian Elections, *The New York Times*, 27 October 1992, p. 10; BRADY/KAPLAN, p. 203.

470 I am very gratefull for Mr. Prof. LIUDAS MAZYLIS' helpful notes, Faculty of Political Sciences and Diplomacy, Vytautas Magnus Univerity Lithuania.

471 Why are the Baltics Still Occupied, *The New York Times*, 15 June 1992, p. 18; Lithuania Backs Quick Pullout of Ex-Soviets, *The New York Times*, 16 June 1992, p. 11.

that autumn. As former First Secretary of the Communist Party of Lithuania (CLP) during the Soviet period, it was thought that BRAZAUSKAS, might not see the Russian troops as an occupying force and might therefore be more conciliatory towards Russia. To avoid such a potential risk, government authorities triggered the referendum on the complete and unconditional withdrawal of the troops, which was also supported by the other parties in the Supreme Council. The parliamentary plebiscite further demanded that Lithuania be compensated for damages resulting from the Soviet occupation. As with the referendum on independence, also this referendum served to strengthen popular resistance in Lithuania and reaffirm the political course already set.[472]

Around 76 percent of 2.5 million eligible voters turned out and an overwhelming 91 percent voted in favour of the referendum, which represents a total of 69 percent of the entire electorate and thus over 50 percent of the eligible voters needed for an approval. The popular endorsement had legitimised the government's claim, which Russia could no longer ignore. It agreed to a withdrawal. However, it maintained that a complete withdrawal from the Baltic states would take up to five years due to housing shortages. The last troops finally left Lithuania on 31 August 1994.[473]

4. The referendum of 25 October 1992 on the constitution

Together with the first round of parliamentary elections to replace the Supreme Council of Lithuania by a new parliament (Seimas), Lithuanians were also asked to vote on their new constitution (mandatory constitutional referendum). The constitution was indeed a compromise between the LDDP and Sajudis after LANDSBERGIS's defeat in the presidential referendum five months before. Both parties agreed on a semi-presidential structure, in which both the president and parliament would be directly elected. Thus, a sophisticated system of checks and balances was put in place, which was designed to ensure that the president's authority would be matched by countervailing powers in the parliament.[474]

The necessary quorum of 50 percent was achieved with a participation rate of 75 percent. Around 56 percent of the entire electorate approved the mandatory referendum on the new constitution. By adopting the referendum, Lithuanians

---

472 KRUPAVICIUS/ZVALIAUSKAS, p. 111; MOLE, pp. 120–122.

473 c2d database, http://c2d.ch/detailed_display.php?lname=votes&table=votes&page=1&parent_id=&sublinkname=results&id=37926 (accessed on 12.12.2013); ROZENVALDS, Baltische Staaten, p. 72.

474 MOLE, p. 94.

had also approved their right to the popular initiative and the right to mandatory referendums for specific constitutional provisions.[475]

As LANDSBERGIS had feared, the parliamentary elections were won by ALGIRDAS BRAZAUSKAS's (formerly communist) party, the LDDP won 73 of 141 seats; its challenger the 'Sajudis' won only 37 seats.

5. The referendum of 27 August 1994 on the law revoking privatisation I–VIII

On 27 August 1994, Lithuanian citizens had to decide on a referendum on economic measures regarding issues of privatisation, including illegal privatisation, compensation of banking savings and distorted justice. For legal reasons, the referendum on the law revoking privatisation was divided into eight parts: 'I. Law on illegal privatisations, devalued accounts, shares, and the failure to respect protective legislation; II. Law on illegal privatisation; III. Abolition of the consequences of illegal privatisation and future privatisations of State property; IV. Re-establishment and reimbursement of devalued private bank accounts; V. Recording the value of long-term capital investments; VI. Restoring the value of devalued assets belonging to the State; VII. Unification and transparency in protective legislation; and VIII. Implementing the law on illegal privatisations, accounts, shares and the failure to respect protective legislation'.

The referendum was initiated as a citizens' initiative by VYTAUTAS LANDSBERGIS's emerging party, the 'Fatherland Union', which was an offshoot of the 'Sajudis', the party that had lost the last parliamentary elections. The party's proposal intended to change the economic policy by stopping privatisation. But in fact, it was also an attempt to advance its campaign to mobilise voters, although many of these eight proposals were impossible to implement.[476] The 'Fatherland Union' was able to collect more than 560,000 signatures over the short time period of two months that was required at that time. The proposed law was to set a new political and economic course in the country by preventing and fighting economic crime. A further aim was to provide benefits to Lithuanians who had suffered in the new market economy after re-independence.

In addition to the government, other oppositional parties such as the Social Democrats and Liberals also encouraged voters to reject all or some of the proposals to avoid the bankruptcy of the nation. The World Bank and International

475 c2d database, http://c2d.ch/detailed_display.php?lname=votes&table=votes&page=1&parent_id=&sublinkname=results&id=57236 (accessed on 12.12.2013).

476 MAZYLIS/JURGELIONYTE, p. 133; MØLLER, p. 287.

Monetary Fund (IMF) had said that implementing LANDSBERGIS's measures would cost an estimated two billion U.S. Dollars, which was enough to severely compromise the national budget and to thrust Lithuania's weak economy into chaos.[477]

On referendum day, only 37 percent of the eligible voters had cast ballots, and according to the LoR, more than half of the country's registered voters needed to take part for the referendum to be valid. 84 percent of those who participated in the ballot voted yes but since the turnout quorum was not reached on any of these eight proposals, the referendum on the law on economic measures was deemed invalid and thus failed.[478]

6. The referendum of 20 October 1996 on the compensation for lost assets prior to 1990

After the eight referendums were defeated, the 'Fatherland Union' (Lithuanian Conservatives) triggered another citizens' initiative (a citizens' initiative on laws and other issues) to restore the savings and pensions that were used up by the Soviet government before 1990. Over 300,000 valid signatures were collected in favour of the draft. After the validation of the signatures by the CECLt, the final act of the proponents, along with the citizens' valid signatures and the committee's conclusions, were submitted to the parliament for deliberation. The parliament declared the initiative valid and submitted it to a popular vote on the same date as the first round of parliamentary elections.

In this case, a turnout and approval quorum of 50 percent of eligible voters was also formally necessary to turn the referendum into law. Indeed, around 52 percent of the eligible voters were not deterred by the turnout obstacle, but this was not enough to overcome the approval quorum. Although the majority of the voters had approved the referendum, it was only 38 percent of the total electorate and, at that time, it was not sufficient to validate the referendum.[479]

---

477 Economic Referendum in Lithuania Fails, *The New York Times*, 28 August 1994, p. 16; Kein Privatisierungsstopp in Litauen. Fiasko für Rechtsopposition, *Neue Zürcher Zeitung*, 29 August 1994, p. 9.

478 See any single result for these 8 referendums in the c2d database, http://www.c2d.ch/votes.php?level=1&country=202&yearr=timeperiods&fromyear=1990&toyear=2013&speyear[]=2013&result=0&terms=&table=votes&sub=Submit_Query (accessed on 13.12.2013).

479 See c2d database, http://www.c2d.ch/detailed_display.php?lname=votes&table=votes&page=1&parent_id=&sublinkname=results&id=37843 (accessed on 13.12.2013).

7. The referendum of 20 October 1996 on parliamentary elections on the second Sunday of April every four years

On the same day as the referendum on the compensation for lost assets prior to 1990, there were three further questions that were put to a popular vote. All three referendums dealt with constitutional provisions (art. 55, art. 57 and art. 131 CLt), including state organisation, the political system and the state budget. But these did not belong to the constitutional provisions of chapters I and XIV, which require that a mandatory referendum be triggered automatically in the case of any alterations.[480]

In contrast to the referendum on the compensation for lost assets, which was asked and triggered from 'below', these three proposals were parliamentary constitutional plebiscites that had been framed and triggered by the governing party, the Lithuanian Democratic Labour Party (LDDP).[481] Thus, collecting signatures was not necessary. The proposals to be submitted to a popular vote had been adopted in parliament by the governing LDDP, which had a total number of 73 seats. At that time, no less than half of the members of parliament (141:2) were necessary to trigger a parliamentary constitutional plebiscite. LDDP's referendums were rather a direct response to the 'Fatherland Union', since at that time the LDDP was on the decline and, hence, afraid to lose in the elections.[482] It was a desperate attempt by the LDDP to mobilise its electorate.[483]

The first measure of these three questions aimed to alter article 57 of the constitution. The parliament was to be elected every four years on the second Sunday of April, instead of in two rounds on varying dates. 52 percent of the eligible voters participated in ballot, which was higher than the required turnout minimum of 50 percent. Approximately 65 percent of those who took part in the ballot said yes to the governmental proposal. However, once again the referendum failed since only 33 instead of the required 50 percent of the total electorate favoured this policy change.[484]

---

480 See art. 148, sec. 2 CLt.

481 Krupavicius, Citizens' Initiatives, p. 143.

482 Møller, p. 287.

483 Mazylis/Jurgelionyte, p. 133.

484 See c2d database, http://www.c2d.ch/detailed_display.php?lname=votes&table=votes&page=1&parent_id=&sublinkname=results&id=37842 (accessed on 13.12.2013).

8. The referendum of 20 October 1996 on the reduction of parliamentary seats from 141 to 111

In addition to the first parliamentary constitutional plebiscite on parliament's term of four years, as outlined under chapter V-B-7, the governing LDDP also intended to reduce parliament's seats from 141 to 111. On 19 September 1996 it ratified the proposal by 62 to 25, with 14 abstentions, and submitted it to a popular vote. The proposal in favour of the reduction of parliamentary seats was supported by 65 percent of the voters. The mandatory turnout quorum was reached by 52 percent of all eligible voters, but due to the low approval quota of 33 percent of the total electorate, this reform too failed to come into force.[485] Today, the Lithuanian parliament still consists of 141 representatives.

9. The referendum of 20 October 1996 on social spending

The third parliamentary reform by the governing party that was submitted to a vote aimed to alter the constitution on issues of social spending (article 131 CLt). This parliamentary constitutional plebiscite required that the annual state budget be deliberated by the parliament and be adopted each year by legislative decree. The parliament further should be able to decide on new expenditures if it specifies the source of capital. Additionally, the proposal foresaw that at least half of the revenue from the public budget should be allocated to social security, medicine, education, science, culture and other social needs of the citizens. Over 50 percent of all voters turned out to vote on the referendum, and 63 percent of these participants voted in favour of the question. But once again, at the time, this quota was not enough to reach the mandatory approval quorum of 50 percent of the total electorate.[486] If this referendum and the three referendums that took place on 20 October 1996 had been held after 2002, all four would have been valid; the new LoR allowed for binding referendums on laws or other issues and constitutional referendums that refer to other provisions than those of chapter I and XIV of the constitution to be deemed approved if not less than one-third of the total electorate votes in favour of them.[487]

485 See c2d database, http://www.c2d.ch/detailed_display.php?lname=votes&table=votes&page=1&parent_id=&sublinkname=results&id=37936 (accessed on 13.12.2013).

486 See c2d database, http://www.c2d.ch/detailed_display.php?lname=votes&table=votes&page=1&parent_id=&sublinkname=results&id=57237 (accessed on 15.12.2013).

487 See art. 7, par. 4 LoR.

10. The referendum of 10 November 1996 on the purchase of agricultural land by certain legal bodies

The referendum on the purchase of agricultural land by certain legal bodies that was held simultaneously during the second round of parliamentary elections dealt with an amendment to the article 47 of the constitution. The issue set to popular vote intended to give foreign corporations the right to acquire agricultural land in Lithuania. In addition to three other referendums as outlined under chapters V-B-7, 8 and 9, the LDDP was also the proponent of this referendum. Collecting signatures was not necessary since the triggering of the referendum in favour of the proposal was supported by the governing majority. At that time, no less than half of the parliament's members (141:2) were required to trigger a parliamentary constitutional plebiscite.

The Law on Referendum required a turnout quorum of at least 50 percent of the eligible electorate and the same quota for an approval. Both requirements failed since participation was much lower: only around 40 percent of the electorate went to the polls and only 43 percent of them (17 percent of the total electorate) voted in favour of LDDP's proposal. Thus, the governing LDDP lost all four plebiscites it had launched before the elections in 1996.[488] But the loss was not only limited to these referendums; the LDDP, which had controlled the Seimas since April 1992, had also lost the parliamentary elections on the same day. Its number of seats fell from 73 to 12, while the 'Fatherland Union' celebrated its comeback by winning 70 of 141 seats.

Six years after the referendum, the right of foreigners to purchase agricultural land was approved by a vote of 90 to 17, with six abstentions by the parliament. The amendment permitted physical and legal entities from EU and NATO countries to purchase farmland in Lithuania after the seven-year transition period stipulated in the Lithuanian EU accession treaty.[489]

11. The referendum of 10 and 11 May 2003 on the accession to the European Union

The EU Accession Treaty was signed in Athens on 16 April 2003. Some months before, on 24 February 2003, leaders of all main parliamentary factions had decided to establish a coordinating council to organise a referendum on Lithuania's

488 See c2d database, http://c2d.ch/detailed_display.php?lname=votes&table=votes&page=1&parent_id=&sublinkname=results&id=37796 (accessed on 04.03.2013).

489 Krupavicius, Lithuania 2004, p. 1062.

future membership in the EU. The decision on the popular vote was supported by 105 of 141 members of parliament. Three days later, the parliament passed a decision to hold a mandatory constitutional referendum on the country's entry into the EU in 2004 on 10–11 May 2003.[490] It was a special version of a mandatory constitutional referendum (mandatory referendum on participation in international organisations), as the newly adopted LoR (June 2002) required. According to par. 1, sec. 5 of article 4 of the LoR, a mandatory popular vote must be held, should Lithuania participate in international organisations and 'should this participation be linked with the partial transfer of the scope of competences of government bodies to the institutions of international organisations and the jurisdictions thereof'.

At that time a positive decision on such a mandatory referendum required more than a 50 percent turnout and at least one third of the eligible voters to be in favour. Although the LoR 2002 was designed to facilitate a positive result by being less restrictive than the LoR 1989, it was still restrictive, especially when compared with the corresponding laws in other EU accession candidate countries.[491] To avoid a negative outcome on the EU accession referendum, the parliament introduced two amendments to the LoR on 27 February 2003. First, it abolished the requirement for a qualified majority of one third of the electorate for a positive decision. From now on, a simple majority of participants was needed for a referendum on participation in international organisations to be approved.[492] But the required turnout of 50 percent still appeared to be a major problem. Therefore, various measures were included in the legislation to facilitate a higher turnout, without changing the turnout quorum itself. In all previous referendums, voting was allowed for one day only. During the EU accession, referendum voting was extended to two days and the polls were to stay open from 6 am to 10 pm, instead of 7 am to 8 pm. In addition, the parliament decided to extend postal voting to 11 instead of 5 days prior to a referendum. In addition to these formal changes, the political establishment had also conducted a well-organised campaign with intensive and innovative information and campaigning to mobilise the voters.[493]

On the ballot, around 63 of the total electorate went to the polls and an overwhelming 91 percent of the voters (57 percent of the total electorate) voted in

490 Krupavicius, Lithuania 2004, p. 1063.

491 Mazylis/Unikaite, p. 3.

492 Art. 7, par. 5 LoR.

493 Mazylis/Unikaite, p. 3, p. 9.

favour of an accession to the European Union.[494] This was a record level of support that would have been valid under all three versions of the LoR (1989: approval threshold >50% of the entire electorate, 2002: >1/3 and 2003[495]: >25%). One can assume that the high level was not only the result of formal changes and well-organised campaigns but also the wish of Lithuanians to be part of the West, and not of the East.[496]

Indeed, procedures enacted by the parliament that encourage more direct, citizen-friendly democracy are welcome, but it is important to note that all changes were promoted by the political elites since they expected positive effects resulting from an accession to the EU. Nevertheless, one should take into account that it was also the same political elite that would reject any other reforms, such as lowering the number of signatures required for citizens' initiatives or extending the collection time that would constrain the elite's capacity to act. To avoid any lowering of the turnout, the parliament took other little measures to make a EU accession possible. It should be noted that there it is still a risk of misuse as long as some important provisions on direct democratic procedures are framed at a level below the constitution, where no qualified majorities are required for their alteration. The possibility that such a misuse can occur is made possible by the Lithuanian parliament itself. Today, apart from the approval quorum, all other changes to the LoR that had been enacted in February 2003 have been reset. The enthusiasm for citizen-friendly procedures lasted for only a short time.

12. The consultative referendum of 12 October 2008 on the service extension for the nuclear power plant 'Ignalina'

The Ignalina nuclear power plant was in operation since 1983. It was built according to a construction design similar to that of Chernobyl. Despite the fact that the plant had another reactor type and was upgraded several times, the European Union considered it too risky and hence, it had to be closed down. The decommissioning of the Ignalina nuclear power plant in 2009 was also one condition for Lithuania to join the European Union, as specified in Lithuania's Treaty of Accession to the EU, which was signed in Spring 2003.

494 See c2d database, http://c2d.ch/detailed_display.php?lname=votes&table=votes&page=1&parent_id=&sublinkname=results&id=37864 (accessed on 05.03.2013).

495 See art. 7, par. 5 LoR.

496 Mazylis/Unikaite, p. 10; Duvold, Making Sense, p. 115f.

The global rise in energy prices sparked a new wave of public discussion to renegotiate a possible extension for keeping the Ignalina plant in operation.[497] To avoid complete dependency on Russian gas, even President VALDAS ADAMKUS believed that Lithuania might be able to convince the European Union of the need to extend the operating period of the Ignalina nuclear power plant. Although he was initially against such a referendum, he changed his opinion and asked Lithuanians to voice their support for remaining a nuclear powered state, which would help secure extra time for the construction of a new plant.

Initially, the non-parliamentary Lithuanian Social Democratic Union actively promoted an idea to pass special legislation to keep the Ignalina nuclear power plant open. It also wanted to hold a national mandatory referendum on extending Ignalina's operation together with the parliamentary elections in October 2008.[498] From 7 March to 7 June 2008, signatures for a corresponding citizen's initiative were collected. However, only 47,000 signatures supporting the service extension were collected, far short of the required 300,000 signatures. While the popular initiative failed,[499] the idea to put the issue to a popular vote remained intact. In 2008, some oppositional parties, among them the Liberal Movement, decided to trigger a referendum that should be held at the same time as the 12 October parliamentary elections.[500] In contrast to the failed citizens' initiative, which was binding, parliament's proposal (parliamentary plebiscite on other issues and laws) should be consultative. It is important to note that the triggering was a tactical choice to increase voter mobilisation during the oncoming general elections that were set for the same date as the referendum, on 12 October 2008.[501]

As for binding referendums, the LoR also requires a turnout threshold of at least half of all eligible voters for consultative referendums.[502] More than 48 percent of the entire electorate took part in the referendum and 91 percent of those who voted in the referendum were in favour of prolonging the Ignalina nuclear power plant's operations. However, 48 percent of the eligible voters who had participated was not enough (turnout threshold: >50%) to validate the referendum

497 Steht Litauen vor einem «Energie-Infarkt»?, *Neue Zürcher Zeitung*, 19 November 2008, p. 7.

498 KRUPAVICIUS, Lithuania 2008, p. 1055; MAZYLIS/JURGELIONYTE, p. 121f.

499 See c2d database, http://c2d.ch/detailed_display.php?lname=votes&table=votes&page=1&parent_id=&sublinkname=results&id=57764 (accessed on 05.03.2013).

500 MAZYLIS/JURGELIONYTE, p. 125.

501 KRUPAVICIUS, Lithuania 2009, p. 1032f.

502 Art. 8, par. 1 LoR.

and thus it too failed.[503] Subsequently, on 31 December 2009 the Ignalina nuclear power plant was closed down as required by Lithuania's entry treaty to the European Union. Without the relatively cheap energy that Ignalina had generated, Lithuania became largely dependent on imported electrical energy.[504] As a consequence, it became particularly reliant on Russia.

13. The consultative referendum of 14 October 2012 on building a new nuclear power plant 'Visaginas'

Before the Ignalina nuclear power plant was closed, the parliament tried to find new ways to diversify its energy sources, enhance energy security and become less dependent on gas from Russia. One option was to build a new nuclear power plant at the same location as the old Ignalina nuclear power plant. The new nuclear power plant, 'Visaginas', was to be a regional project along with Estonia and Latvia would replace the old one, which was closed down as a condition of joining the European Union. Most importantly, it would make Lithuania less dependent on Russia, which supplied not only gas but also electricity to Lithuania.[505] The relevant law on building a new atomic power plant had already been in force since 2007, but it was controversially discussed by society and finally recalled by the new parliamentary majority.[506]

Due to discussions in Lithuanian society, the Green Party and some environmental associations started to collect signatures for a popular vote to veto the plans for the new power plant. However, they failed to collect the minimum number of required signatures.[507] Although the citizens failed to bring the issue to the popular arena, opposition parties compelled the parliament to vote on the issue on 16 July 2012, which resulted in a vote in favour (62 to 39 with 18 abstentions) of holding a consultative referendum on the construction of the new plant

---

503 See c2d database, http://c2d.ch/detailed_display.php?lname=votes&table=votes&page=1&parent_id=&sublinkname=results&id=57764 (accessed on 06.03.2013); Litauen vor einem Regierungswechsel, *Neue Zürcher Zeitung*, 14 October 2008, p. 3.

504 Krupavicius, Lithuania 2010, p. 1072f.

505 Steht Litauen vor einem «Energie-Infarkt»?, *Neue Zürcher Zeitung*, 19 November 2008, p. 7; Litauen lässt sich seine Energie etwas kosten, *Neue Zürcher Zeitung*, 18 October 2012, p. 21; Lithuania's Final Sprint, *The Economist* [online], http://www.economist.com/blogs/easternapproaches/2012/09/lithuania (accessed on 06.03.2013).

506 Mazylis/Jurgelionyte, p. 120.

507 This example proves that Lithuanians are also entitled to use their right of referendum according to article 9 of the constitution to veto parliamentary decisions in favour of the status quo.

(parliamentary plebiscite on other issues and laws). The referendum was to be held on 14 October 2012. Once again, the referendum was set on the same day as first-round parliamentary elections.[508] The governing parties of the Fatherland Union and the Lithuanian Christian Democrats, who were in favour of the new atomic power station, had opposed the proposal by accusing the opposition parties of seeking political gain from the issue prior to the elections.

On ballot day, 52 percent of all eligible voters went to the polls, and the required turnout quorum of 50 percent of the total electorate was reached. Around 65 percent of the voters and, thus, 32 percent of the total electorate rejected the government's plans of building a new nuclear plant.[509] Voters' negative attitudes on nuclear energy were clearly influenced by the recent Fukushima Daiichi nuclear disaster in Japan.[510] Due its advisory character, however, the parliament was not obliged to follow the people's decision.

The Social Democrats, who had won the parliamentary elections 2012 and were initially sceptical of a new nuclear power plant, have made less of an effort to uphold the voters' decision. Indeed, for the new government, avoiding any energy dependency from abroad, namely from Russia, seems to be more of a priority than a total moratorium on a possible new nuclear power plant. However, Algirdas Butkevičius, leader of Lithuanian Social Democratic party, promised that his party had no intention of making hasty decisions regarding a new power plant project. Until now, the construction plans remained uncertain.[511]

14. The referendum of 29 June 2014 regarding the amendment of articles 9, 47 and 147 of the constitution

Between 29 August and 29 November 2013, there was a signature collection for a formulated constitutional initiative to amend articles 9, 47 and 147 of the constitution.[512] The initiative was framed by a group of 26 members from the National Union and the Lithuanian Greens, as well as some citizens. According

508 Krupavicius, Lithuania 2013, p. 144, 147.

509 See c2d database, http://c2d.ch/detailed_display.php?lname=votes&table=votes&page=1&parent_id=&sublinkname=results&id=132717 (accessed on 14.12.2013); Machtwechsel in Litauen, *Neue Zürcher Zeitung*, 16 October 2012, p. 5; Krupavicius, Lithuania 2013, p. 147.

510 Krupavicius, Lithuania 2013, p. 147.

511 Krupavicius, Lithuania 2013, p. 147.

512 See http://www3.lrs.lt/pls/inter3/dokpaieska.showdoc_l?p_id=468761&p_tr2=2 (accessed on 26.05.2014) and documentation under http://www3.lrs.lt/pls/inter3/dokpaieska.showdoc_l?p_id=454839&p_query=&p_tr2=2 (accessed on 20.10.2014).

to the initiative group's indication at the registration procedure, its result would be binding.[513] Unlike three failed initiatives on the same issue in the past, this time the proponents succeeded in gathering over 300,000 (320,818 were collected, 7393 thereof electronically)[514] valid signatures required within a time frame of three months. Consequently, after parliament's consideration and its doubtful admissibility check of the popular initiative the referendum on the issue was held on 29 June 2014.[515] Around 380,000 people (15 % of electorate) voted in the referendum and 269,049 of them voted in favour of the proposed constitutional amendments (72,8 % yes-votes). The referendum failed, however, due to the record low turnout, which was around 15 percent.[516] Legally, at least 50 percent of electorate needed to have voted in the referendum for it to be deemed valid.

With regard to its subject matter, the initiative aimed to amend three different constitutional provisions by pursuing different targets. According to the first draft amendment to article 9 of the constitution, in the future a decision adopted by referendum should be changed only by a referendum. Further, the number of signatures for a citizen-initiated referendum should be reduced from 300,000 to 100,000. The same number should also be applied to constitutional initiatives according to article 147 of the constitution. Finally, according to the amendments to the article 47 CLt, land, internal waters, forests and parks should only belong to the Republic of Lithuania and Lithuanians in order to preserve Lithuania's territorial integrity. In contrast to the current provision,[517] foreigners would not be permitted to buy these types of lands.[518] However, banning the sale of land to foreigners and foreign legal entities would have undoubtedly breached Lithuania's EU commitments (violation of material requirements: the conformity of initiatives with the norms and principles of higher legal force).

Pursuant to the draft in question, citizens had to vote on all amendments with a single answer. Surprisingly, there was no option to give separate answers, despite the fact that the submitted drafts attempted to achieve different objectives.

---

513 Art. 10, par. 2 LoR.

514 http://www.vrk.lt/ankstesnes1 (accessed on 20.10.2014).

515 For procedure of legal assessment of citizens' initiatives see chapter V-A-4.

516 See http://www.2013.vrk.lt/2014_referendumas/output_en/rinkimu_diena/index.html and http://www.vrk.lt/naujienos/-/content/10180/1/referendumas-neivyko-rinkeju-aktyvumas-itin-mazas (accessed on 04.07.2014 and 03.10.2014).

517 See art. 47, par. 3 CLt.

518 See http://www3.lrs.lt/pls/inter3/dokpaieska.showdoc_l?p_id=468761&p_tr2=2 (accessed on 26.05.2014).

Citizens were asked to give a single answer to all unrelated issues simultaneously. Accordingly, the single question could not be answered unambiguously.

Noticeable is that there is not always a logical material link between the three parts and the measures of the proposal do not necessarily serve for the regulation of the same issue. Factually, a voter who favours the reduction of the signature numbers (art. 9 CLt.) could at the same time reject the amendment to article 47 CLt intending to restrict for land purchases by foreigners. However, due to the single answer option, the voter is not able to freely express him or herself. He or she cannot answer separate questions either affirmatively or negatively. Hence, in order to avoid distortion of the expression of free will, issues without a logical material link to each other should be separated not only in the ballot questions but also even before starting with the signature collection. Accordingly, to keep the principle of unity of subject matter (formal requirement), each issue that is not necessarily linked to each other in a logical sense would require a separate signature collection process and consequently a separate referendum.

15. Popular initiatives without sufficient signatures

According to the Central Election Commission of Lithuania, between 1995 and 2014 there were a total of 23 popular launches, which either failed to obtain the required 300,000 signatures or did not meet other formal requirements to be proceeded further.[519] There is no comprehensive information available for those citizens' initiated referendums that failed before 1994.

The initiatives without sufficient signatures dealt with different issues. In 1995, a group of people intended to change the election law, however, within the two months that was granted to an initiative committee at that time, only 200,000 signatures could be gathered. An interesting case refers to the citizens' initiative of the Lithuanian National Progress Party on soil policy that was launched in 1996. It intended to enable foreigners and international organisations to own Lithuanian land. Proponents narrowly missed collecting 300,000 signatures in favour of their proposal. However, 65,000 signatures were stolen from the headquarters of the referendum organisers. Furthermore, the initiative committee was met with intense opposition from other political parties. Of the 600 individuals who had started collecting signatures, only around 30 were left at the end, due to being openly hassled and threatened. One year later, in 1997, an initiative intended to

519 See http://www.vrk.lt/documents/10180/432567/2340_referendumai2012-06.pdf/84adb4dc-41c4-44c3-896d-2aff437125d3 (accessed on 26.05.2014) and http://www.vrk.lt/ankstesnes1 (accessed on 22.09.2014).

privatize infrastructure of state-owned strategic companies (e.g. oil, gas, nuclear power, thermal energy, shipping, transport and telecommunication enterprises), but only 180,000 signatures were obtained. A 1998 initiative on electing municipal mayors also failed to obtain the required number of signatures. In 1999, the initiative of a group of citizens to reform the parliamentary election procedure also failed to collect enough signatures.[520] In the new millennium, the following signature drives were also ultimately unsuccessful: a constitutional initiative to amend the composition of parliament (2000); an initiative concerning referendum rights and economic structural policies (2002); an initiative on the NATO membership (2002); initiatives on the law of electing municipal mayors (2003) and on the election procedure of the Seimas (to introduce the majoritarian electoral system and to reduce the number of parliamentary seats) (2003); a constitutional initiative on retirement regulations (2004); a constitutional initiative to reduce the required number of signatures for bottom-up referendums from 300,000 to 100,000 (2004); an initiative to introduce a mandatory referendum on the introduction of the Euro in Lithuania (2005); a constitutional initiative to enable citizens to recall parliament (2008 and once again in 2009); an initiative on extending the operation of the Ignalina nuclear power plant station by the Lithuanian Social Democratic Union (2008);[521] and a constitutional initiative on reducing the number of signatures required for citizen-initiated referendums from 300,000 to 100,000 as well as on introducing the right for local referendums in each administrative unit of Lithuania (2009). The same initiative launch once again failed to get enough signatures between June and September 2012.[522] In January 2010, the initiative to introduce the right to recall parliament was brought up for the third time by the New Union (Social Liberals). Once again, the initiative group fell short of obtaining the 300,000 required signatures by 50,000.[523] Also the fourth trial between June and September 2012 missed the necessary amount of 300,000 signatures.[524] After the parliamentary agreement on the construction of a new nuclear power station in Lithuania, a consultative citizens' initiative was launched between March and June 2012. Proponents of the initiative wanted the issue of building a new nuclear power plant to be decided by the people. But

---

520 See also KRUPAVICIUS/ZVALIAUSKAS, p. 116f.

521 See also MAZYLIS/JURGELIONYTE, p. 121f.

522 See documentation under http://www3.lrs.lt/pls/inter2/dokpaieska.showdoc_l?p_id=427370&p_query=&p_tr2=2 (accessed on 20.10.2014).

523 KRUPAVICIUS, Lithuania 2011, p. 1055.

524 See documentation under http://www3.lrs.lt/pls/inter2/dokpaieska.showdoc_l?p_id=427370&p_query=&p_tr2=2 (accessed on 20.10.2014).

as mentioned in chapter V-B-13, they failed to gather the necessary minimum number of signatures.[525] Almost at the same time, between 17 April and 17 July 2012 there was another ineffective initiative launch. According to the mandatory initiative at statutory level (submitted as general suggestion) nuclear power plants should be prohibited in Lithuania and the government should be charged to promote renewable energy and energy supply from safe sources.[526] Once again in 2012, between May and August there was a further attempt to change the election procedure of parliament by amending articles 55 (to lower the number of seats to 101 members and to raise the term of office to five years), 56 (time limit for re-election) and 57 (to change the regular election month from October to April) of the constitution.[527] In 2014, another two ineffective initiative were launched. On 17 April 2014, a group filed their application with the Central Electoral Commission, aiming at the election of municipal mayors through direct elections only.[528] However, the initiative group was not able to gather 300,000 signatures within the time limit of three months.[529] Finally, prompted by the impending introduction of the Euro as Lithuania's new official currency from 1 January 2015, a group of 13 members demanded on 25 June 2014 that the question of the adoption of the Euro be decided by the people. Since the group could not form a group of at least 15 eligible citizens, as the LoR requires,[530] the Central Electoral Commission had to reject the group's registration.[531] Accordingly, Lithuania will become the 19th member of the Euro-zone, after Estonia and Latvia. The introduction of the Euro is seen as a further step towards deeper European integration. As in Estonia and Latvia, its adoption is more than an economic matter in Lithuania.[532]

---

525 Mazylis/Jurgelionyte p. 120, see documentation under http://www3.lrs.lt/pls/inter2/dokpaieska.showdoc_l?p_id=420458&p_query=&p_tr2=2 (accessed on 20.10.2014).

526 See documentation under http://www3.lrs.lt/pls/inter3/dokpaieska.showdoc_l?p_id=422357&p_query=&p_tr2=2 (accessed on 20.10.2014).

527 See documentation under http://www3.lrs.lt/pls/inter2/dokpaieska.showdoc_l?p_id=424403&p_query=&p_tr2=2 (accessed on 20.10.2014).

528 See documentation under http://www3.lrs.lt/pls/inter2/dokpaieska.showdoc_l?p_id=469592&p_tr2=2 (accessed on 20.10.2014).

529 See http://www.vrk.lt/naujienos/-/content/10180/1/iniciatyvine-grupe-sudaryta (accessed on 13.10.2014).

530 Art. 10, par. 1 LoR.

531 See http://www.vrk.lt/naujienos/-/content/10180/1/atsisakyta-registruoti-iniciatyvine-grupe-surengti-referenduma-del-euro-ivedimo (accessed on 13.10.2014).

532 Litauen ist fit für den Euro, *Neue Zürcher Zeitung*, 5 June 2014, p. 23; Der Weg zum Euro ist offen. Freude bei Litauens Politikern, Skepsis im Volk, *Neue Zürcher Zeitung*,

C. Explanations for the Lithuanian practice

1. Legal constraints

One of the most influential factors that determines the use and outcome of Lithuanian referendums stems from the institutional settings stipulated by the constitution and the LoR. After almost a quarter of a century of experience, the Lithuanian law on referendums is still not favourable enough for the development of direct democracy. Firstly, the formal obstacles of collection time requirements and number of signatures needed for citizen initiated referendums make using such democratic tools very difficult. Allowing only three months to collect 300,000 signatures, which represents around 12 percent of the electorate, is not an easy initial position for the common people to launch a popular initiative. Within twenty years, there were around 23 popular launches that did not result in a referendum. In contrast to the citizens, large political parties such as the Fatherland Union or the LDDP mostly succeeded in collecting signatures in support of a particular issue or in triggering a referendum through the parliament.[533] As mentioned previously, there were several initiative launches in the last decade that intended to decrease the number of signatures from 300,000 to 100,000. After several failures, the fourth initiative launch on that issues finally succeeded in gathering the 300,000 required signatures needed to trigger a national referendum. However, the hurdle to trigger a referendum could not be lowered after the referendum results on 29 June 2014 (see chapter V-B-14). Too few citizens went to the polls and thus turnout quorum was not reached.

With regard to the outcome of referendums, the turnout and approval are decisive obstacles. The high turnout quorum of 50 percent of all eligible voters for all kinds of referendums and the high threshold of yes votes necessary (from one-quarter to three-quarter) to pass a decision by referendum obstructs the will of the people. In the opinion of the constitutional court, the high quorums are justified on the one hand by the fact that 'direct participation of citizens in the government of their state is a very important expression of the supreme sovereign power, therefor referendum shall be a testimony of the real will of the people', and on the other hand by the fact that democratic decisions are adopted by the majority principle. Since the first article of the constitution establishes that 'the State of Lithuania shall be an independent and democratic republic', it would

5 June 2014, p. 24; Litauen wird zum Euro-Land, *Neue Zürcher Zeitung*, 24 July 2014, p. 19.

533 See also Krupavicius, Citizens' Initiatives, p. 139.

consequently require that decisions felt by the people are also made according to the majority rule.[534]

For Lithuanians, it might be understandable that a vote by three-quarters of citizens is needed to amend the first article of the constitution, but is a qualified majority of the whole electorate really necessary for other issues too?[535] Regarding the success of the 21 referendums that have been held in Lithuania since 1991, this question can be answered with a 'no'. 15 of the 19 referendums that were actually supported by the majority of voters had to be invalidated because they failed to fulfil the formal restrictions on turnout or approval.

As SCHILLER argues, the framers of the constitution wanted to consolidate the country after re-independence by enacting high obstacles on policy change from citizens. It was in the interest of Lithuania that referendums were decided by the majority of Lithuanians and not by the Russian minorities.[536] But nowadays fewer hurdles would be more helpful in strengthening civil society by encouraging a participatory culture and promoting the people's participation in referendums. Any further hurdles are a source of distrust towards these direct democratic institutions, which undermines people's belief in their power to influence politics.

Consideration must also be given to the provisions that regulate the turnout and approval quorums. Apart from the threshold for an amendment of the provision of article 1 of the constitution,[537] it is surprising that in Lithuania all other referendum quorums are only framed at the statutory level and not further in the constitution, as is the case in Latvia.[538] Consequently, the threshold provisions as indicated under article 7 par. 1, 3, 4, 5 and article 8 LoR can be changed by parliament more easily, since no qualified majority is needed for an alteration of such a law.[539] It is possible for parliament to impede the direct legislation if the results of referendums do not serve their interest.

2. Informal constraints

In addition to the institutional framework, there are also informal procedures that define the use and outcome of popular votes. In many cases, these are caused

---

534 See JLtCC 1994-07-22, point 8.

535 DAGYS, Participatory Democracy, p. 10.

536 SCHILLER, Direct Democracy, p. 85.

537 See art. 148 CLt and art. 7, par. 2 LoR.

538 See also the approval provisions for referendums in Estonia, which are at the statutory level for referendums that are required by the law (art. 2 ERA) and at constitutional level for referendums from above (art. 105 CE).

539 False interpretation in EWERT, Potentiale, p. 123 and footnote 166.

by the tactical manoeuvres of the Lithuanian political elites themselves. One of the most commonly used tactics is opposing a referendum. A referendum can have no chance of success if its opponents encourage electors to abstain. Another strategy has to do with the ballot day. As GIEDRIUS ZVALIAUSKAS in his interview with BENJAMIN EWERT states, 'voter's turnout is less than 50 percent and it means that Lithuanian parties' capabilities to mobilize voters are weak'.[540] Therefore, it is not surprising that referendums have often been held at the same time as parliamentary elections. This scheduling has become a supplementary tool used in the most important campaigns to mobilize the party electorate.[541] To avoid mixing up party politics and issue politics, a referendum should not be held on the same day as general elections to the parliament.

Referendums have only in a few cases been used to solve domestic political deadlocks or to consolidate Lithuania's statehood (referendum on independence; referendum on withdrawal of the Soviet troops; referendum on the accession to the EU). In other cases, referendums have mostly been initiated for political mobilisation of the supporters of one party or another. The role of political parties in the triggering of referendums is still prevalent in Lithuania. According to LUISE PAPE MØLLER, it is the Lithuanian polarised party system that gave rise to party incentives in framing and triggering referendums. She notes that a high degree of polarisation between the parties makes it difficult to reach an agreement through negotiation. As a result, parties would rather by-pass parliamentary decision-making and trigger referendums to reach their goals by putting pressure on the other political wing.[542] As the authors ALGIS KRUPAVISCIUS and GIEDRIUS ZVALIAUSKAS correctly note, no single successful referendum has been implemented without the active role of political parties. 21 referendums were held in Lithuania between 1991 and 2014 and none of them was really citizen initiated. Also, intermediary organisations such as non-governmental organisations (NGOs), associations or unions are still weak in using direct democratic tools. They are still underdeveloped and there is also an historical mistrust towards interest groups such as unions. Finally, until 1990 they were ruled by the communist regime.[543]

These facts do not conform to the conventional notion that the referendum is an instrument of policy-making, which allows citizens or social groups to make

540 EWERT, Potentiale, p. 153.

541 MAZYLIS/JURGELIONYTE, pp. 117–120, p. 132.

542 MØLLER, p 282, pp. 284–289.

543 EWERT, Potentiale, p. 88; KNEUER, Transformationsstaaten, p. 88; LINDÉN, Zivilgesellschaft, p. 254.

political decisions directly and over the heads of their representatives.[544] Until now, Lithuanian direct democracy could not fulfil its function of expressing popular sovereignty and political equality. It did not bring about new decisions to which the political elites would disagree. To some extent, this outcome can be explained by the lack of practice on the part of Lithuanian civil society. According to GIEDRIUS ZVALIAUSKAS 'Citizens do not consider themselves as a force, which could be real actor within political system. [...] [They] are not satisfied how things are going, but do not think that they could influence politics'.[545] Considering the last referendums and initiative launches (nuclear power plant),[546] one can at least note an emergence of post-material values and movements within the Lithuanian civil society. Thus, it is possible that direct democracy tools will be used more frequently by groups outside parliament.

However, it should also be noted that framing and triggering a referendum and reaching a positive outcome is a costly undertaking and out of the reach of many citizens. It can only be hoped that lowering some hurdles at the beginning of the procedure will increase people's interest in direct democracy.

---

544 KRUPAVICIUS/ZVALIAUSKAS, p. 123.

545 Statement of GIEDRIUS ZVALIAUSKAS in his interview with BENJAMIN EWERT, see EWERT, Potentiale, p. 153.

546 See chapters V-B-12, 13 and 15.

VI. The quality of direct democracy in the Baltic states

A. A comparison of use and success of Baltic referendums

To illustrate the use and performance of direct democracy in the Baltic states, all 35 referendums held between 1991 and 2014 have been put into one figure (see *Figure 4* and also *Table 4*). A timeframe of almost 25 years is a solid period with which to make a judgement about the practical value of Baltic popular rights. Within two decades there were only four required referendums and most referendums (18) held in the Baltic republics were triggered from above – by the public authorities. However, in at least four cases it was a semi-plebiscite and thus the referendum was promoted by the joint action of both authorities and citizens.

Despite the large number of top-down referendums, it should be noted that authorities' referendums in the Baltic states were almost never used to empower governing majorities or the president (in the sense of extending the term, altering the balance between the government/president and parliament), as is the case in less democratic societies (e.g. Belarus).[547] Baltic top-down referendums were instead used strategically for partisan purposes in order to strengthen the parties' public image before parliamentary elections. Within 24 years, there was one plebiscite that might be considered critical, namely the Lithuanian failed plebiscite on the restoration of the presidential institution (see chapter V-B-2). Indeed, there are three main reasons that explain the absence of empowering referendums. As previously stated, first is the criterion of a controlling feature of a referendum. In the sense of checks and balances, referendums from above are mainly framed and triggered by different political actors, or they depend on joint action.[548] Secondly, as in citizen-initiated referendums, further procedural settings, such as restrictions on subject matter (e.g. the Latvian presidential plebiscite only for recalling the parliament) along with turnout and approval quorums also diminish the effect of referendums from above. A further reason for the absence of empowering referendums results from the party system (i.e. Estonia

547 See c2d database, http://c2d.ch/detailed_display.php?lname=votes&table=votes&page=1&parent_id=&sublinkname=results&id=39265 (accessed on 20.12.2013).

548 For instance the Latvian presidential plebiscite on recalling the parliament is framed and triggered by the president. Nevertheless, he or she is constrained by other institutional settings regulating the referendum; a negative outcome causes a removal of the president from office.

Figure 4: Referendums held in the Baltic states

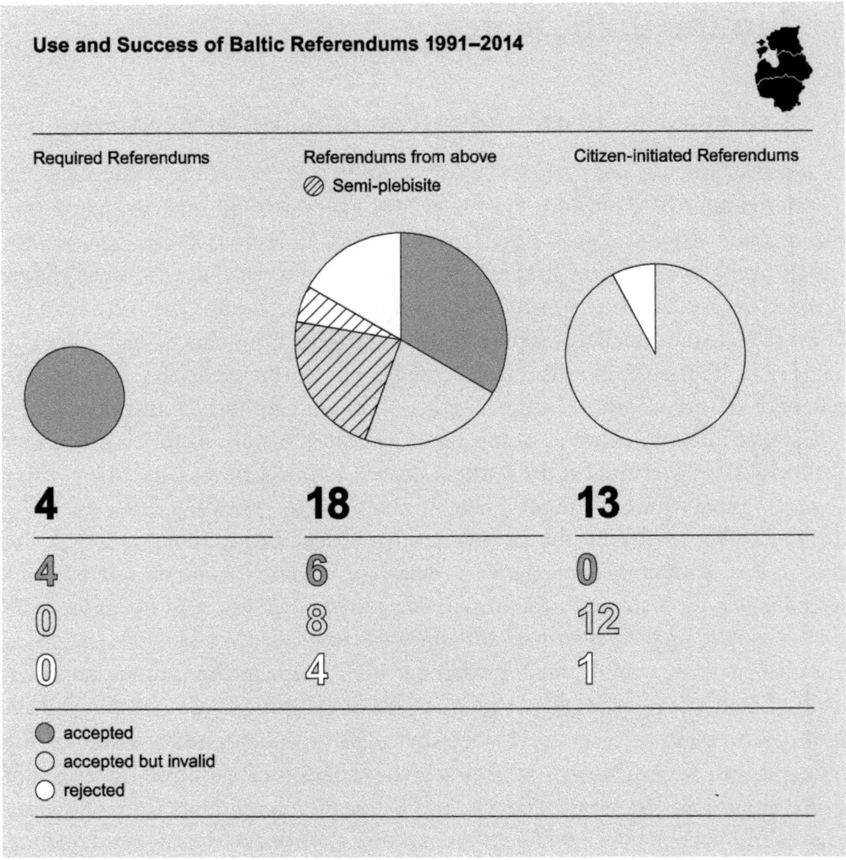

Source: Author's own calculations based on the data from www.c2d.ch and Central Electoral Commissions of three Republics

and Latvia's volatile multi-party system, Lithuania's polarised and volatile party system) in the Baltic republics. As explained, volatile and polarised party systems make it difficult to reach agreements on such critical resolutions.

Citizen-initiated referendums are the second largest group of referendums held in the Baltic states, but in all 13 cases political parties played a prominent role in the triggering of citizen-initiated referendums. As with referendums from above, citizen-initiated referendums were also a strategic tool used to bypass the parliament in order to eventually get the necessary popular support. But even more than the required popular support for a specific issue, citizens' initiatives were also an important tool in promoting party campaigns, especially by holding them on the same day as the elections.

With regard to performance, required referendums were the most effective referendums, since all four succeeded in full. Less formal effect (one-third) has been achieved in referendums from above and no formal success at all (in the sense of changing the legal order) has been achieved through citizen-initiated referendums. Indeed, as illustrated above, almost all (12 of 13) citizen-initiated referendums had been adopted by the people. Nevertheless, they failed to fulfil the minimum turnout or approval quorum and were thus not passed into law. Similar cases happened in referendums from above.

Figure 5: Policy areas of Baltic referendums

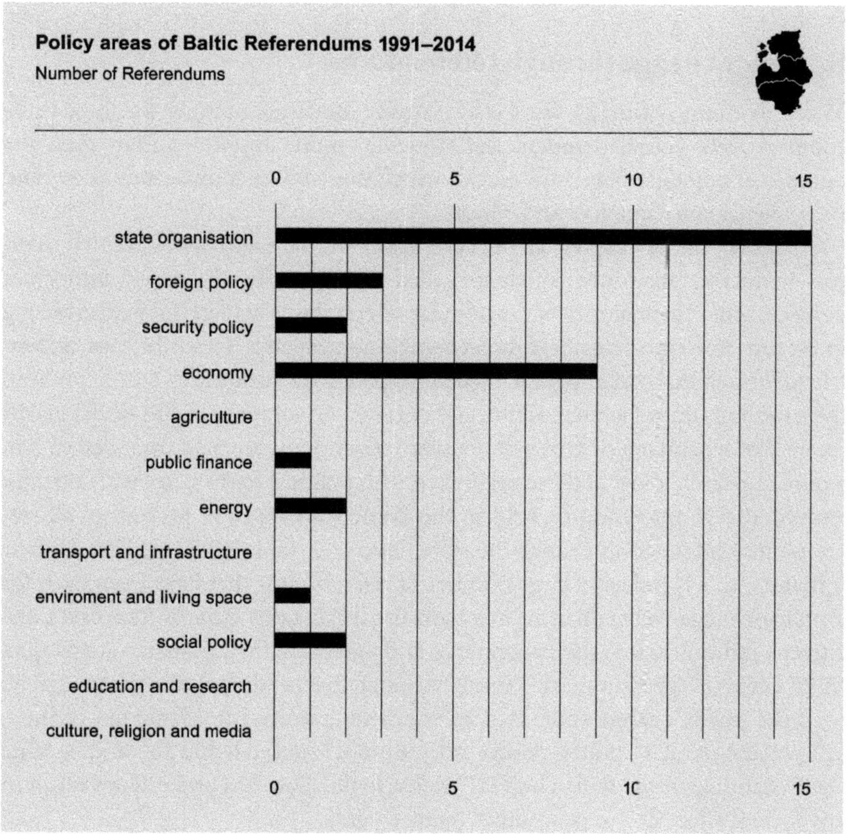

Source: Author's own calculations based on data from www.c2d.ch and Central Electoral Commissions of three Republics

Regarding policy areas (see Figure 5), it is not surprising that most referendums that have been held in the Baltic states dealt with issues of state organisation, including national identity, legal and political systems and citizens' rights, as the Figure 5 illustrates. Referendums were helpful tools in overcoming the Soviet trauma and re-establishing a country's crucial legal framework, particularly during the transitional period. However, in both Estonia and Latvia, the re-establishment of the nation state happened at the expense of Russian-speaking minorities. This persistent ethnic cleavage in each country is also apparent among the citizens' initiatives that did not succeed during the signature collection procedure (see chapters IV-B-12 and V-B-15). A second large topic for referendums concerned questions on economics. Other policy areas were seldom or never subject to Baltic referendums.

B. Policy change through referendums

35 referendums within 24 years is a relatively moderate number for these three comparatively young democracies. However, more important than even the number of popular votes is the way in which these referendums came about and their formal consequences and effects.

As shown under chapters III-A, IV-A and V-A, the Baltic states are rich in direct democratic instruments that are called automatically – by public authorities or by citizens. The majority of the popular referendums held in the Baltics belong to the top-down mechanism of direct democracy, which is in fact the least citizen-friendly of all direct democratic mechanisms. Public authorities decide on both the issue and time of a referendum, and citizens cannot make public decisions directly. The second major group of popular referendums are held from below. But, as already stated, most of these originated with political parties, not with citizens. Among the 35 referendums held in the Baltic states, 31 (89 percent of all referendums) intended to change the status quo (see Table 4). Regardless of their initiators, this is indeed a large number of referendums that have been used for a policy change rather than to maintain the legal status quo. In four cases, the citizens did not follow the proponents and voted for the legislative status quo. In 27 cases (87 percent of all 31 policy change referendums), the voters agreed with the policy change submitted to vote and approved it. While ten of them (32 percent of all 31 policy change referendums) succeeded in full and became legally binding, more than a half (17) failed to pass into law and did not result in any formal effect due to procedural requirements.

By analysing these results, we can argue that direct democracy in the Baltic states did not effectively empower the citizens or spread the political power

Table 4: Overview of referendums in three Baltic States, 1991–2014

Country	Name and Date of Referendum	Mechanism of DD	DD Institution	Intention	Approval	In Force
ESTONIA	Referendum on Estonia's independence (3 March 1991)	*top-down*	parliamentary plebiscite	policy change	yes	yes
	Referendum on the constitution (28 June 1992)	*top-down*	parliamentary constitutional plebiscite	policy change	yes	yes
	Referendum on voting rights for those who did not yet have citizenship status, (28 June 1992)	*top-down*	parliamentary constitutional plebiscite	policy change	no	no
	Referendum on the accession to the EU (14 September 2003)	*required*	mandatory constitutional referendum	policy change	yes	yes
LATVIA	Referendum on Latvia's independence (3 March 1991)	*top-down*	parliamentary plebiscite	policy change	yes	yes
	Referendum on the repeal of the facilitated naturalisation amendment (3 October 1998)	*top-down (+citizens)*	semi-plebiscite on repealing a law	status quo	no	no
	Referendum on the repeal of the pension system reform amendment (13 November 1999)	*top-down (+citizens)*	semi-plebiscite on repealing a law	status quo	yes	no
	Referendum on the accession to the EU (21 September 2003)	*required*	mandatory referendum on EU-Accession	policy change	yes	yes
	Referendum on the repeal of amendments to the law on state security services (7 July 2007)	*top-down (+citizens)*	semi-plebiscite on repealing a law	status quo	yes	no
	Referendum on the repeal of amendments to the law on state security authorities (7 July 2007)	*top-down (+citizens)*	semi-plebiscite on repealing a law	status quo	yes	no

Country	Name and Date of Referendum	Mechanism of DD	DD Institution	Intention	Approval	In Force
LATVIA	Referendum on the dissolution of parliament by popular vote (2 August 2008)	*bottom-up*	citizens' constitutional initiative	policy change	yes	no
	Referendum on a limited increase of public pensions (23 August 2008)	*bottom-up*	citizens' legislative initiative	policy change	yes	no
	Referendum on the early dissolution of the Saeima (Parliament) (23 July 2011)	*top-down*	presidential plebiscite on recalling parliament	policy change	yes	yes
	Referendum on Russian as the second official language (8 February 2012)	*bottom-up*	citizens' constitutional initiative	policy change	no	no
LITHUANIA	Referendum on Lithuania's independence (9 February 1991)	*top-down*	parliamentary plebiscite on other issues	policy change	yes	yes
	Referendum on the restoration of the presidential institution (23 May 1992)	*top-down*	parliamentary constitutional plebiscite	policy change	yes	no
	Referendum on the withdrawal of Soviet troops (14 June 1992)	*top-down*	parliamentary plebiscite on other issues	policy change	yes	yes
	Referendum on the constitution (25 October 1992)	*required*	mandatory constitutional referendum	policy change	yes	yes
	Referendum on the law revoking privatisation I–VIII (8 parts) (27 August 1994)	*bottom-up*	citizens' legislative initiative (8 issues!)	policy change	yes	no

Country	Name and Date of Referendum	Mechanism of DD	DD Institution	Intention	Approval	In Force
LITHUANIA	Referendum on the compensation for lost assets prior to 1990 (20 October 1996)	*bottom-up*	citizens' legislative initiative	policy change	yes	no
	Referendum on parliamentary elections on the second Sunday of April every four years (20 October 1996)	*top-down*	parliamentary constitutional plebiscite	policy change	yes	no
	Referendum on the reduction of parliamentary seats from 141 to 111 (20 October 1996)	*top-down*	parliamentary constitutional plebiscite	policy change	yes	no
	Referendum on social spending (20 October 1996)	*top-down*	parliamentary constitutional plebiscite	policy change	yes	no
	Referendum on the purchase of agricultural land by certain legal bodies (10 November 1996)	*top-down*	parliamentary constitutional plebiscite	policy change	no	no
	Referendum on the accession to the EU (10 and 11 May 2003)	*required*	mandatory referendum on participation in Int. Org.	policy change	yes	yes
	Consultative referendum on the service extension for the nuclear power plant 'Ignalina' (12 October 2008)	*top-down*	parliamentary plebiscite on other issues	policy change	yes	no
	Consultative referendum on building of a new nuclear power plant 'Visaginas' (14 October 2012)	*top-down*	parliamentary plebiscite on other issues	policy change	no	no
	Referendum regarding the amendment of articles 9, 47 and 147 of the constitution (reform of referendum rights and land sale) (29 June 2014)	*bottom-up*	citizens' constitutional initiative	policy change	yes	no

more widely across their societies. In the beginning of this book, it was stated that direct democratic mechanisms with binding results theoretically introduce the people as one additional veto player into public legislation and that any additional actor would diminish the potential for policy change. At first glance, the results confirm this assumption. A closer look at Table 4, however, illustrates that most policy changes were made through provisions allowing required referendums, indeed, within a direct democratic mechanism in which many actors with veto player status prevail. This is contrary to the predictions of veto-player model. However, it should be noted that the number of cases here (4 required referendums) is relatively small to be statistically significant. Contrary to this assumption, these referendums, which were under full control of the citizens, remained completely ineffective.

In fact, according to the theory of HUG/TSEBELIS, under such institutional provisions with which the citizens control both the asking of the question in the popular vote and the triggering of the process of the referendum, it is expected that citizens would actually individually determine the outcome of the referendum. This occurs because such referendums cancel out the other veto players, resulting in a decrease in the number of political actors. In turn, the potential of policy change preferred by the citizens should increase.[549] Factually, as one can see, there was a strong popular effort towards new policies but in 12 of 13 cases (all of them citizens' initiatives, see also Figure 4), the citizens failed to form the veto player. Accordingly, policy outcomes favoured the status quo.

C. Quality of direct democracy

Possible reasons for the low performance of direct democracy in the Baltic states have been evaluated for each republic. Generally speaking, there are many procedural hurdles that diminish the will of the people and affect the nature of the popular veto player, so that in most cases citizens fail to form the veto player. What follows thereafter is disappointment and distrust in direct legislation.

In order to avoid such developments and to establish a more citizen-friendly direct democracy, a number of formal factors have to be taken into account when drawing up a direct democratic mechanism. The authors KAUFMANN/BÜCHI/BRAUN name some important criteria, such as signature thresholds, collection periods, collection places, turnout and approval quorums, restriction of subject matter, type of authorities' involvement and legal consequences of referendums,

549 HUG/TSEBELIS, pp. 477–492.

where attention should be paid to designing a reasonable direct democracy that encourages rather than prevents citizen participation.[550] At the same time, improving the quality of direct democracy by designing more citizen-friendly procedures is not the only solution for ensuring a better-performing direct democracy. A well-functioning direct democracy is also dependent on a motivated and self-confident *demos*. The role of civic society and of civic education cannot be neglected. Further aspects, such as finances and transparency in ballot campaigns are also essential in achieving fair direct democratic procedures that can realise their full potential.

The following table (Table 5) lists a selection of the most fundamental institutional and procedural criteria of direct democracy. Without claiming to be exhaustive, a tentative judgment of the quality of direct democracy in the Baltic states has been undertaken following these elements and criteria.[551] The quality-check list is not definite; nevertheless, it is a useful tool with which to make a comparison between the three models of direct democracy in the Baltic states. To better explain the deficiencies of the direct democratic system, a summary reference of the institutions and procedures of direct democracy in Switzerland has also been made.

550 KAUFMANN/BÜCHI/BRAUN, pp. 92–94.

551 The criteria to judge the quality of Baltic direct-democratic design are mostly derived from the IRI's conceptualisation that is recommended to assess a better performing direct democracy; see KAUFMANN, Monitor, pp. 26–29.

Table 5: Quality of direct democracy in the Baltic states in comparison with Switzerland (2014)

		Factors / Criteria	IRI's Reccommendation, with Author's Supplements / Max. ✓	Estonia	Latvia	Lithuania	Switzerland
MECHANISM OF DIRECT DEMOCRACY Institutional Provisions	REQUIRED	Mandatory constitutional referendum / Mandatory referendum on other issues	yes, but it should not solely be restricted to specific provisions, ✓✓	✓	✓	✓	✓✓
	TOP-DOWN	from parliamentary minority	IRI no recommendation, ✓	×	(✓)	✓	×
		from parliamentary majority or president	no recommendation, IRI rather critical, (✓)	(✓)	(✓)	(✓)	×
	BOTTOM-UP	Citizens' facultative referendum	yes, should be available, ✓✓	×	(✓)	✓	✓✓
		Citizens' constitutional and legislative initiative as formulated draft / general suggestion, or both	yes, should be available, ✓✓✓	×	✓✓(✓)	✓✓✓	✓(✓)✓
	Other Instruments	Citizens' recall on parliament	no recommendation, ✓	×	✓	×	(×)

		Factors / Criteria	IRI's Reccommendation, with Author's Supplements / Max. ✓	Estonia	Latvia	Lithuania	Switzerland
PROCEDURES OF DIRECT DEMOCRACY Procedural Provisions	Procedure of signature collection	Number of signatures	in order to force a referendum, the entry hurdles should not exceed 5% of the electorate, ✓	✗	✗	✗	✓
		Collection time	a minimum of 6 months should be allowed, ✓	✗	✗[A]	✗	✓
		Collection place	should be free at every public place, ✓	✗	✗	✓	✓
	Validation of the vote	Turnout quorum	participation quorum higher than 25% should be avoided, much better no participation quorum at all, ✓	✓	✗	✗	✓
		Approval quorum	approval requirements as a proportion of the entire electorate should be avoided, ✓	✓	✗	✗	✓
		Character	binding results, ✓	✓	✓	✓	✓
	Initiative procedure	Direct or Indirect	indirect: parliament should be obliged to debate all popular initiatives and should have the right to present a counter-proposal; the initiative group should also be able to withdraw its proposal, ✓✓	✗	(✓)	(✓)	✓✓

		Factors / Criteria	IRI's Reccommendation, with Author's Supplements / Max. ✓	Estonia	Latvia	Lithuania	Switzerland
		Restriction on subject matter	there should be no exclusion on issues in the direct democratic process, ✓	×	×	✓	✓
	Coordinator / Supervisor	Central Electoral / Referendum Commission	a referendum electoral body should be available to advise the initiative committees, make a preliminary examination of the proposal, verify signatures, supervise the campaign and monitor and evaluate a referendum, ✓	✓	✓	✓	(✓)
Number of 'points' (tick marks)			**Max. = 19.5**	**5.5**	**9**	**11**	**16.25**

Source: Author's analysis

Remarks

✓ fulfilled (1), if a factor is of great significance to direct democracy then it is valued with more points (tick marks)
(✓) partially fulfilled or constrained by other provisions, and consequently a less citizen-friendly element (0.5)
× not fulfilled, not available (0)
(×) not fulfilled, but to some part available (0.25)
Max = the more points a country gets, the more citizen-friendly and well designed its direct democracy
A: Starting from 1 January 2015, signature collection of one tenth of the electorate will last for 12 months in Latvia

As is well known, the Federal State of Switzerland has the longest, most detailed and most comprehensive experience of citizens' law-making in the world. This also becomes obvious when we consider the referendums that were held in Switzerland between 1991 and 2014. In comparison to the same time period in the Baltic states, Swiss citizens were asked to decide on a total of 211 different referendums (without counter-proposals) and almost one half (97) of which succeeded in full and became legally binding.[552]

The table on quality of direct democracy (Table 5) consists of two parts divided into 'institutional' and 'procedural provisions'. For each section, there are certain fundamental 'factors' that are required for a direct democratic system to work. Derived from the recommendations of the Initiative and Referendum Institute Europe (IRI)[553] and my supplements based on theoretical and even practical explanations in chapters II–V, for each factor there is a maximum number of 'points' (tick marks) distributed. The more points a factor has, the more essential it is for direct democracy. And the more points a country gets, the better designed and citizen-friendly its direct democracy is.

1. Quality in Estonia

Among the three Baltic states, Estonia has the lowest score (5.5 points) of 'direct democratic quality'. Considering the availability of institutional provisions, it can be argued that Estonia is weak in terms of direct democratic instruments. The most serious shortcoming of its mechanisms is that there are no citizen-initiated referendums. Indeed, as already described in detail, there is a mandatory constitutional referendum but it can only be applied to a few issues (to alter the provisions of chapters I and XV of the Estonian Constitution) and the parliamentary plebiscite remains an exclusive right of a majority in parliament. A special point here is that any negative outcome of a parliamentary plebiscite for draft acts causes the dissolution of the parliament itself. Thus, this additional restriction makes the right of parliament to submit referendums on draft acts superfluous.

Regarding procedural provisions, Estonia still lags behind the recommendations established here. Some of the procedural deficiencies result from the

---

552 See c2d, http://c2d.ch/votes.php?level=1&country=1&yearr=timeperiods&fromyear=1991&toyear=2014&speyear[]=2014&result=0&terms=&group[]=26&group[]=28&group[]=30&group[]=31&group[]=33&group[]=35&table=votes&sub=Submit_Query (accessed on 23.10.2014) = 208, in addition three further referendums will be held on 30 November 2014.

553 KAUFMANN, Monitor, pp. 26–29.

missing bottom-up mechanism itself. The most positive procedural factor is the majority requirement for both the participation and approval of the vote. There is no turnout quorum that would put the validity of the referendum vote into question; the referendum simply becomes legally binding if the majority of the voters approves it. These theoretical aspects are also compatible with Estonian practice. Within this restricted legal framework, over twenty years only four referendums could be held. However, the success of these four popular votes was very high, as three referendums became legally binding and no referendum was invalidated.

2. Quality in Latvia

In Latvia, which scored 9 points, one can see that almost all direct democratic institutions, including the right to a popular initiative for constitutional and legislative amendments, are available to Latvian citizens. However, there is a weakness in the restrictions on subject matter here. Issues regarding the budget and laws concerning loans, taxes, custom duties, railroad tariffs and military conscription are excluded from the process of direct legislation. With regard to citizens' initiatives, Latvian law states that only elaborated drafts can be forwarded to a national referendum. General suggestions that would also enable citizens without legal knowledge to launch legislation are not provided for, which means that without professionalization, it is difficult for common people to legislate. Therefore, the full number of the possible points was not awarded here. In addition to citizens' initiatives, Latvians also have the citizens' right to veto a parliamentary resolution. This, however, still has relatively low value in the calculation because a joint action with the president or one-third of the members of parliament is still needed. Without a first action by the authorities, the popular veto to repeal a law cannot be triggered. This is also why this tool has been classified as a top-down instrument instead. A special and unique institutional feature that was recently given to Latvians is the right to recall parliament and set new elections for it. Still, it must be noted that such a right allows for making decisions about a public body, not about substantive issues.

Despite the availability of several direct democratic tools, Latvia scores very poorly in procedural provisions. For all types of referendums, there are restrictive rules that exclude certain issues from direct legislation. Additionally, a high number of signatures (10 percent of the total electorate) within a very short time period are required in order to force a citizen-initiated referendum. However, starting from 1 January 2015, the collection time for the same amount of signatures will last for 12 months. Options for signature gathering are limited since the collection cannot be done at every public place. With regard to the initiative procedure Latvia provides, to a certain degree, an indirect initiative process which obliges the Latvian parliament to debate all popular initiatives before they can be advanced to the people's decision. In its considerations, parliament generally rejects the citizens' initiative and calls a referendum on it. In fact, the parliament has also the possibility to adopt a citizens' proposal directly without submitting it to a referendum. Through parliament's involvement in citizens' legislation, a link is made between representative democracy and direct democracy because citizens and representatives come closer together. However, at that stage, there are no provisions in the Latvian system for counter-proposals or withdrawals that would lead to a compromise between parliament and the initiators. Therefore, only one-quarter of the possible points is given to Latvia. In the matter of turnout and approval quorums, Latvia does not perform very well either. To validate a popular vote for almost each kind of referendum, a different majority requirement is asked. For a mandatory constitutional referendum and a citizens' constitutional referendum, indeed, no formal turnout requirement is given but in fact, a high turnout quorum nevertheless occurs, since for an approval of such a referendum more than a half of all eligible voters are needed. Other approval quorums are mostly coupled with the number of electors who participated in the previous parliamentary elections. The unique positive aspect on procedural criteria is that the outcome of a referendum is binding. Nevertheless, this provision alone did or does not actually enable the people to become a veto player within the decision-making process, nor does it particularly facilitate their use of these direct democratic tools in practice. As stated before, ten referendums on almost all possible types have been held in practice. But, only three votes succeeded in full and five others failed to become legally binding, despite their adoption by the people.

3. Quality in Lithuania

Lithuania, the western neighbour of Latvia, performs a bit better in terms of the quality of direct democracy, with 11 points. Citizens of the third Baltic republic can participate in referendums that are triggered automatically, whether by a minority of the parliament or by the citizens themselves. Required referendums can only be applied for those issues that are explicitly determined by the constitution (therefore it gets only one tick mark). In contrast, there are no restrictions on subject matter for parliamentary plebiscites and citizens' initiatives. A citizens' proposal to be adopted by referendum can be proposed either as a preliminary or final text to the Central Election Committee. The possibility of both proposal forms has to be seen as positive, since it better allows for the integration of citizens who may do not have skilled knowledge about legislation into decision-making process.

Despite its wide range of direct democratic institutions, Lithuania does not perform very well on procedural conditions. Regarding the procedure of signature collection, neither the criteria of signature numbers nor the time limits to gather the required signatures are met. Signatures of nearly 12 percent of the electorate have to be collected within three months.[554] At this stage, the proponents of a citizens' initiative are at least free to collect signatures in support of their proposal anywhere they choose. Nevertheless, it is not surprising that around 23 popular initiatives failed to gather the necessary number of signatures and that all citizens' initiatives held in Lithuania were the products of established political parties rather than coming from groups of citizens. A major deficiency inherent to Lithuanian direct democracy stems from the validation of the votes. To get valid results, at first a minimum of 50 percent of the entire electorate has to participate. This rule applies to all referendum types. In addition to turnout quorums, there are also high approval requirements demanded by law. These two criteria have produced negative results, since 15 of 19 referendums that were adopted by the people had to be invalidated. As mentioned before, turnout and approval quorums not only cause invalidation but also false incentives, so that some parties and their supporters do not contribute to the political dialogues that would be vital for the success of a direct democratic process. Another negative aspect that the Lithuanian practice has revealed is the combination of referendum days with parliamentary elections. Referendums were mostly used for particular interests before general elections. To avoid mixing up party politics and issue politics, new democracies should avoid such voting days. One positive aspect in addition to the absence of restrictions on subject matter and binding referendum results is the indirect procedure of initiatives and the central role of the parliament in them. The parliament is obliged to deliberate the citizens' final act, but as in Latvia there are also no legal provisions for counter-proposals in Lithuania. Indeed, members of the initiative group are allowed to withdraw their signatures from an application to register the group. However, the withdrawal is not conditional upon a possible alternative proposal by the parliament. Just before signature collection, the initiative process is interrupted if fewer than

554 The required number of signatures was not reduced to 100,000 after the referendum on 29.06.2014.

15 members remain in the group.[555] As in the two other republics, referendums are also supervised by a central election commission in Lithuania. An independent committee can fulfil an informative and supportive function for the citizens and keep direct democratic procedures from being dominated by the parliament or government. It might be also responsible for legal validation of initiatives submitted by the citizens. It is important that in all three countries, decisions by the central election commission or another authority that may undermine the democratic rights of the people can be appealed against in court. A mechanism for assessing the legality of the decisions adopted by such institutions should also be available.

4. The most striking variation between the Baltic states

Looking at the direct democratic institutions and procedural provisions in each Baltic state listed in the Table 5, one notices several differences that are either of great or small importance. The ways in which the three republics differ from each other decisively quickly become clear, particularly given the absence of citizen-initiated referendums in Estonia. Hence, the question is: what are the reasons for these differences? As mentioned above, all three neighbour states already established direct democratic institutions in the interwar period (1918–1939) and they were all exposed to same historical events, such as occupation by the Soviets and independence in 1991. In contrast to Latvia and Lithuania, after independence Estonia did not introduce provisions for bottom-up direct democracy. Instead, it confined itself to referendums that were either required by law or called by parliament. The first reason for the absence of citizen-initiated referendums might be explained by negative experiences with direct democratic rights that Estonia experienced during the interwar years. As KOMÁROMI notes, the Estonian Constitution of 1920 allowed the citizens not only to participate in mandatory referendums but also to launch initiatives. During a volatile period with serious economic crises and frequent cabinet changes, however, popular rights were not conducive to the State Assembly's ability to solve the state's economic and political problems. On the contrary, mandatory referendums tended to hinder reforms to the state system and the citizens' initiative had become a tool of anti-parliamentary radical forces (League of Veterans). Their constitutional initiative intending establishing a presidential regime adopted in the referendum of 16 October 1933 actually paved the way for the provisional head of state KONSTANTIN PÄTS to establish his authoritarian regime. In September 1935,

555 Art. 10, par. 7 LoR.

PÄTS abolished citizen-initiated and required referendums and used plebiscitary tools to stabilise and extend his own power, much like Hitler did in Germany during the same time.[556]

In addition to these historical experiences, another reason to not introduce a bottom-up mechanism may have been due to the lack of efforts on the part of the elites. As explained previously, after independence Estonian elites preferred to consolidate the new democracy without any interruption or input from the people, especially when other ethnic groups constituted around one-third of the Estonian population at that time.[557] After the end of Soviet-era, the Baltic countries had to, on the one hand, build and expand democracy and urgently secure their nation on the other hand, particularly in Estonia and Latvia.[558] Faced with such a dilemma, it becomes understandable that a country may renounce a particular direct democratic right. However, after the consolidation of Estonian democracy, there is still no consensus among different parties to introduce such instruments and the effective constitutional order still does not provide any incentives for them after 24 years. In contrast to Estonia, in Lithuania for instance direct democratic instruments were not only linked with positive experiences in the sense of mass mobilisation for the peaceful transition from the beginning of re-independence, but also with the mobilisation of the electorate for particular party goals.[559] Today, attitudes of Lithuanian political parties towards direct democracy are still supportive.[560] Considering the 15 invalidated results of 19 approved referendums (total number of referendums held: 21, see Table 3 and Figure 3 under chapter V-A and B) it becomes clear why: as long as for the parliamentary elites there is no risk of policy change through referendums (high turnout and approval thresholds) that would have been controversial to representative policies, and as long as direct democratic instruments can be used in a manipulative way allowing parties an additional stage to place themselves more frequently in the agenda, there is also no reason for not supporting them.

556 KOMÁROMI, Volkswille, p. 452f.; KOMÁROMI, Popular law-making, pp. 69–74; see also KASEKAMP, The Radical Right, pp. 43–48, 120–128.

557 LAGERSPETZ/MAIER, Estland, p. 80.

558 DUVOLD, Making Sense, p. 92.

559 See ALGIS KRUPAVICIUS' interview statement, EWERT, Potentiale, p. 152 and MAZYLIS/JURGELIONYTE, p. 117f.

560 See GIEDRIUS ZVALIAUSKAS' interview statement, EWERT, Potentiale, p. 154.

D. More than instruments

No matter how many direct democratic instruments are available to the citizens, a direct democratic mechanism cannot work within a poorly designed framework, nor can it encourage the people to participate in direct legislation. To illustrate the importance of direct democracy's design, we must briefly consider the case of Switzerland. Swiss direct democracy provides for referendum instruments that are either automatically derived or from the citizens (without a citizens' legislative initiative). At national level, the absence of referendums triggered by authorities is not seen as a deficiency. The quality of Swiss direct democracy and its performance (211 referendums within 24 years) are determined by its procedural rather than its institutional provisions (16.25 points).

As illustrated in the table, Switzerland performs best in the procedural section; all criteria that are listed are fulfilled. There is enough time (18 months for citizens' initiatives and 100 days for citizens' facultative referendums) to collect 100,000 signatures (2 percent of the entire electorate) in support of citizens' initiatives and 50,000 signatures (1 percent of the whole electorate) to veto parliamentary decrees.[561] Signatures can also be collected everywhere and no special majority requirements are applied to referendum decisions. A referendum becomes legally binding if the majority of the voters approves it. For constitutional amendments, however, a qualified approval quorum – double majority of people and cantons – is required because Switzerland is a federal state. Here, in order to be adopted, the majority of both the voters and cantons must vote in favour. Decisions that have been approved by the people can be altered by the parliament at a later date. This is not necessarily a disadvantage. On the one hand, any constitutional amendment that is launched by the parliament has to be automatically submitted to popular vote and, on the other hand, the amendment might be conducive to promoting a functional legal setting, instead of a legal deadlock.

In Switzerland, no policy areas are excluded from being subject to a popular vote. Another citizen-friendly procedure results from the manner in which initiatives are treated before they are placed on the ballot. Swiss initiative procedure is an indirect process by which popular initiatives must be considered and deliberated by the government and parliament. The parliament is entitled to accept the initiative or to present a counter-proposal as an alternative to the proposal contained in a citizens' initiative. The proponents of an initiative can also withdraw their proposal if they agree with the alternative proposed by the parliament. If not, the counter-proposal (if there is any) and the citizens' initiative are

561 See art. 138, 139 and 141, Swiss Federal Constitution of 18 April 1999 (Cst-CH).

placed on the ballot simultaneously, and citizens have a choice between these two possibilities. The advantage of an indirect initiative procedure, in which representative and direct democracy are linked, lies in the fact that initiatives are debated longer and citizens and their representatives come into closer contact with each other. In many cases, the parliament recognises the need for legal action and enacts counter-proposals, which can also increase the efficiency of citizens' initiatives by other means. As Gabriela Rohner has established, almost half of citizens' constitutional initiatives have caused a change in the Swiss federal legislative status, resulting either from the direct adoption of citizens' initiatives, or the adoption of counter-proposals.[562] Nevertheless, in spite of these citizen-friendly provisions, a major imperfection remains in terms of the procedures on the validity check of Swiss initiatives. It might be determined that adopted initiatives do not comply with the provisions of both Switzerland's constitution and its international agreements.

Considering the legal framework in which direct legislation could flourish, it can be argued that direct democracy is more than the sum of its instruments. In order to assess a qualitative and citizen-friendly direct democracy, several procedural provisions have to be taken into account. The time allowances given for each stage of the direct democratic process should not be underestimated. Solutions adopted through direct democratic procedures should not be hastily made decisions. The collection of signatures, responses from authorities, campaigns and public debate need an appropriate period of time to develop interactively and enact functional laws. It does not matter how many people have turned out in the last stage of direct democratic legislation to achieve a final decision that is considered as legitimate. As long as the procedural design is legitimate (citizen-friendly provisions, accessibility, parliamentary debates on the issue, determination of the results, judicial review, legal protection of political rights), it will also generate legitimate outcomes, whether the popular decision is 'wrong or right'.

562 Rohner, p. 282.

VII. Conclusions

A. Rich in instruments, moderate in use, poor in performance

Independently of the grade of direct democracy, referendums in all three Baltic states have been helpful tools in carrying the transition trough peacefully and in legitimising nation-building decisions after the fall of the Soviet Union in the beginning of the 1990s. All three countries showed how democracy could be peacefully restored with various forms of direct democracy, in accordance with international law. After the Soviet trauma, the people not only elected their representatives but also decided on fundamental policy issues with regard to independence, the constitution, the re-establishment of statehood and accession to supranational organisations, such as the European Union. One may note that Estonia, Latvia and Lithuania are currently the only EU member states that were formerly republics of the Soviet Union.

Currently, the Baltic states have a large number of direct democratic instruments that were set up in difficult circumstances. Thanks to direct democratic tools with binding results, the citizens are partly introduced into the legislative process as one additional veto player, whose agreement is needed for a change in the legislative status quo. Following the conceptualisation of direct democratic mechanisms, many different types of referendums have been determined that are constitutionally provided in these three republics. Despite common experiences in the interwar, as well as in the immadiate post-war period, the overview of their referendum rights has illustrated that all three Baltic states have established direct democratic mechanisms to different extents after they regained their independence in 1991. Required referendums exist in all three Republics. However, in all three countries policy areas that are subject to such mandatory referendums are very restricted. Several constitutional issues do not make up a part of the required referendums. In addition to required referendums, referendums that are derived from the authorities also exist in each country, but they are considered less democratic since they are fully subject to the control of the authorities. Here, the citizens are only asked to go to polls and cast their votes for a proposal that has been framed and triggered by the public authorities. Top-down referendums can have somewhat more of a democratising effect, even if, as is the case in Lithuania, a parliamentary minority triggers the referendum. Without doubt, the largest effect that the people can have is through referendums that are from below. Unlike Estonians, Latvians and Lithuanians are entitled to initiate referendums in order to amend the constitution, statutory provisions and other issues or to veto parliamentary resolutions. Since recently, Latvians are even entitled to trigger a referendum on recalling the parliament.

Despite having many direct democratic tools, the Baltic states perform only moderately well in terms of their application. Between 1991 and 2014, 35 referendums have been held in these three republic: 21 in Lithuania, 10 in Latvia and 4 in Estonia. Among these 35 referendums, 31 were intended to cause a policy change in the legislative status quo. Referendums from above are the leading group, followed by citizens' initiatives and automatic referendums. In all three direct mechanisms, political parties were the most active users, but referendums have seldom been applied to reach solutions on deadlocked policies. On the contrary, parties often used referendums strategically (on the same day as parliamentary elections) in order to promote partisan interests and campaigns. Despite their active partisan use, however, it should be noted that direct democratic instruments have not been exploited to enlarge political power in favour of governing majorities or the president.

In terms of performance, the results in this book show that the Baltic states do not rank well. Only one-third (10 of 30) of the referendums approved by the people have been passed into law. In contrast, two-thirds (20) of all approved referendums deemed to be invalid since they failed to achieve turnout or approval requirements (see Figure 4 and Table 4). It should also be noted that none of citizen-initiated referendums became legally binding. Here, the model of veto player did not work at all. Despite the fact that citizens were in full control of the referendums (framing/triggering), they failed to become an oppositional power against the representative state organs and to reach political decisions on issues in which they were in disagreement with the political elite. Above all, citizens were not able to determine the outcome of public decisions individually. Regardless of the mechanism employed, direct democracy fails to fulfil the desired effect of allowing citizens to make political decisions directly and over the heads of their representatives. Too weak is the integration of concerns of 'outsiders' and not sufficiently effective the control over representative policy making.

B. A better design for a better balance

The weak performance of direct democratic mechanisms in the Baltic states – in the sense of giving citizens additional possibilities of making proposals or of political control independently of their representatives – is determined by informal and formal factors. As already mentioned, the Baltic states are comparatively young democracies that have travelled a difficult path towards democracy. Until their re-independence in 1991, they had experienced several non-democratic regimes. The Soviet occupation, which lasted for over 50 years, was enough to suppress any development of individual and self-confident people. The Soviet model imposed on these three republics undoubtedly left profound marks on society and the people lived under it. Under the all-encompassing institutional framework of the Soviet Union, neither a distinct civil society nor liberal individualism could emerge.[563] Consequently, adequate time is needed to develop a strong civil society that places its trust in participatory democracy rather than an elite-dominated government. Hence, each referendum that is held in these countries may contribute to promoting collective learning and trust in direct democratic procedures. Another informal reason for the poor performance of referendums originates with the elites. They still act within a legal framework that favours their interests, and in some cases, referendums have been part of their strategic calculations. In addition, as noted previously, the Baltic party system without distinct roots in civil society is a very unstable, and within a volatile party landscape, it is difficult to find majorities that would reform the current legal order.

In addition to the informal aspects, the weak performance is also influenced by formal settings, specifically by the less citizen-friendly procedural design of direct democracy. It is true that the implementation of direct democratic provisions was made within volatile economic, social, and technical circumstances. But it is also true that until now, less effort has been made by the elites to make participatory democracy more citizen friendly. In each republic, there are various formal constraints, such as restrictions on subject matter, high signature numbers, short collection periods, and high turnout and approval quorums, all of which diminish the sovereignty of the people in terms of more citizens' participation and the correction of policy course of democratically legitimized elites. Any referendum that is ruled out due to formal restrictions makes people less than keen about this mechanism of decision-making. Citizens simply get tired of them. To close the gap between representative democracy and the various types of direct democracy, such procedural obstacles should be reduced. Another possibility to enchance direct democracy and its practice is the introduction of an indirect initiative process, potentially enabling a rapprochement of elites and citizens. Counter-proposals and the option of withdrawal of citizens' initiatives are helpful tools to lead both sides to negotiate with each other. Also,

563 See also DUVOLD, Making Sense, pp. 150–154, 256f; ROSENVALDS, Baltische Staaten, p. 60; LINDÉN, Zivilgesellschaft, p. 243f., p. 254.

promotion of participation rights at sub-national level can contribute to a better performing direct democracy. Decision taking at the local level would not only promote a sense of responsibility for each citizen, it would also contribute to a societal learning and, thus, social trust in direct legislation.

The introduction of direct democratic tools into constitutional law in order to give citizens the means to play an active role in politics is indeed a positive step forward. However, regarding the settings and results outlined in this book, we can conclude that the Baltic states have not yet risen to the challenge of striking a balance between representative and direct democracy. To reach this goal, it is not enough to provide citizens with all different direct democratic mechanisms. It is also essential to ensure that they are well designed. Many obstacles and high hurdles are less helpful in developing a strong civil society and encouraging the people to more actively participate in direct legislation. Such constraints tend to impede deliberative dialogues and cause distrust in direct democratic polities.

VIII. References

Books and Journals

ALTMAN DAVID, *Direct Democracy Worldwide* (Cambridge 2010), (cit. ALTMAN).

AUER ANDREAS, National Referendums in the Process of European Integration: Time for Change, in: ALBI ANNELI/ZILLER JACQUES (eds.), *The European Constitution and National Constitutions. Ratification and Beyond* (Amsterdam 2007), pp. 261–271 (cit. AUER, National Referendums).

AUER ANDREAS/BÜTZER MICHAEL (eds.), *Direct Democracy. The Eastern and Central European Experience* (Aldershot et al. 2001), (cit. AUER/BÜTZER, Direct Democracy).

AUER ANDREAS/MALINVERNI GIORGIO/HOTTELIER MICHEL, *Droit constitutionnel suisse. Volume I: L'Etat*, 3rd edition (Bern 2013), (cit. AUER/MALINVERNI/HOTTELIER, Volume I).

AUERS DAUNIS, An Electoral Tactic? Citizens' Initiatives in Post-Soviet Latvia, in: SETÄLÄ MAIJA/SCHILLER THEO (eds.), *Citizens' Initiatives in Europe. Procedures and Consequences of Agenda-Setting by Citizens* (Basingstoke 2012), pp. 53–68 (cit. AUERS).

BIAGGINI GIOVANNI, Demokratietheorie – rechtswissenschaftlich betrachtet, in: GOOD ANDREA/PLATIPODIS BETTINA (eds.), *Direkte Demokratie. Herausforderungen zwischen Politik und Recht. Festschrift für Andreas Auer zum 65. Geburtstag* (Bern 2013), pp. 1–13 (cit. BIAGGINI, Demokratietheorie).

BRADY HENRY E./KAPLAN CYNTHIA S., Eastern Europe and the Former Soviet Union, in: BUTLER DAVID/RANNEY AUSTIN (eds.), *Referendums around the World. The Growing Use of Direct Democracy* (Washington D.C. 1994), pp. 174–217 (cit. BRADY/KAPLAN).

BUTLER DAVID/RANNEY AUSTIN (eds.), *Referendums around the World. The Growing Use of Direct Democracy* (Washington D. C. 1994), (cit. BUTLER/RANNEY, Growing Use).

DAGYS REMANTAS, Participatory Democracy in the Baltic States, before and after the Communist Regime, in: COUNCIL OF EUROPE (ed.): *Seminar on Participatory Democracy in Central and Eastern Europe Toady: Challenges and Perspectives* (Vilnius 1997), pp. 9–16 (cit. DAGYS, Participatory Democracy).

DUVOLD KJETIL, *Making Sense of Baltic Democracy. Estonia, Latvia and Lithuania between Soviet Union and the European Union* (Saarbrücken 2010), (cit. DUVOLD, Making Sense).

Ewert Benjamin, *Potentiale der direkten Demokratie in Litauen, Slowenien und Ungarn unter besonderer Berücksichtigung der politischen Kultur* (Frankfurt am Main et al. 2007), (cit. Ewert, Potentiale).

Feldhune Gita, Latvia, in: Kaufmann Bruno/Waters Dane M. (eds.), *Direct Democracy in Europe. A Comprehensive Reference Guide to the Initiative and Referendum Process in Europe* (Durham 2004), pp. 77–83 (cit. Feldhune).

Haab Richard, *Das Verfahren mit bedingter Eventaulabstimmung (Doppel-Ja mit Stichfrage). Die Einführung im Kanton Basel-Landschaft anlässlich der Erprobung an der Doppelabstimmung über das Sonntagsschiessverbot* (Zürich 1989), (cit. Haab, Verfahren).

Hall Peter A./Taylor Rosemary C. R., Political Science and the Three New Institutionalism, in: *Political Studies* 44/1996, pp. 936–957 (cit. Hall/Taylor, New Institutionalism).

Hangartner Yvo/Kley Andreas, *Die demokratischen Rechte in Bund und Kantonen der Schweizerischen Eidgenossenschaft* (Zürich 2000), (cit. Hangartner/Kley).

Hofer Bruno, Die Volksinitiative als Verhandlungspfand, in: Schweizerische Vereinigung für politische Wissenschaft, SVPW Jahrbuch (eds): *Abstimmungen und Wahlen*, Bern 27/1987, pp. 207–235 (cit. Hofer, Verhandlungspfand).

Hoffmann Thomas, Sachunmittelbare Demokratie im Baltikum (Estland, Lettland, Litauen), in: Neumann Peter/Renger Denise (eds.), *Sachunmittelbare Demokratie im interdisziplinären und internationalen Kontext 2010/2011* (Baden-Baden 2012), pp. 309–327 (cit. Hoffmann, Baltikum).

Hug Simon/Tsebelis George, Veto Players and Referendums around the World, *Journal of Theoretical Politics* 14(4)/2002, pp. 465–515 (cit. Hug/Tsebelis).

Ikstens Janis, Latvia, *European Journal of Political Research* 42/2003, pp. 1003–1049 (cit. Ikstens, Latvia 2003).

Ikstens Janis, Latvia, *European Journal of Political Research* 43/2004, pp. 1054–1058 (cit. Ikstens, Latvia 2004).

Ikstens Janis, Latvia, *European Journal of Political Research* 44/2005, pp. 1077–1085 (cit. Ikstens, Latvia 2005).

Ikstens Janis, Latvia, *European Journal of Political Research* 47/2008, pp. 1039–1047 (cit. Ikstens, Latvia 2008).

Ikstens Janis, Latvia, *European Journal of Political Research* 48/2009, pp. 1015–1021 (cit. Ikstens, Latvia 2009).

IKSTENS JANIS, Latvia, *European Journal of Political Research* 49/2010, pp. 1049–1057 (cit. IKSTENS, Latvia 2010).

IKSTENS JANIS, Latvia, *European Journal of Political Research Political Data Yearbook* 51/2012, pp. 175–186 (cit. IKSTENS, Latvia 2012).

IKSTENS JANIS, Latvia, *European Journal of Political Research Political Data Yearbook* 52/2013, pp. 134–139 (cit. IKSTENS, Latvia 2013).

IMMERGUT ELLEN M., The Logic of Health Policy-making in France, Switzerland and Sweden, in: STEINMO SVEN [et al.] (eds.), *Structuring Politics. Historical Institutionalism in Comparative Analysis* (Cambridge 1992), pp. 57–89 (cit. IMMERGUT, Policy-making).

IMMERGUT ELLEN M., Health Politics. *Interest and Institutions in Western Europe* (Cambridge 1992), (cit. IMMERGUT, Health Politics).

KAISER ANDRÉ, Types of Democracy. From Classical to New Institutionalism, *Journal of Theoretical Politics* 9(4)/1997, pp. 419–444 (cit. KAISER, Types).

KASEKAMP ANDRES, *The Radical Right in Interwar Estonia* (Basingstoke 2000), (cit. KASEKAMP, The Radical Right).

KASEKAMP ANDRES, *A History of the Baltic States* (Basingstoke 2010), (cit. KASEKAMP, History).

KAUFMANN BRUNO (ed.), *Initiative & Referendum Monitor 2004/2005* (Amsterdam 2004), Initiative and Referendum Institute Europe, pp. 1– 47 (cit. KAUFMANN, Monitor).

KAUFMANN BRUNO/BÜCHI ROLF/BRAUN NADJA (eds.), *Guidebook to Direct Democracy in Switzerland and beyond* (Marburg 2008), (cit. KAUFMANN/BÜCHI/BRAUN).

KAUFMANN BRUNO/WATERS M. DANE (eds.), *Direct Democracy in Europe. A Comprehensive Reference Guide to the Initiative and Referendum Process in Europe* (Durham 2008), (cit. KAUFMANN/WATERS).

KOMÁROMI LÁSZLÓ, Volkswille und Legitimation. Direktdemokratische Erfahrungen aus der Zwischenkriegszeit, in: *Beiträge zur Rechtsgeschichte Österreichs BRGÖ* 2013, pp. 447–455 (cit. KOMÁROMI, Volkswille).

KOMÁROMI LÁSZLÓ, Parliaments and Popular Law-making: the German and Estonian Experience in the Interwar Years, in: *Parliaments, Estates and Representation* 34(1)/2014, pp. 55–75 (cit. KOMÁROMI, Popular Law-making).

KNEUER MARIANNE, Die baltischen Staaten als Transformationsstaaten, in: KNODT MICHÈLE/URDZE SIGITA (eds.), *Die politischen Systeme der baltischen*

Staaten. Eine Einführung (Wiesbaden 2012), pp. 75–96 (cit. KNEUER, Transformationsstaaten).

KREUZE MARCUS/PETTAI VELLO, Patterns of Political Instability: Affiliation Patterns of Politicians and Voters in Post-Communist Estonia, Latvia and Lithuania, in: *Studies in Comparative International Development* 38(2)/2003, pp. 76–98 (cit. KREUZE/PETTAI, Instability).

KRIESI HANSPETER/BERNHARD LAURENT, Die Referendumsdemokratie, in: SCHOLTEN HEIKE/KAMPS KLAUS (eds.), *Abstimmungskampagnen. Politikvermittlung in der Referendumsdemokratie* (Wiebaden 2014), pp. 3–18 (cit. KRIESI/BERNHARD, Referendumsdemokratie).

KRUPAVICIUS ALGIS/ZVALIAUSKAS GIEDRIUS, Lithuania, in: AUER ANDREAS/BÜTZER MICHAEL (eds.), *Direct Democracy. The Eastern and Central European Experience* (Aldershot et al. 2001), p. 109–128 (cit. KRUPAVICIUS/ZVALIAUSKAS).

KRUPAVICIUS ALGIS, Lithuania, *European Journal of Political Research* 42/2003, pp. 1010–1020 (cit. KRUPAVICIUS, Lithuania 2003).

KRUPAVICIUS ALGIS, Lithuania, *European Journal of Political Research* 43/2004, pp. 1059–1069 (cit. KRUPAVICIUS, Lithuania 2004).

KRUPAVICIUS ALGIS, Lithuania, *European Journal of Political Research* 47/2008, pp. 1048–1059 (cit. KRUPAVICIUS, Lithuania 2008).

KRUPAVICIUS ALGIS, Lithuania, *European Journal of Political Research* 48/2009, pp. 1022–1036 (cit. KRUPAVICIUS, Lithuania 2009).

KRUPAVICIUS ALGIS, Lithuania, *European Journal of Political Research* 49/2010, pp. 1058–1075 (cit. KRUPAVICIUS, Lithuania 2010).

KRUPAVICIUS ALGIS, Lithuania, *European Journal of Political Research* 50/2011, pp. 1045–1057 (cit. KRUPAVICIUS, Lithuania 2011).

KRUPAVICIUS ALGIS, Lithuania, *European Journal of Political Research* Political Data Yearbook 52/2013, pp. 140–151 (cit. KRUPAVICIUS, Lithuania 2013).

KRUPAVICIUS ALGIS, Citizens' Initiatives in Lithuania: Initiative Institutions and Their Political Impact in a New Democracy, in: SETÄLÄ MAIJA/SCHILLER THEO (eds.), *Citizens' Initiatives in Europe. Procedures and Consequences of Agenda-Setting by Citizens* (Basingstoke 2012), pp. 134–151 (cit. KRUPAVICIUS, Citizens' Initiatives).

LAGERSPETZ MIKKO/MAIER KONRAD, Das politische System Estlands, in: ISMAYR WOLFGANG (eds.), *Die politischen Systeme Osteuropas*, 3rd edition (Wiesbaden 2010), pp. 79–121 (cit. LAGERSPETZ/MAIER, Estland).

LeDuc Lawrence, *The Politics of Direct Democracy: Referendums in Global Perspective* (Ontario 2003), (cit. LeDuc, Politics of Direct Democracy).

Lijphart Arend, *Democracies. Patterns of Majoritarian and Consensus Government in Twenty-One Countries* (New Haven/London 1984), (cit. Lijphart, Democracies).

Lijphart Arend, *Patterns of Democracies. Government Forms and Performance in Thirty-Six Countries*, 2nd edition (New Haven/London 2012), (cit. Lijphart, Patterns).

Lindén Tove, Interessenverbände und Zivilgesellschaft in den baltischen Staaten, in: Knodt Michèle/Urdze Sigita (eds.), *Die politischen Systeme der baltischen Staaten. Eine Einführung* (Wiesbaden 2012), pp. 241–257 (cit. Lindén, Zivilgesellschaft).

Linder Wolf, *Schweizerische Demokratie. Institutionen – Prozesse – Perspektiven*, 3rd edition (Bern 2012), (cit. Linder, Schweizerische Demokratie).

Linder Wolf/Lutz Georg, Direkte Demokratie, in: Klöti Ulrich [et al.] (eds.), *Handbuch der Schweizer Politik*, 4th edition (Zürich 2006), pp. 103–124 (cit. Linder/Lutz, Direkte Demokratie).

Liivik Ero, Legitimacy through Direct Democracy in the EU Member State. Direct Democratic Initiatives in the Estonian Parliament, *Proceedings of the Institute for European Studies* 8/2010, p. 89 (cit. Liivik, Legitimacy).

Liivik Ero, Referendum in the Estonian Constitution: Historical and Comparative Constitutional Aspects, in: *Juridica International* XVIII/2011, pp. 17–26 (cit. Liivik, Referendum).

Liivik Ero, Direct Democracy and its Indirect Neutralization in Political Systems: Learning from the Case of Estonia, *Baltic Journal of Law & Politics* 6(1)/2013, pp. 27–44 (cit. Liivik, Learning).

Marxer Wilfried, *Wir sind das Volk. Direkte Demokratie – Verfahren, Verbreitung, Wirkung*, Beiträge (24)/2004 Liechtenstein-Institut (Bendern 2004), (cit. Marxer, Wir sind das Volk).

Marxer Wilfried/Pállinger Zoltán Tibor, System Context and System Effects of Direct Democracy – Direct Democracy in Liechtenstein and Switzerland Compared, in: Pállinger Zoltán Tibor [et al.] (eds.), *Direct Democracy in Europe. Developments and Prospects* (Wiesbaden 2007), pp. 12–39 (cit. Marxer/Pallinger, System).

Mazylis Liudas/Jurgelionyte Ausrine, The Lithuanian Referendum on Extending the Working of the Ignalina Nuclear Power Station: The Rationality of Actors within (Un-)changing Structures, *Baltic Journal of Law & Politics* 5(1)/2012, pp. 117–136 (cit. MAZYLIS/JURGELIONYTE).

MAZYLIS LIUDAS/UNIKAITE INGRIDA, The Lithuanian EU Accession Referendum 10–11 May 2003. *Referendum Briefing No. 8 for European Parties Elections and Referendums Network* EPERN, pp. 1–11, in: http://www.sussex.ac.uk/sei/research/europeanpartieselectionsreferendumsnetwork/epernreferendumbriefings (accessed on 10.06.2013), (cit. MAZYLIS/UNIKAITE).

MIKKEL EVALD/PRIDHAM GEOFFREY, Clinching the 'Return to Europe': The Referendums on EU Accession in Estonia and Latvia, *West European Politics* 27(4)/2004, pp. 716–748 (cit. MIKKEL/PRIDHAM).

MÖCKLI SILVANO, Direkte Demokratie in den Gliedstaaten der USA, in: FREITAG MARKUS/WAGSCHAL UWE (eds.), *Direkte Demokratie. Bestandaufnahmen und Wirkungen im internationalen Vergleich* (Berlin 2007), pp. 19–39 (cit. MÖCKLI, Gliedstaaten).

MOLE RICHARD C. M., *The Baltic States from the Soviet Union to the European Union. Identity, Discourse and Power in the Post-Communist Transition of Estonia, Latvia and Lithuania* (London/New York 2012), (cit. MOLE).

MØLLER LUISE PAPE, Moving Away from the Ideal: The Rational Use of Referendums in Baltic States, *Scandinavian Political Studies* 23(3)/2002, pp. 281–293 (cit. MØLLER).

MÜLLER GEORG/UHLMANN FELIX, *Elemente einer Rechtssetzungslehre*, 3rd edition, (Zürich/Basel/Genf 2013), (cit. MÜLLER/UHLMANN, Rechtssetzungslehre).

NEIDHART LEONHARD, *Plebiszit und pluralitäre Demokratie: Eine Analyse der Funktion des schwezerischen Gesetzesreferendums* (Bern 1970), (cit. NEIDHART, Plebiszit).

NEUMANN PETER/RENGER DENISE (eds.), *Sachunmittelbare Demokratie im interdisziplinären und internationalen Kontext 2010/2011* (Baden-Baden 2012), (cit. NEUMANN/RENGER).

NOYES HENRY S.; *The Law of Direct Democracy* (Durham, North Carolina 2014), (cit. NOYES, Law of Direct Democracy).

PALLINGER ZOLTAN TIBOR/KAUFMANN BRUNO/MARXER WILFRIED/SCHILLER THEO (eds.), *Direct Democracy in Europe. Developments and Prospects* (Wiesbaden 2007), (cit. PALLINGER et al., Direct Democracy).

PETTAI VELLO, Estonia, *European Journal of Political Research* 43/2004, pp. 993–999 (cit. PETTAI).

PAPADOPOULOS YANNIS, How Does Direct Democracy Matter? The Impact of Referendum Votes on Politics and Policy-making, in: *West European politics* 2/2001, pp. 35–58 (cit. PAPADOPOULOS, Matter).

QVORTRUP MATT (ed.), *Referendums around the World: The Continued Growth of Direct Democracy* (Basingstoke/New York 2014), (cit. QVORTRUP, Continued Growth).

ROHNER GABRIELA, *Die Wirksamkeit von Volksinitiativen im Bund. 1848–2010* (Zürich/Basel/ Genf 2012), (cit. ROHNER).

ROZENWALDS JURIS, Baltische Staaten und ihre Gesellschaften nach dem Zweiten Weltkrieg, in: KNODT MICHÈLE/URDZE SIGITA (eds.), *Die politischen Systeme der baltischen Staaten. Eine Einführung* (Wiesbaden 2012), pp. 55–74 (cit. ROZENVALDS, Baltische Staaten).

RUUS JÜRI, Estonia, in: AUER ANDREAS/BÜTZER MICHAEL (eds.), *Direct Democracy. The Eastern and Central European Experience* (Aldershot et al 2001), pp. 47–62 (cit. RUUS, Estonia).

RUUS JÜRI, Estonia, in: KAUFMANN BRUNO/WATERS DANE M. (eds.), *Direct Democracy in Europe. A Comprehensive Reference Guide to the Initiative and Referendum Process in Europe* (Durham 2004), pp. 54–58 (cit. RUUS in KAUFMANN/WATERS).

SCHMID STEFAN G., Alte Unbekannte. Das Behördenreferendum und das ausserordentliche Referendum im kantonalen Staatsrecht, in: *Schweizerisches Zentralblatt für Staats- und Verwaltungsrecht ZBl* 114/2013, pp. 127–158 (cit. SCHMID, Unbekannte).

SAULIUS ARLAUSKAS, Sovereignty of a Nation in the Parliamentary System of Lithuania. Problems and Proposals, *Limes* 3(2)/2010, pp. 99–109 (cit. SAULIUS, Sovereignty).

SCHILLER THEO, Direct Democracy in Europe: Comparing Initiatives Instruments, in: KAUFMANN BRUNO [et al.] (eds.), *Initiative for Europe: A Roadmap for Transnational Democracy: IRI Europe Handbook 2007 on the Prospects for the Development of Citizens' Initiative Tools across Europe after the Failure of the EU Constitutional Treaty* (Marburg 2006), pp. 80–91 (cit. SCHILLER, Direct Democracy).

SERDÜLT UWE/WELP YANINA, Direct Democracy Upside Down, in: *Taiwan Journal of Democracy* 8(1)/2012, pp. 69–92 (cit. SERDÜLT/WELP).

SIKK, ALLAN, How Unstable? Volatility and the Genuinely New Parties in Eastern Europe, in: *European Journal of Political Research* 44/2005, pp. 391–412 (cit. SIKK, How Unstable).

SMITH GORDON, The Functional Properties of the Referendum, in: *European Journal of Political Research 4/1976*, pp. 1–23 (cit. SMITH, Functional).

SOMER EVREN, Das Initiativverfahren – Indirekt, dafür wirkungsvoll, in: GOOD ANDREA/PLATIPODIS BETTINA (eds.), *Direkte Demokratie. Herausforderungen zwischen Politik und Recht. Festschrift für Andreas Auer zum 65. Geburtstag* (Bern 2013), pp. 359–376 (cit. SOMER, Initiativverfahren).

TAUBER JOACHIM, Das politische System Litauens, in: ISMAYR WOLFGANG (ed.), *Die politischen Systeme Osteuropas*, 3rd edition (Wiesbaden 2010), pp. 171–208 (cit. TAUBER, Litauen).

TAUBER JOACHIM, Die Geschichte der baltischen Staaten bis 1945, in: KNODT MICHÈLE/URDZE SIGITA (eds.), *Die politischen Systeme der baltischen Staaten. Eine Einführung* (Wiesbaden 2012), pp. 17–33 (cit. TAUBER, Geschichte).

TSEBELIS GEORGE, Decision Making in Political Systems: Veto Players in Presidentialism, Parliamentarism, Multicamerialism and Multipartyism, in: *British Journal of Political Science* 25/1995, pp. 289–325 (cit. TSEBELIS, Decision Making).

TSEBELIS GEORGE, *Veto Players. How Political Institutions Work* (Princeton 2002), (cit. TSEBELIS, Veto Players).

UŠACKA ANITA, Latvia, in: AUER ANDREAS/BÜTZER MICHAEL (eds.), *Direct Democracy. The Eastern and Central European Experience* (Aldershot et al. 2001), pp. 94–108 (cit. UŠACKA).

VANAGS EDVINS/VILKA INGA, Local Democracy in the Baltic Countries: A New Beginning?, in: BALDERSHEIM HARALD/ILLNER MICHAL/WOLLMANN HELMUT (eds.), *Local Democracy in Post-Communist Europe* (Opladen 2003), pp. 123–156 (cit. VANAGS/VILKA, Local democracy).

VATTER ADRIAN, *Das politische System der Schweiz* (Baden-Baden 2014), (cit. VATTER, Politisches System).

VETIK RAIVO, Elite vs. People? Eurosceptic Public Opinion in Estonia, *Cambridge Review of International Affairs*, 16(2)/2003, pp. 257–271 (cit. VETIK).

VON ARX NICOLAS, *Ähnlich aber anders. Die Volksinitiative in Kalifornien und in der Schweiz* (Geneva 2002), (cit. VON ARX, Ähnlich).

WERDER HANS, *Die Bedeutung der Volksinitiative in der Nachkriegszeit* (Bern 1978), (cit. WERDER, Bedeutung).

Newspapers

The Economist

The Grip on Lithuania, *The Economist* [London, England], 21 April 1990, p. 13.

Backdown, *The Economist* [London, England], 2 February 1991, p. 50.

Thunderballot, *The Economist* [London, England], 16 February 1991, pp. 54–55.

Loser Gorbachev, *The Economist* [London, England], 9 March 1991, p. 16.

The Referendum Scorecard, *The Economist* [London, England], 23 March 1991, p. 62.

Leftovers, *The Economist* [London, England], 18 July 1992, p. 41.

A Long Hot Summer, *The Economist* [online], http://www.economist.com/ (15.07.2011).

Lativia's Failed Referendum, *The Economist* [online], http://www.economist.com/ (20.11.2012).

Lithuania's Final Sprint, *The Economist* [online], http://www.economist.com/ (13.12.2012).

Echoes of the Sudetenland. The Baltics look to NATO for protection, The Economist [online], http://www.economist.com/ (29.03.2014).

Latvia and the Euro. Lat go, *The Economist* [online], http://www.economist.com/ (05.06.2014).

Neue Zürcher Zeitung

Kein Privatisierungsstopp in Litauen. Fiasko für Rechtsopposition, *Neue Zürcher Zeitung*, 29 August 1994, p. 9.

Litauen vor einem Regierungswechsel, *Neue Zürcher Zeitung*, 14 October 2008, p. 3.

Steht Litauen vor einem «Energie-Infarkt»?, *Neue Zürcher Zeitung*, 19 November 2008, p. 7.

Valdis Zatlers plant Comeback, *Neue Zürcher Zeitung*, 23 July 2011, p. 7.

Die Letten für baldige Wahlen, *Neue Zürcher Zeitung*, 25 July 2011, p. 2.

Die Linksopposition siegreich in Lettland, *Neue Zürcher Zeitung*, 19 September 2011, p. 3.

Dombrovskis bleibt im Amt, *Neue Zürcher Zeitung*, 12 October 2011, p. 7.

«Es gibt kein stärkeres Mittel, um uns wütend zu machen», *Neue Zürcher Zeitung*, 18 February 2012, p. 7.

Russisch wird nicht zweite Amtssprache in Lettland, *Neue Zürcher Zeitung*, 20 February 2012, p. 3.

Machtwechsel in Litauen, *Neue Zürcher Zeitung*, 16 October 2012, p. 5.

Litauen lässt sich seine Energie etwas kosten, *Neue Zürcher Zeitung*, 18 October 2012, p. 21.

Litauen ist fit für den Euro, *Neue Zürcher Zeitung*, 5 June 2014, p. 23.

Der Weg zum Euro ist offen. Freude bei Litauens Politikern, Skepsis im Volk, *Neue Zürcher Zeitung*, 5 June 2014, p. 24.

Litauen wird zum Euro-Land, *Neue Zürcher Zeitung*, 24 July 2014, p. 19.

Die Ukraine Krise wirft ihren Schatten auf Lettland, *Neue Zürcher Zeitung*, 26 September 2014, p. 5.

Keine politischen Experimente in Lettland, *Neue Zürcher Zeitung*, 6 October 2014, p. 5.

New York Times, The

Leader Fails to Win Vote, *The New York Times*, 25 May 1992, p. 5.

Why are the Baltics Still Occupied, *The New York Times*, 15 June 1992, p. 18.

Lithuania Backs Quick Pullout of Ex-Soviets, *The New York Times*, 16 June 1992, p. 11.

The Ex-Communists Ahead in Lithuanian Elections, *The New York Times*, 27 October 1992, p. 10.

Economic Referendum in Lithuania Fails, *The New York Times*, 28 August 1994, p. 16.

Official Documents

EU

European Commission, http://ec.europa.eu/.

Standard Eurobarometer 80, *Public Opinion in the European Union – Report Autumn 2013* (cit. EB80), http://ec.europa.eu/public_opinion/archives/eb/eb80/eb80_en.htm (accessed on 01.06.2014).

Estonia

Law on the Application of the Constitution of June 28, 1992 (LAC).

Constitution of Republic of Estonia of 15 June 1920.

Constitution of Republic of Estonia of 3 July 1992, as last amended on 13 April 2011 (CE).

Estonian Referendum Act of 6 April 2002, as last amended on 17 October 2012 (ERA).

Riigikogu Rules of Procedures and Internal Rules Act of 11 February 2003, (RRPIRA).

Response to Memoranda and Request for Explanations and Submission of Collective Addresses Act of 10 November 2004 (CAA).

The Estonian National Electoral Committee (NEC), http://www.vvk.ee.

Latvia

Constitution of the Republic of Latvia of 15 February 1922, as last amended 08 April 2009 (CLv).

Law on National Referendums, Initiation of Laws and European Citizens' Initiative of 31 March 1994, as last amended on 8 November 2012 (LoNRILaECI).

Law on National Referendums, Initiation of Laws and European Citizens' Initiative of 31 March 1994, in force as of 1 January 2015 (LoNRILaECI-2015, after all revisions from 8 November 2012 come into force).

Judgement of 19 December 2012 by the Latvian Constitutional Court in Case No. 2012-03-01 "On the Compliance of the first part of Section 11 and the first part of Section 25 of the Law 'On National Referendums and Legislative Initiatives' with Article 1, 77, and 78 of the Satversme" (cit. JLvCC 2012-03-01).

Judgement of 18 December 2013 by the Latvian Constitutional Court in Case No. 2013-06-01 "On Compliance of Para 2 of Section 23(5) and Section 23^1(1) of Law on National Referendums, Legislative Initiatives and European Citizens' initiative with Article 1 of the Satversme of the Republic of Latvia" (cit. JLvCC 2013-06-01), http://www.satv.tiesa.gov.lv/upload/spriedums_2013-06-01_ENG.pdf (accessed on 29.05.2014).

The Central Election Commission of Latvia (CECLv), http://web.cvk.lv/pub/public/28361.html.

The Constitutional Court of the Republic of Latvia, http://www.satv.tiesa.gov.lv/?lang=2.

Lithuania

Constitutional Law of the Republic of Lithuania on the State of Lithuania of 11 February 1991.

Constitutional Act of the Republic of Lithuania on the Non-alignment of the Republic of Lithuania to Post-Soviet Eastern Unions of 8 June 1992.

Constitution of the Republic of Lithuania of 25 November 1992, as last amended on 25 April 2006 (CLt).

Seimas of the Republic of Lithuania Statute of 17 February 1994.

Law on Citizens' Legislatives of the Republic of Lithuania of 22 December 1998 (LoCLt).

Law on Petitions of the Republic of Lithuania of 7 July 1999 (LoP).

Law on Referendums of 4 June 2002, as last amended on 6 May 2014 (LoR).

Law on Electronic Signature of 11 July 2000 (LoES).

The Central Electoral Commission of the Republic of Lithuania (CECLt), http://www.vrk.lt.

Judgement of 22 July 1994 by the Lithuanian Constitutional Court "On the compliance of the provisions of items 1, 9, 11 and 39 of the Law 'On Amending and Appending the Law of Republic of Lithuania on Referendum' of 15 June 1994, by Articles 1, 9, 12 and 32 of the Law on Referendum have been amended or appended, with the Constitution of the Republic of Lithuania" (cit. JLtCC 1994-07-22), http://www.lrkt.lt/dokumentai/1994/n4a0722a.htm (accessed on 07.06.2014).

The Constitutional Court of the Republic of Lithuania, http://www.lrkt.lt/index_e.html.

Switzerland

Swiss Federal Constitution of 18 April 1999 (Cst-CH).
Constitution of Canton of Aargau of 25 June 1980, (Cst-AG).
Constitution of Canton of Bern of 6 June 1993 (Cst-BE).
Constitution of Canton of Solothurn of 8 June 1986 (Cst-SO).
Constitution of Canton of Zug of 31 January 1894 (Cst-ZG).
Constitution of Canton of Zürich of 27 February 2005 (Cst-ZH).
Centre for Research on Direct Democracy (c2d), http://www.c2d.ch.

Studien des Instituts für Ostrecht München

Begründet von Professor Dr. Reinhart Maurach
Herausgegeben von Professor Dr. Friedrich-Christian Schroeder,
Dr. h.c. (Breslau), Regensburg

Band 41 Manfred Gratzl: Die Reform der tschechischen Strafprozeßordnung nach 1989. Im Spannungsfeld von Rechtsstaatlichkeit, Verfahrensökonomie und Effizienz. 2002.

Band 42 Thomas Paintner: Die Insolvenz des Unternehmers in Polen. 2003.

Band 43 Niels von Redecker (Hrsg.): Deutsch-Estnische Rechtsfragen. 2003.

Band 44 Niels von Redecker: Die polnischen Vertreibungsdekrete und die offenen Vermögensfragen zwischen Deutschland und Polen. 2003. 2., durchgesehene Auflage 2004.

Band 45 Niels von Redecker: Das polnische Beamtenrecht. Entwicklung und Stand beim Beitritt Polens zur Europäischen Gemeinschaft. 2003.

Band 46 Cornelia Stefanie Wölk: Das Deliktsrecht Rußlands nach dem neuen Zivilgesetzbuch. 2003.

Band 47 Petr Bohata: Untersuchungshaft im deutschen und tschechischen Recht. 2003.

Band 48 Attila Széchényi: Das neue ungarische Strafprozessrecht im Spannungsverhältnis zwischen Rechtsstaatsprinzip, Verfahrensökonomie und Effizienz. 2003.

Band 49 Agnes Balawejder: Das polnische Telekommunikationsrecht. Umsetzungsbemühungen und -stand des telekommunikationsrechtlichen acquis communautaire im polnischen TK-Recht vor dem Unionsbeitritt Polens. 2004.

Band 50 Sven I. Oksaar / Niels von Redecker (Hrsg.): Deutsch-Estnische Rechtsvergleichung und Europa. 2004.

Band 51 Friedrich-Christian Schroeder (Hrsg.): Justizreform in Osteuropa. 2004.

Band 52 Herbert Küpper: Kollektive Rechte in der Wiedergutmachung von Systemunrecht. Teil I und Teil II. 2004.

Band 53 Sören Langner: Der GmbH-Geschäftsführer im tschechischen Recht. Organstellung und Anstellung im Rechtsvergleich. 2005.

Band 54 Herbert Küpper: Einführung in die Rechtsgeschichte Osteuropas. 2005.

Band 55 Anja Spitzweg: Das russische föderale Gesetz „Über Investmentfonds". 2007.

Band 56 Herbert Küpper: Die ungarische Verfassung nach zwei Jahrzehnten des Übergangs. Einführung mit Textübersetzung. 2007.

Band 57 Axel Boës: Die Gesellschaft mit beschränkter Haftung im russischen und deutschen Recht. 2007.

Band 58 Katrin Heinritz: „Defekte Demokratisierung" – ein Weg zur Diktatur? Turkmenistan und die Republik Sacha (Jakutien) in der Russischen Förderation nach dem Ende der Sowjetunion. 2007.

Band 59 Stefan Hülshörster: Recht im Umbruch. Die Transformation des Rechtssystems in der Ukraine unter ausländischer Beratung. 2008.

Band 60 Carsten Dewald-Werner: Versicherungsmarkt und Versicherungsaufsicht in der Russischen Föderation. 2008.

Band 61 Oleksiy Feliv: Die Hypothek im deutschen und ukrainischen Recht. Der systematische Vergleich des Hypothekenrechts in Deutschland und der Ukraine einschließlich der rechtstheoretischen Grundlagen und der Ausblicke für das gemeinsame Hypothekenrecht. 2009.

Band 62 Christoph Kurzböck: Die Abwicklung deutsch-tschechischer Erbfälle. 2010.

Band 63 Friedrich-Christian Schroeder / Herbert Küpper (Hrsg.): Die rechtliche Aufarbeitung der kommunistischen Vergangenheit in Osteuropa. 2010.

Band 64 Herbert Küpper / Wolfgang Brenn (Hrsg.): Rechtstransfer und internationale rechtliche Zusammenarbeit. Deutsche und japanische Erfahrungen bei der Kooperation mit Osteuropa und Zentralasien. 2010.

Band 65 Daniela Horner / Dragan Bataveljić: Grundeigentum und Registrierung von Liegenschaften in Serbien. Eigentumsschutz in der Praxis. 2010.

Band 66 Nail Mammadov: Die Straffreistellungsgründe im russischen und aserbaidschanischen Strafrecht im Vergleich zur deutschen Strafrechtsdogmatik. 2010.

Band 67 Matthias Farian: Dingliche Nutzungsrechte an fremden Grundstücken im russischen Recht. 2010.

Band 68 Manuchehr Kudratov: Die Straftatausschließungsgründe nach tadschikischem Strafrecht. Eine Analyse aus deutscher Perspektive. 2011.

Band 69 Michael Holland: Die Staatsanwaltschaft im russischen Strafprozess. 2012.

Band 70 Herbert Küpper: Ungarns Verfassung vom 25. April 2011. Einführung – Übersetzung – Materialien. 2012.

Band 71 Friedrich-Christian Schroeder / Manuchehr Kudratov (Hrsg.): Das strafprozessuale Vorverfahren in Zentralasien zwischen inquisitorischem und adversatorischem Modell. 2012.

Band 72 Tina de Vries (Hrsg.): Mediation als Verfahren konsensualer Streitbeilegung. Die deutsche, polnische und ukrainische Perspektive. 2012.

Band 73 Monika Lipińska: Die Sexualstraftaten im polnischen Strafkodex im Vergleich zum deutschen Strafgesetzbuch. 2013.

Band 74 Mirona Marisch: Das System der Arbeitnehmervertretung und des Sozialen Dialogs im rumänischen Recht im Vergleich zum deutschen Recht. 2013.

Band 75 Friedrich-Christian Schroeder / Manuchehr Kudratov (Hrsg.): Die strafprozessuale Hauptverhandlung zwischen inquisitorischem und adversatorischem Modell. Eine rechtsvergleichende Analyse am Beispiel des deutschen und des zentralasiatischen Strafprozessrechts. 2014.

Band 76 Evren Somer: Direct Democracy in the Baltic States. Institutions, Procedures and Practice in Estonia, Latvia and Lithuania. 2015.

Band 77 Florian Plagemann: Die russische Aktiengesellschaft. Darstellung aus Sicht des ausländischen Investors. 2014.

www.peterlang.com

www.ingramcontent.com/pod-product-compliance
Ingram Content Group UK Ltd.
Pitfield, Milton Keynes, MK11 3LW, UK
UKHW021833100926
8556IPUK00004B/306

9 783631 652985